AF478935

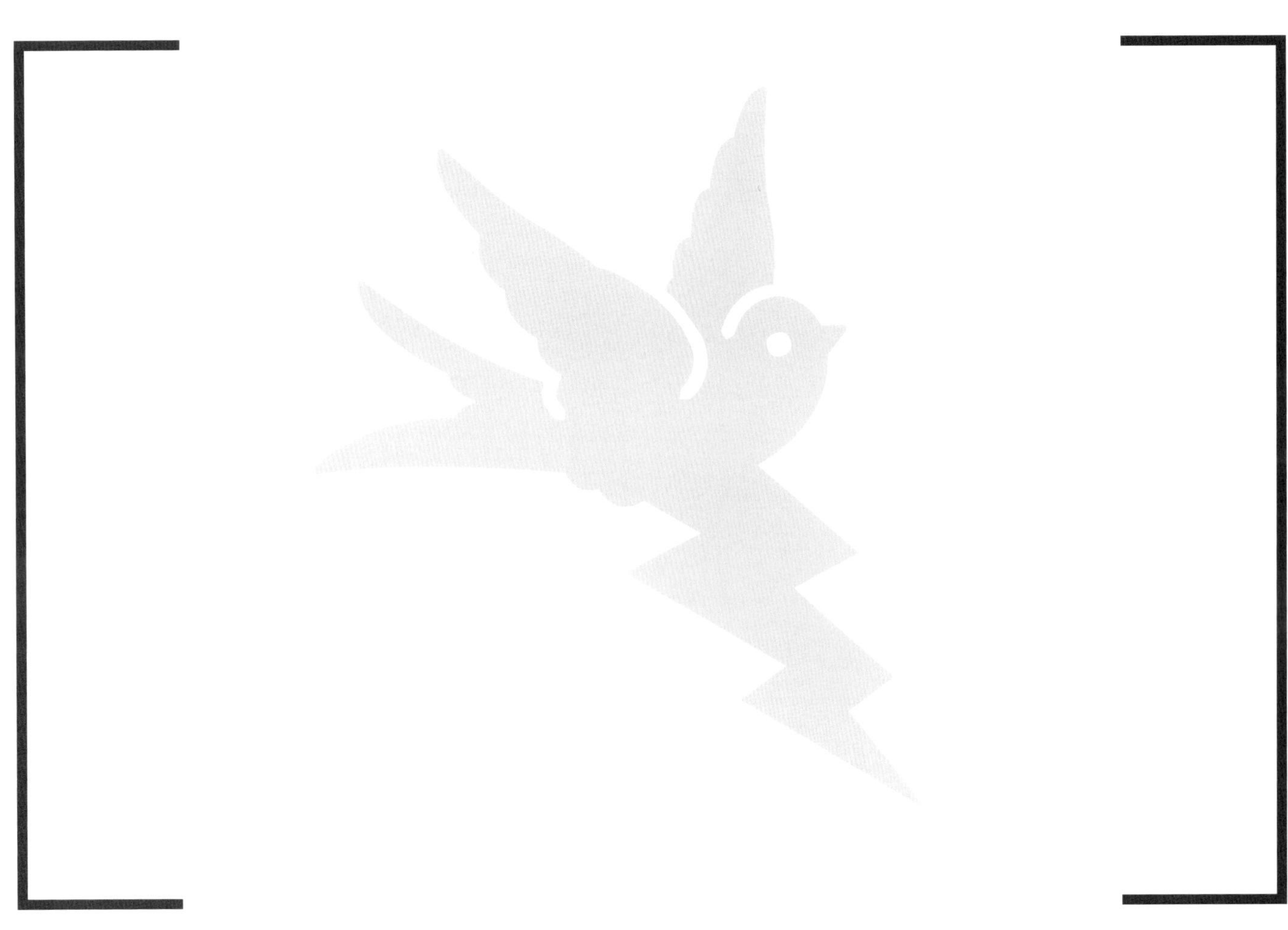

LORENZO BONINI

RAPTUZ - MOTHER ROAD

DAMIANI

RAPTUZ - MOTHER ROAD

Design: Raptuz Creative Services
www.raptuz.com

Words: Lorenzo Bonini - Luigi "Raptuz" Muratore.

DAMIANI

Damiani Editore
Via Zanardi, 376
40131 Bologna
t. +39 051 63 56 811
f. +39 051 63 47 188
info@damianieditore.it
www.damianieditore.com

Photo credits:
Cover portrait - DANIELE BARRACO.
DANIELE BARRACO - The best! - www.danielebarraco.com
on pages: 15, 110,112, 113, and from 120 to141.
ADRIANO ALECCHI - Thanx to my friend Adriano for using his photos.
on pages: 12, 31, 32, 33, 36, 40.
CBS CREW - For the family portrait 2011.
LUIGI "RAPTUZ" MURATORE - for all the other images.

Printed in February 2012 by Grafiche Damiani, Bologna, Italy.

Printed on Hello Silk - grs. 250
First Edition 2012
ISBN 978-88-6208-229-7

Supported by

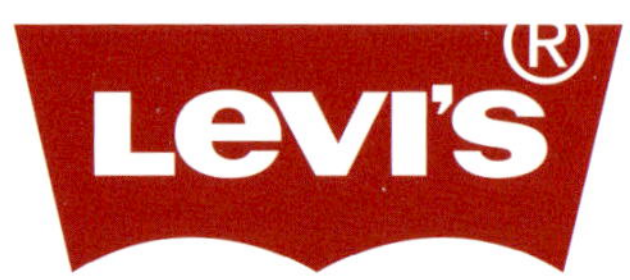

Also supported by

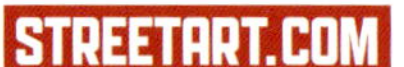

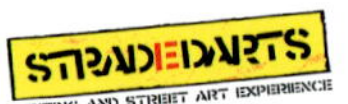

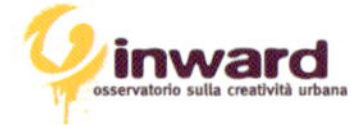

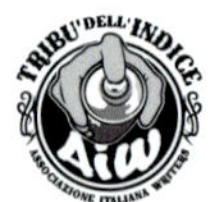

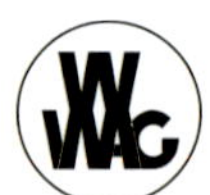

This book is heartfeltly dedicate to all my family and friends
expecially to my love and wife Rossana, my dogs Adolf & Heidi
and all the CBS and TDK brothers.

Thanx for the precious support to
Vittorio Sacchi, Lorenzo Bonini, Stefano Tei, Giuseppe Iavicoli.

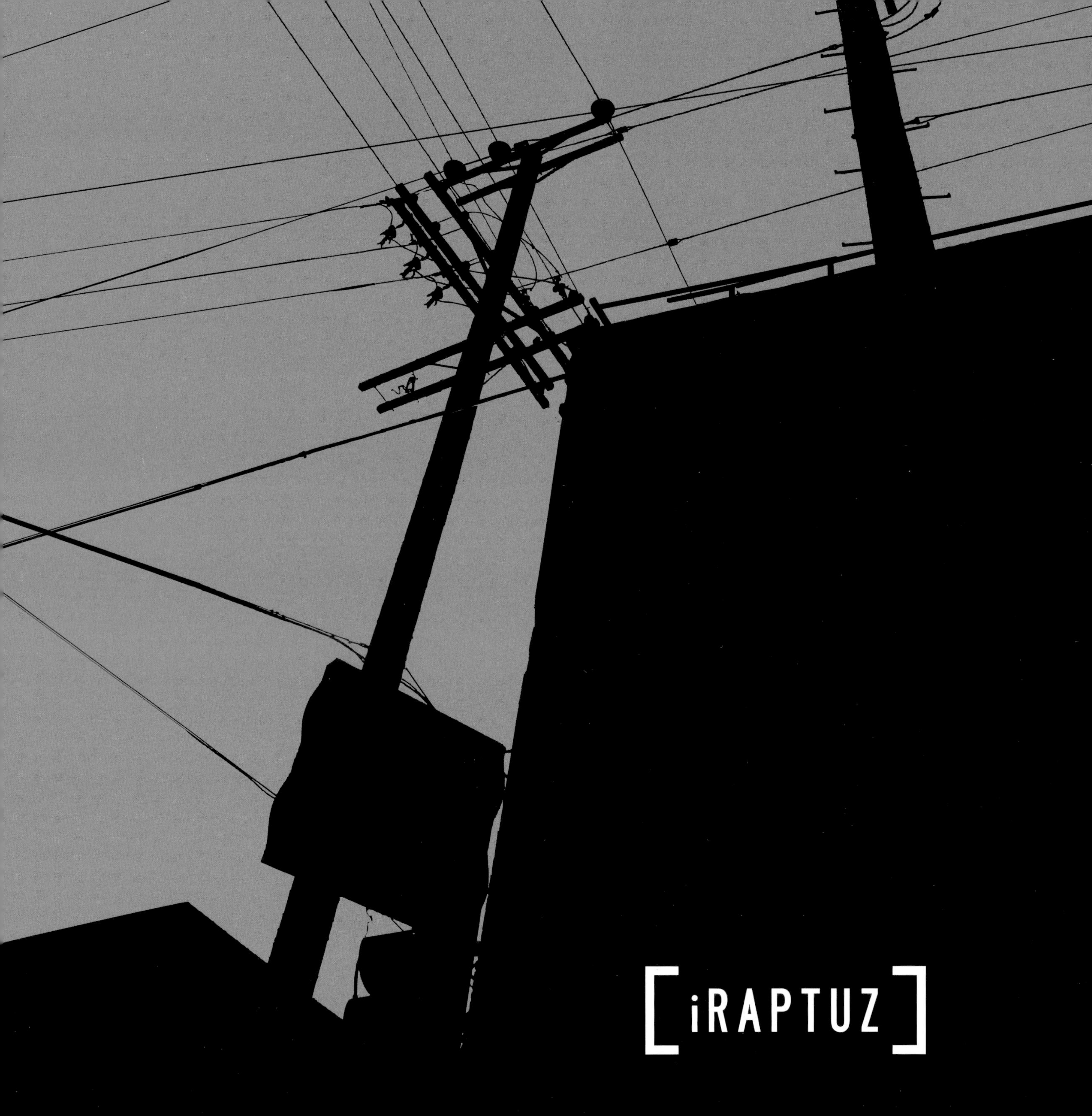

[iRAPTUZ]

Artist by chance

by Luigi "Raptuz" Muratore.

I did not want to become an artist and I do not belong to a rich family, and therefore I do not smile easily, I am a bit hot-tempered and I hate people's lies.

It happens to people like me who live in Milan's hinterland and do not know how to spend their time, I remember very well it was a very hot and muggy day of July 1987, a three hundred sixty degree-dead calm, not even a shadow of money for a vacation. What can you do with too much free time and without any dime in your pocket? Sometimes fate helps you, you meet your usual friends who are totally bored and suffer existential distress, Paul and Michele, at the end of a hot day, were holding a book that had just been printed, full of absolutely new things that stun you in just a second. It is also possible that an American kid, with a strange blond forelock, come to town for a *study tour*, then you watch a couple of movies on TV that really get you exited. Well, this is how it all started, by chance; you find a large piece of chalk at a building yard which is closed for the summer holidays and you begin drawing something on any kind of wall, without even thinking too much about it, freely without prejudice.

By saving money and doing odd jobs I was able to buy the first spray cans for bodyworks, after you start looking for your wall you want to *humanize* and make become *the bearer of news*, and then you finally reach the wall of an abandoned farmstead which is full of stories, you create the first real piece: *night prowler*. From this moment things get serious.

The next thing that happens to you is you start taking a liking to it and begin wandering around the neighboring towns at night, loaded with spray cans and adrenaline, then go around the great city of Milan and finally you "discover" the railroad. Shit! Kilometers and kilometers of tracks running with massive walls on their sides, trains inside garages and stations, and buildings which have more or less been forgotten about. Shit! A ready to use giant canvas.

Then you serve the army (183rd Battalion "NEMBO" Paratroops), and if you get back home as a *skinhead* more than a *writer*, you are also more "*trained*" for certain situations and to shout out: "*As Lightning from the sky, as a storm cloud,* " nobody can stop you, Milan is yours! You meet the first *writers*, those who will later become your "*cousins*" and with whom you will share everything. Massimo (MEC), Dimitri (STEN), Danilo (REO), Dario (SKAH), and Renato (RENDO), the myth of the TDK Crew (*The Damage Kidz*) is born. The more you paint and the more you only think about painting, and so you start out with the neighborhood walls, with

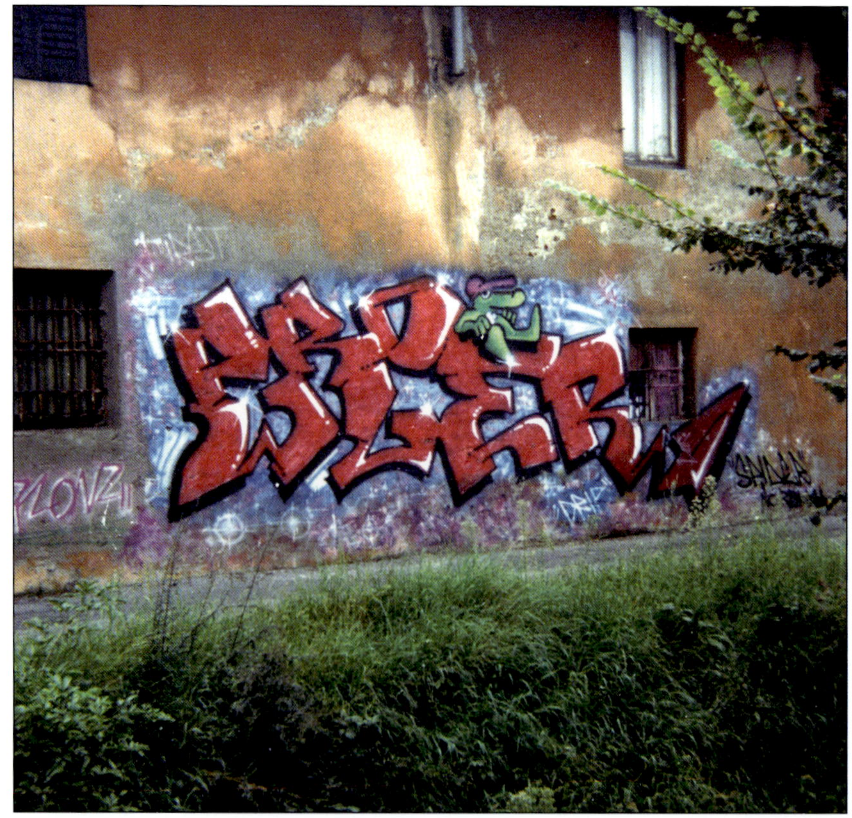

the *hall of fames*, with bombings on roofs, trains, platforms, aqueducts, and whatever you'll need to show your work to as many people as possible, and you discover your true gift: The Underground. The few lights lit on along the platform at night which far from the tunnel appear like – the Crystal Cathedral - of Santana, the rustling of ventilation fans blowing in the dark is deafening, but you only hear your heart beating, and so you do all of them, I mean all of them, *the Green Line, the Red Line, and even "the new" yellow line.*

Anyway, whatever you do you'll be out of money, and so then you decide to leave for Los Angeles, with the intention of doing any for a living, you'll also find a job, as a waiter in an Italian restaurant, on the first day you'll show up wearing your nice vest, a black bow tie, a white shirt, and occasionally between a plate and another you start understanding how to guess, you try to show your drawings to the owner of the place who quickly assigns you with another duty: "Would you be able to paint *Trinita Dei Monti* on that wall? "-" Of course, I can! "

The event, once it has been finished spreads around quickly, in a short time I end up having to paint for thousands of Italian restaurants in Southern California. I was invited to take part in some important artistic events, such as "*Vargas Awards*" in Las Vegas, and the "*Festival of Arts*" in Laguna Beach.
But the call to the (*forest*) road is too strong, in the meantime I had met

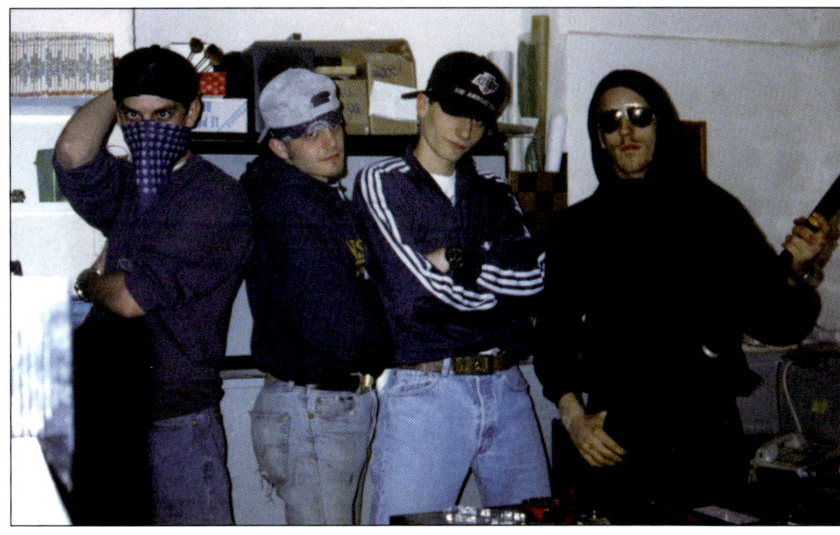

some famous *writers*: HEX, SLICK, SK8, and when you see their *creations* you are fascinated by the power, the colors and the light that the pieces give off, you leave everything and make a rush for them. You paint illegal walls in Santa Ana, Venice, Hollywood, Downtown, East LA, Long Beach, back and forth for a decade and then? Then go back to Milan and take back that exhilarating adventure full of experiences. As you get back home, in the meantime, you discover that some of your friends have become famous singers and nostalgia punctually come backs once again and you start travelling around Italy with them (J-AX and SPACE ONE) on a tour painting and signing "*Spaghetti Funk*".

Then you start thinking about that land across the ocean again, which you haven't forgotten about, in particular you won't forget those kids who sign themselves as the CBS Crew (*California Bomb Squad*); then

you decide to leave again – nostalgia - you know *writers* such as: NATOE, DYTCH66, MERS, HASTE, ANGER, UNEK, and you naturally feel like one of them, as if you've always been a part of their family, you become an integral part of the CBS and it is a great honor to be part of it. All of this is the fun part.
Now I remember the warm and sultry nights spent in the suburbs of Lombardy, many things have changed in my first 25 years, with my head facing the wall, here come the works on demand, live performances, graphics, paintings, exhibitions, sponsors and everything strangely seems very natural to me. Ah! I forgot… my friend Michele, he has made his way through, he has become famous as ASSO, and the book we went through on that day hot and sultry day, was: "*Subway Art*" by Henry Chalfant, while the boy with the strange blond forelock, was Tim Colavito, who together with my friend Paul (DRIP), was one of the pioneers of *skateboarding*

in Milan and the films in question that were seen: "*Turk 182*" and "*The Warriors.*"

Now deep in my heart, without evening knowing it, I wonderingly discover being an artist, but perhaps I am still a cruel thug.

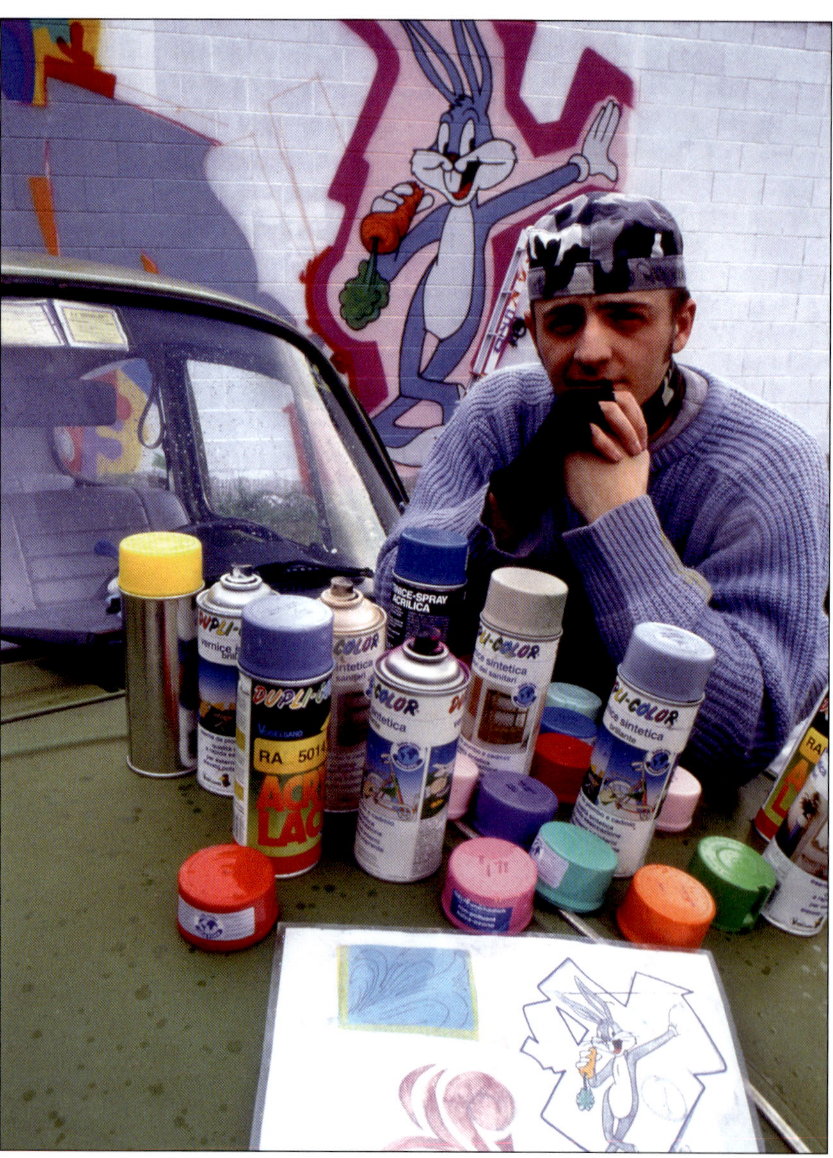

Artista per caso

Luigi "Raptuz" Muratore.

Non volevo fare l'artista non sono ricco di famiglia e pertanto non ho facili sorrisi, sono un po' iracondo e non sopporto la falsità della gente.

Capita a quelli come me che vivono nell'hinterland milanese che non sappiano come passare il tempo. Ricordo molto bene: era un caldissimo e afoso mese di luglio del 1987, calma piatta a trecentosessanta gradi, soldi per andare in vacanza nemmeno l'ombra. Cosa si può fare con troppo tempo libero e senza denaro? A volte il destino ti aiuta. Incontri i tuoi soliti amici, pieni di noia e come te di disagio esistenziale; Paul e Michele, sul calare della rovente giornata, avevano in mano un libro fresco di stampa, pieno di cose assolutamente nuove che ti folgorano all'istante. Succede pure che arrivi in paese per delle vacanze-studio un ragazzotto americano, con uno strano ciuffo biondo; poi vedi in televisione un paio di film che ti gasano un sacco… Ecco, tutto è iniziato così, per caso: trovi un grosso pezzo di gesso in un cantiere fermo per le ferie estive, e inizi a disegnare qualcosa su un muro qualsiasi, senza nemmeno pensarci troppo, libero senza pregiudizi.

Risparmiando e facendo piccoli lavori riesci a procurarti le prime bombolette spray per carrozzeria, dopo di che vai alla ricerca del tuo muro da umanizzare e far diventare portatore di novità: ecco finalmente sul muro di una cascina diroccata piena

di storie abbandonate, tu crei il primo vero pezzo: *night prowler*.
Da qui in poi la cosa si fa seria.

Dopodiché succede che ci prendi gusto e che inizi a girovagare di notte carico di spray e di adrenalina per i paesi limitrofi e poi per la grande Milano e alla fine "scopri" la ferrovia. Cazzo! Chilometri e chilometri di binari costeggianti muraglioni continui, treni in rimessaggio e stazioni, ed edifici più o meno dimenticati. Cazzo! Una gigantesca tela pronta all'uso.

Capita poi che tu vada a fare il militare (183° Btg. Paracadutisti "NEMBO"), e se quando torni sei più *skinhead* che *writer*, in più sei anche "addestrato" a certe situazioni e al grido di: "*Come Folgore da cielo, come Nembo di tempesta*", non ti ferma più nessuno: Milano è tua! Conosci i primi *writers*, quelli che poi diventeranno i tuoi "cugini" e con i quali condividerai tutto. Massimo (MEC), Dimitri (STEN), Danilo (REO), Dario (SKAH), e Renato (RENDO) con loro nasce il mito della TDK Crew (*The Damage Kidz*). Più dipingi e più pensi solo a dipingere, e allora si parte con i muri di quartiere, con le *hall of fames*, con i *bombing* sui tetti, sui treni, sulle banchine, sugli acquedotti, e con quant'altro serva a far vedere le tue opere a più gente possibile. E scopri la tua vera vocazione: la Metropolitana. Le poche luci accese nella notte della banchina, viste in lontananza dal tunnel sembrano la *Crystal Cathedral* di Santa Ana, il fruscio del soffio delle ventole d'aereazione nel buio è assordante, ma tu senti solo il battito del tuo cuore, e allora te le fai tutte; ma proprio tutte;

Linea verde, Linea rossa, e perfino la "neonata" *Linea gialla.*

Qualsiasi cosa tu faccia comunque resti sempre senza soldi. E allora decidi di partire per Los Angeles, con l'intenzione di fare un lavoro qualsiasi. Lo trovi anche il lavoro, come cameriere in un ristorante italiano: il primo giorno ti presenti con il tuo bel gilet, il farfallino di colore nero con la camicia bianca, e occasionalmente tra un piatto e l'altro cominci a comprendere a intuire, ti sbilanci mostrando i tuoi disegni al proprietario del locale che t'impiega subito in un altro modo: "Mi sapresti dipingere *Trinità Dei Monti* su quella parete?" - "*Certo che SI!*".

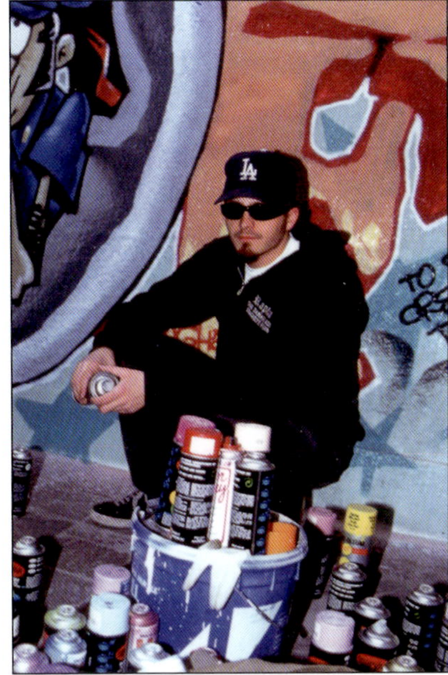

L'evento, una volta finito si diffonde con rapidità e tempestività, in breve tempo ti ritrovi a dover dipingere un'infinità di ristoranti italiani nel sud della California, e sei invitato a partecipare a manifestazioni artistiche importanti, come i "*Vargas Awards*" a Las Vegas, e il "*Festival of Arts*" a Laguna Beach.
Ma, il richiamo della (*foresta*) strada è troppo forte, avevi nel frattempo conosciuto *writers* famosi: HEX, SLICK, SK8, e quando vedi le loro *creazioni* ne resti affascinato dalla forza, dai colori e dalla luce che emanano i pezzi. E allora lasci tutto e torni all'arrembaggio. Dipingi muri illegali a Santa Ana, Venice, Hollywood, Downtown, East LA, Long Beach, avanti e indietro per un decennio e poi? Poi torni a Milano con addosso quell'entusiasmante avventura piena di esperienze. Al tuo rientro scopri che alcuni tuoi amici nel frattempo sono diventati dei cantanti famosi e di nuovo il richiamo non tarda a farsi sentire e assieme

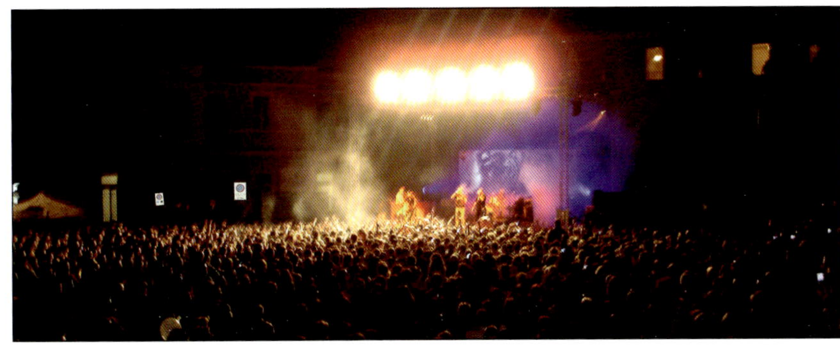

a loro (J-AX e SPACE ONE) ti rimetti a girare per l'Italia in tour dipingendo e firmando "*Spaghetti Funk*".

Poi ti succede di pensare alla terra oltre l'oceano, che ti è rimasta dentro. In particolare non ti togli dalla testa quei ragazzi che si firmano CBS *Crew* (*California Bomb Squad*); allora decidi di ripartire - un altro richiamo - e conosci *writers* come: NATOE, DYTCH66, MERS, HASTE, ANGER, UNEK, e nel modo più naturale ti senti uno di loro, della loro famiglia da sempre, diventando parte integrante dei CBS ed è un grandissimo onore farne parte.

Ora mi ricordo le notti calde e afose trascorse nella periferia lombarda. Molte cose sono passate nel corso dei miei primi 25 anni con la faccia rivolta al muro, ora arrivano i lavori su commissione, le esibizioni live, le grafiche, i quadri, le mostre, gli sponsor e stranamente tutto mi sembra molto naturale. Ah! Dimenticavo... il mio amico Michele, ha fatto strada; è diventato noto col nome di ASSO, e il libro che sfogliammo quel giorno caldo e afoso, era: "*Subway Art*" di Henry Chalfant, mentre il ragazzotto dallo strano ciuffo biondo, era Tim Colavito, che assieme al mio amico Paul (DRIP), è stato uno dei pionieri dello *skate-boarding* a Milano. Quanto ai film visti, erano: "*Turk 182*" e "*I Guerrieri della Notte*".

Ora nel profondo del mio cuore a mia insaputa scopro con meraviglia di essere un artista, mentre forse sono rimasto ancora solo un barbaro teppista.

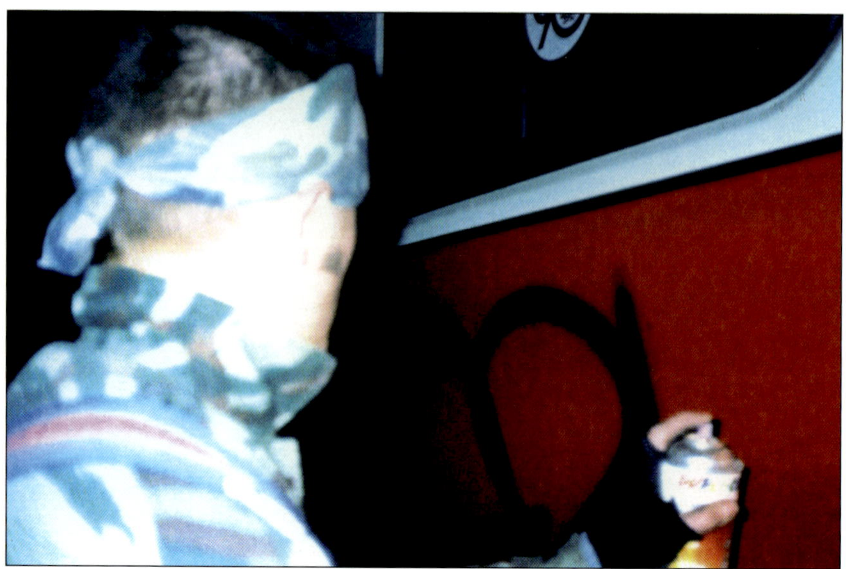

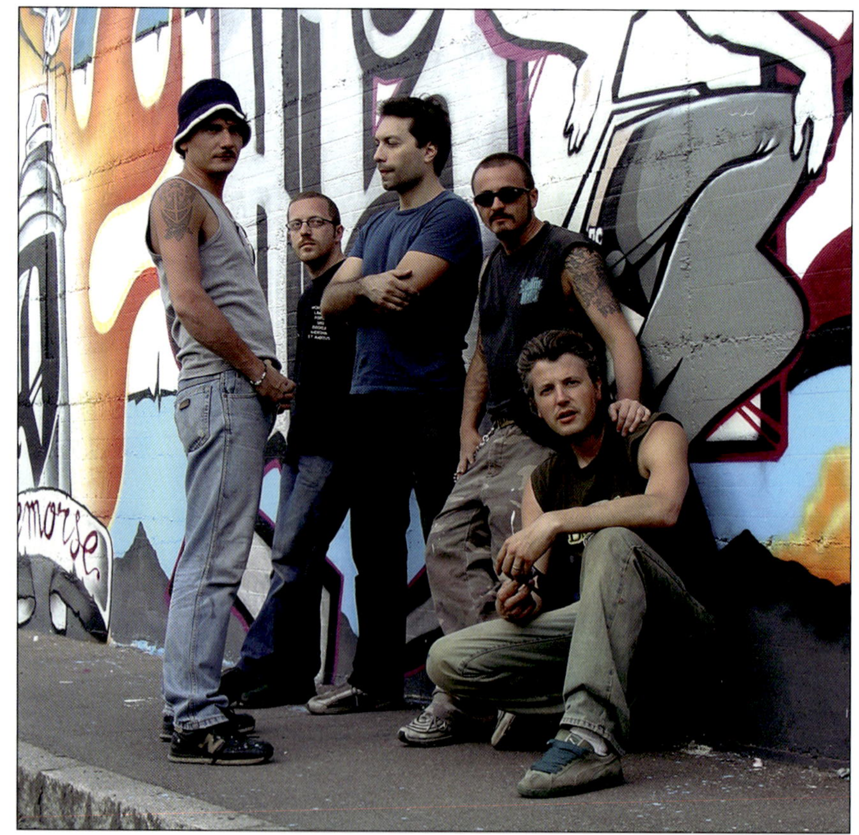

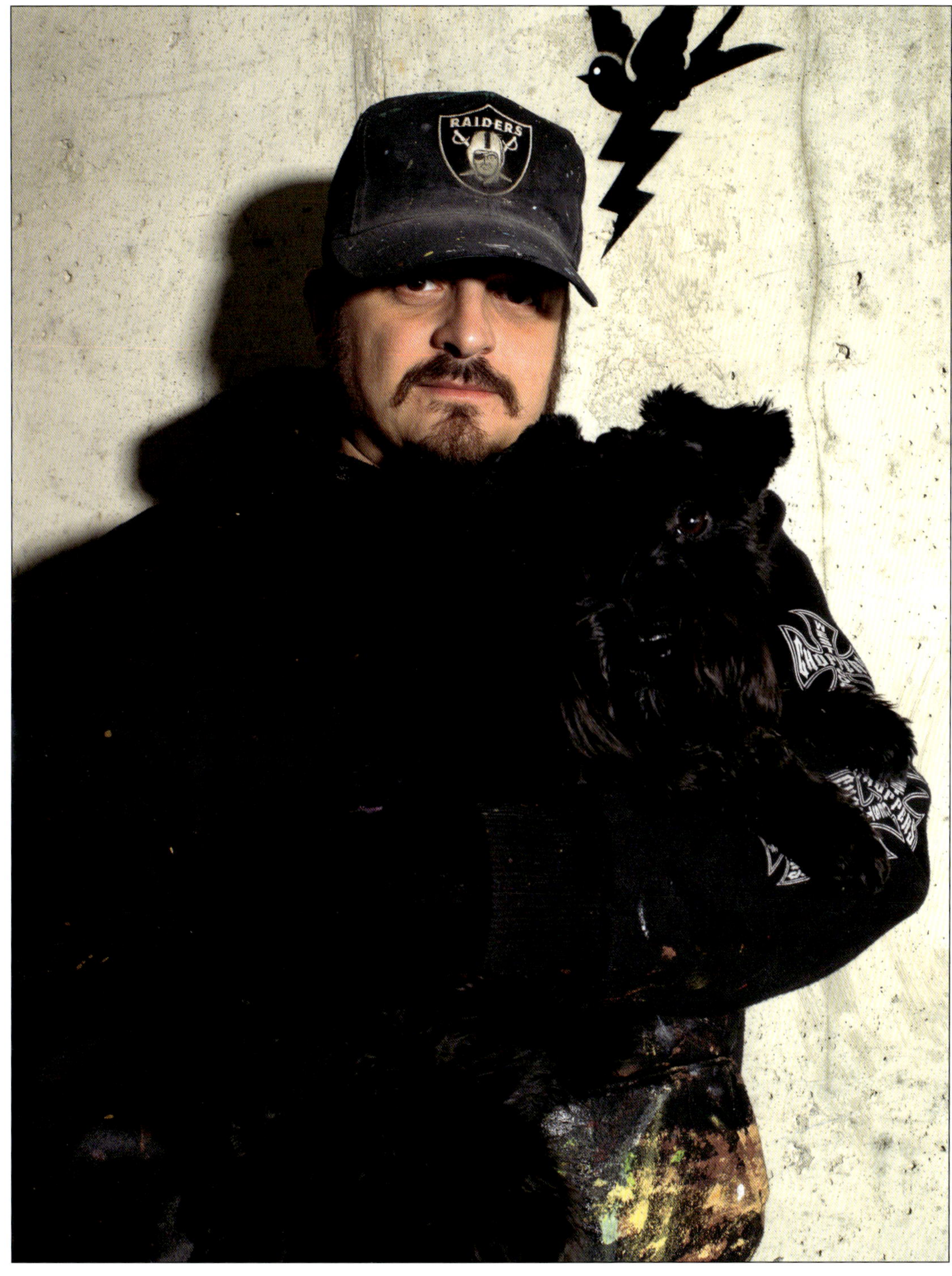

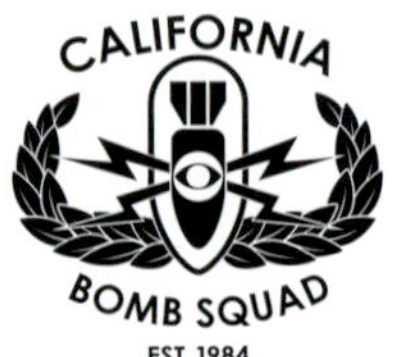

CBS Family - Hollywood 2011

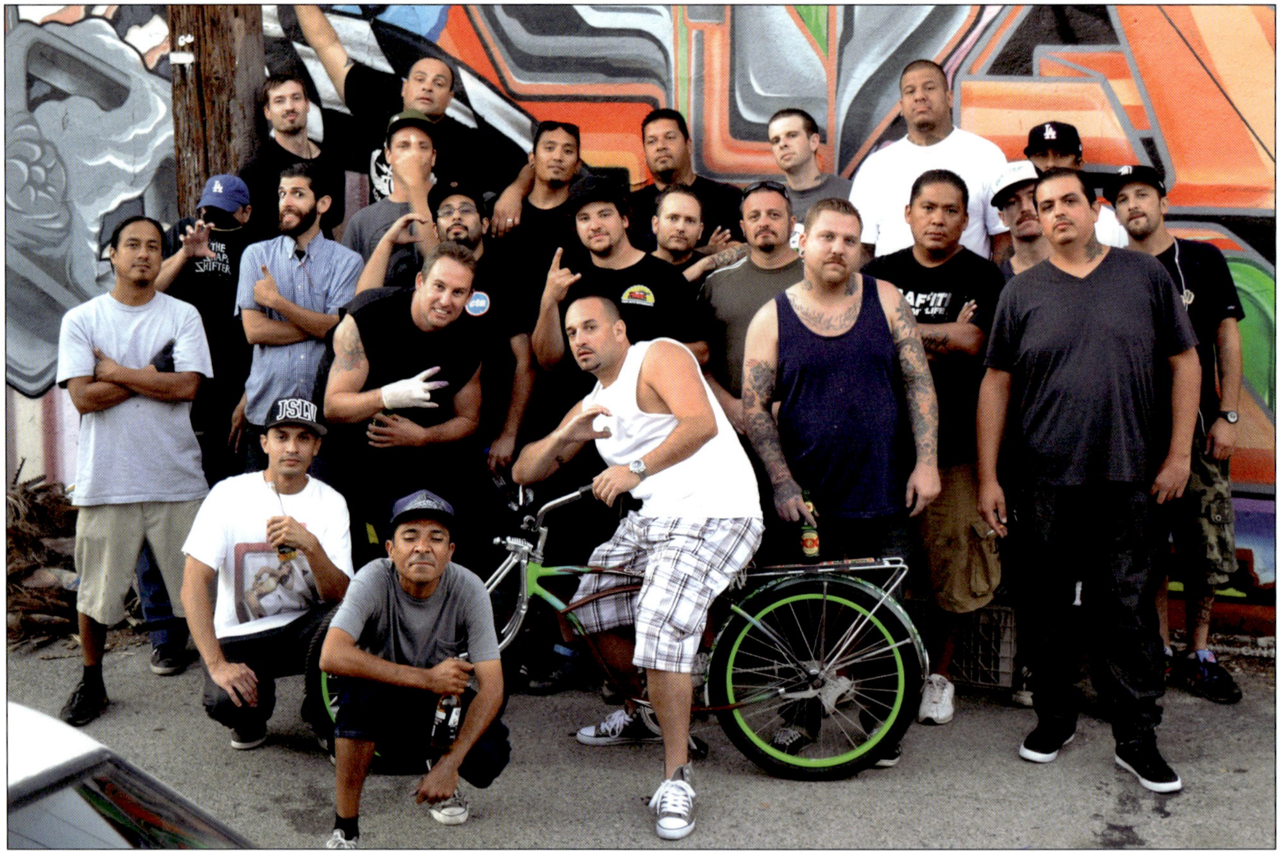

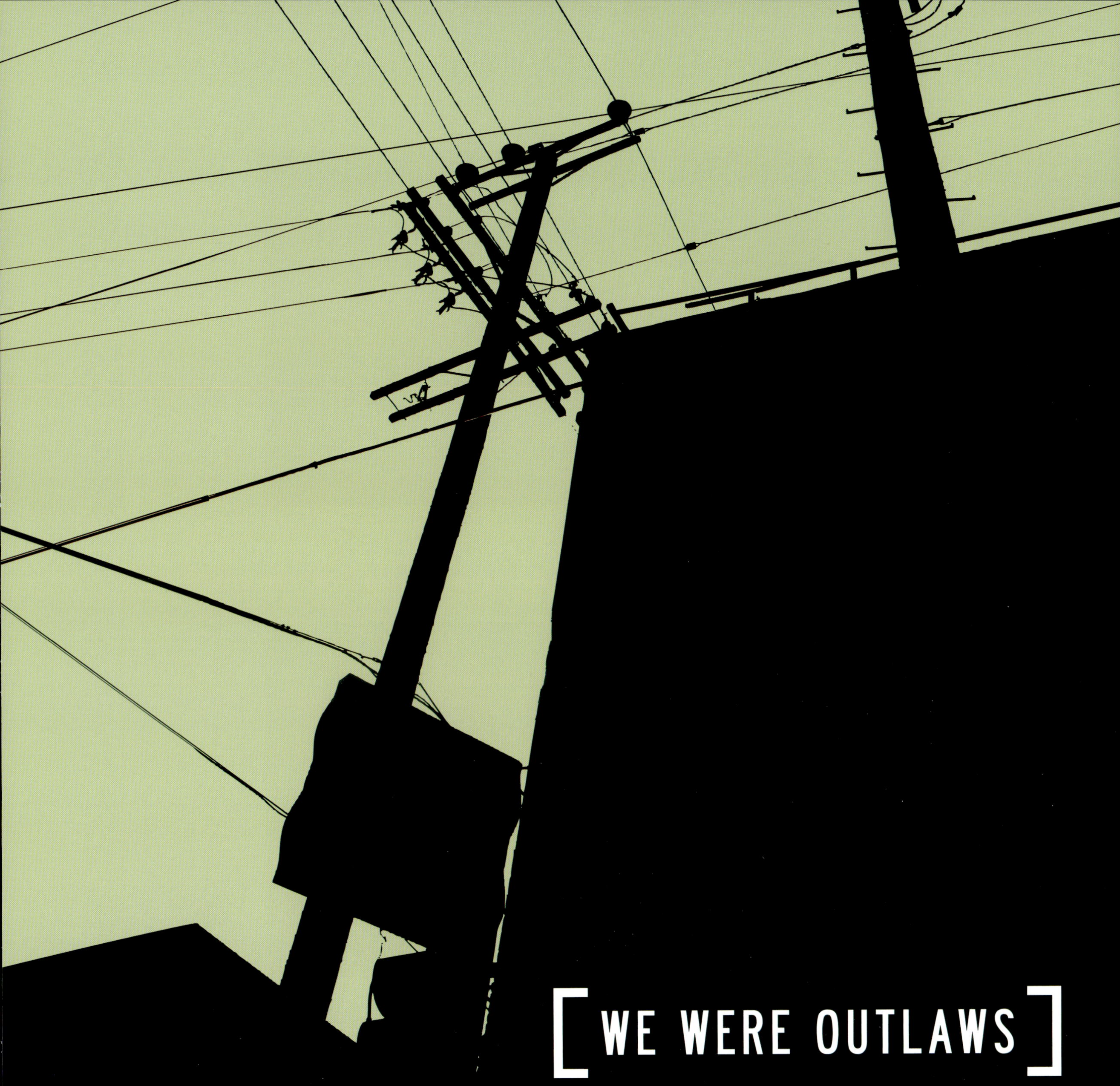

[WE WERE OUTLAWS]

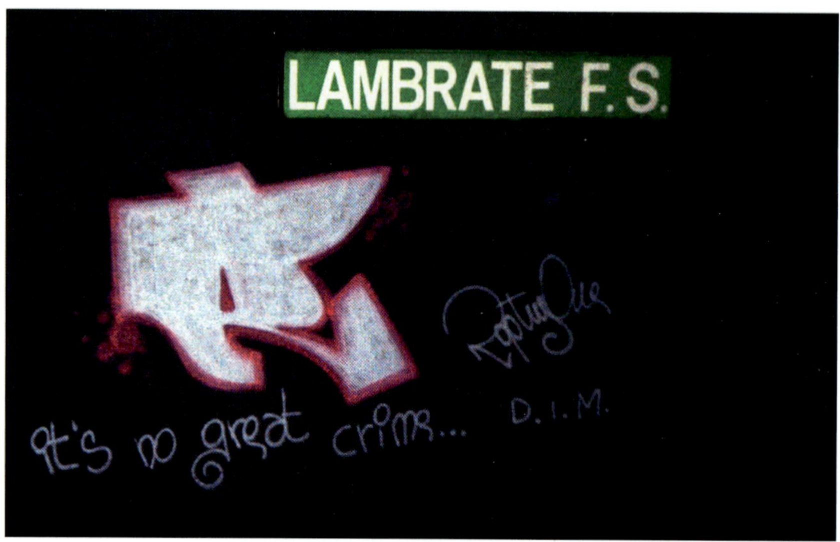

First subway crime - 1988

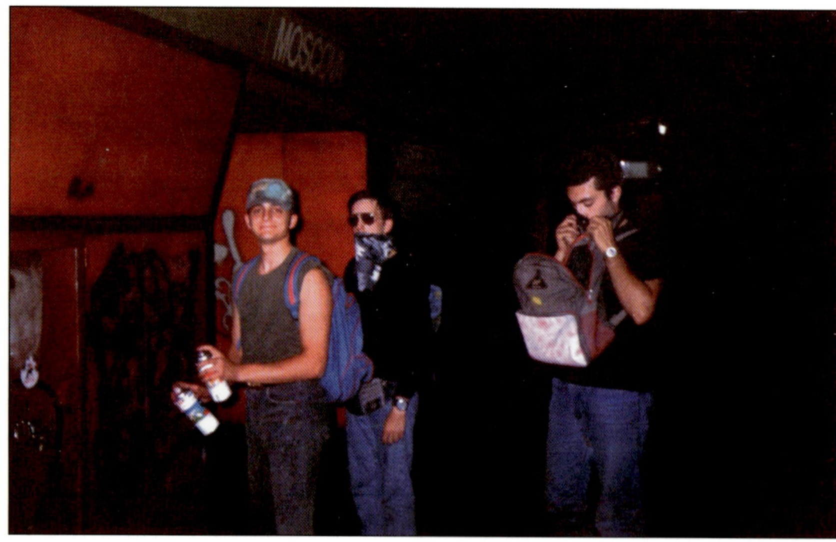

MM1 Moscova - 1990

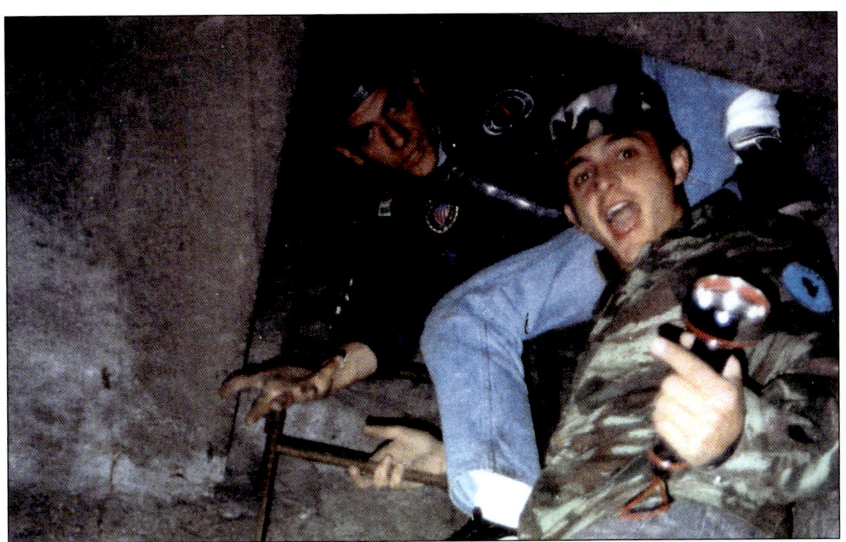

Exploring subway tunnels - 1990

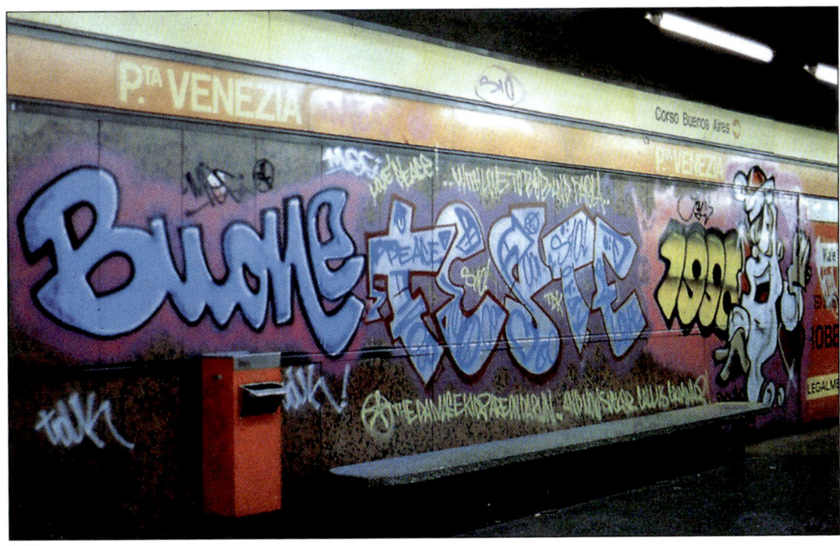

MM1 P.ta Venezia - 1990

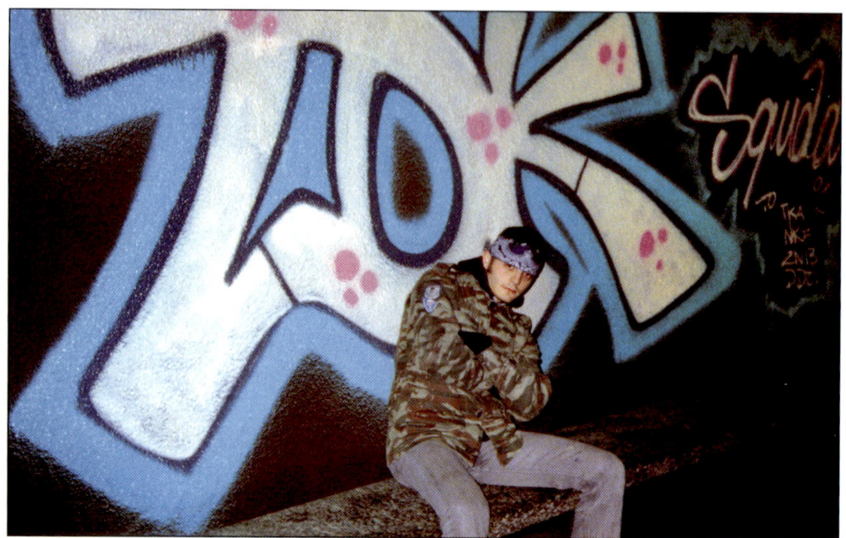

MM1 Pasteur - 1991

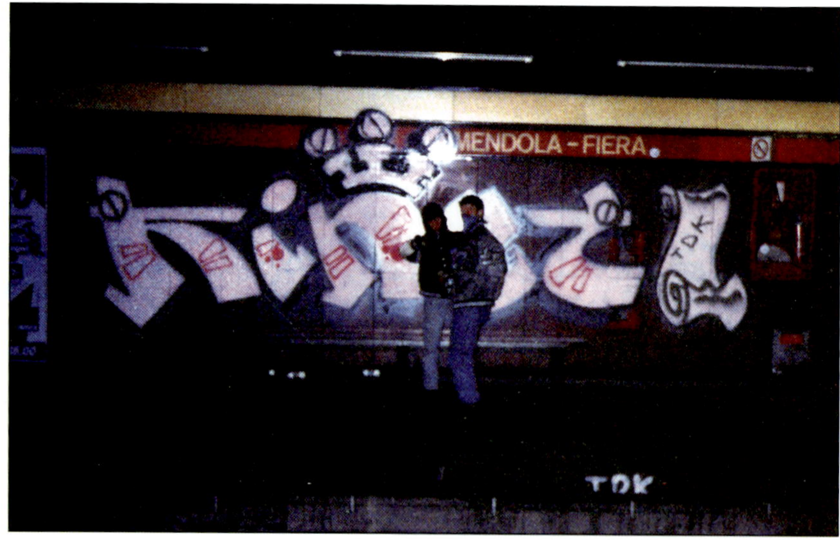

MM1 Amendola-Fiera - 1991

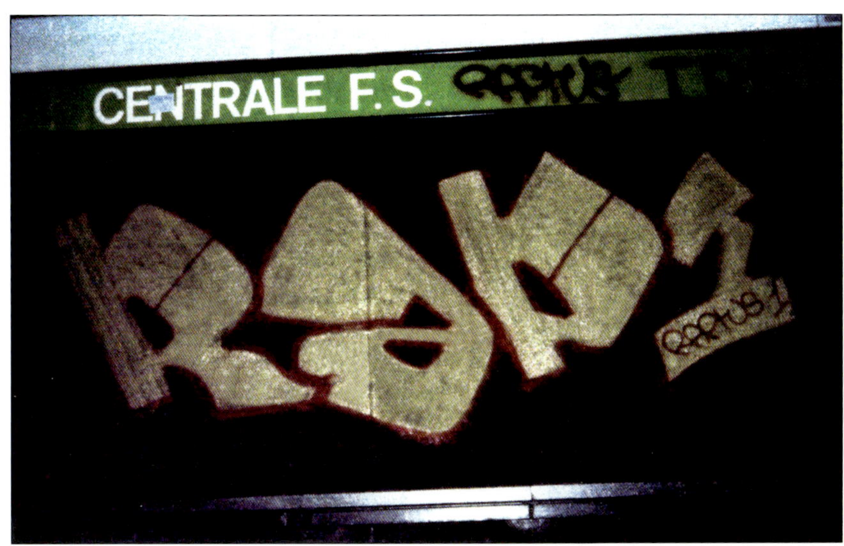

MM2 Centrale FS - 1991

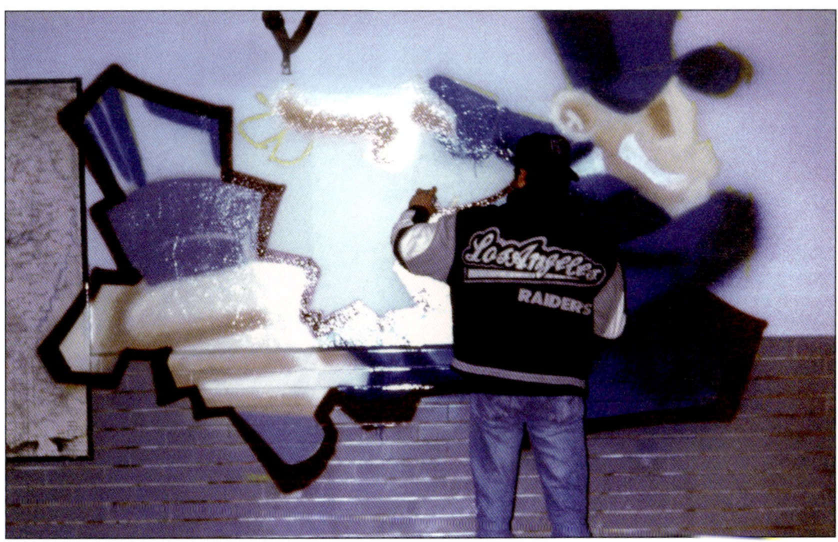

MM2 Cernusco SN - 1991

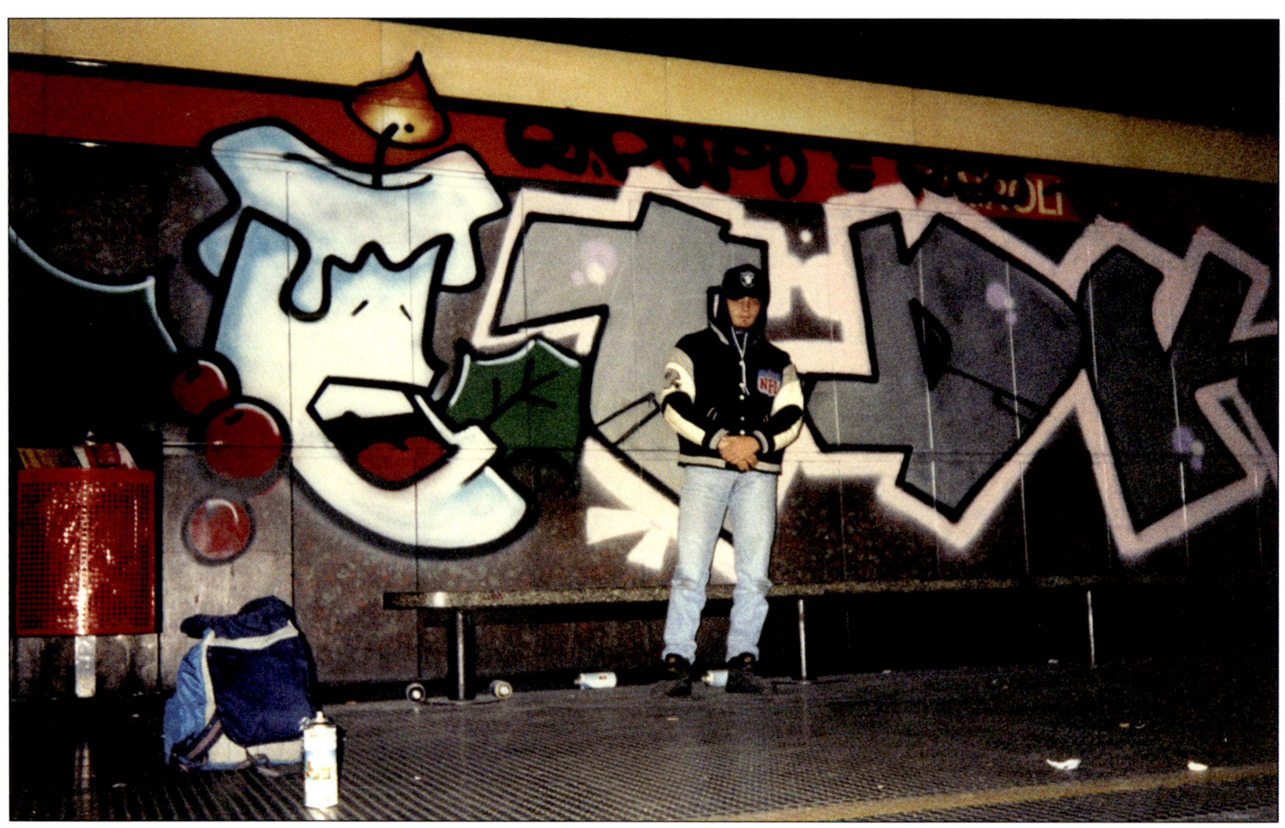

MM1 Cairoli - 1992

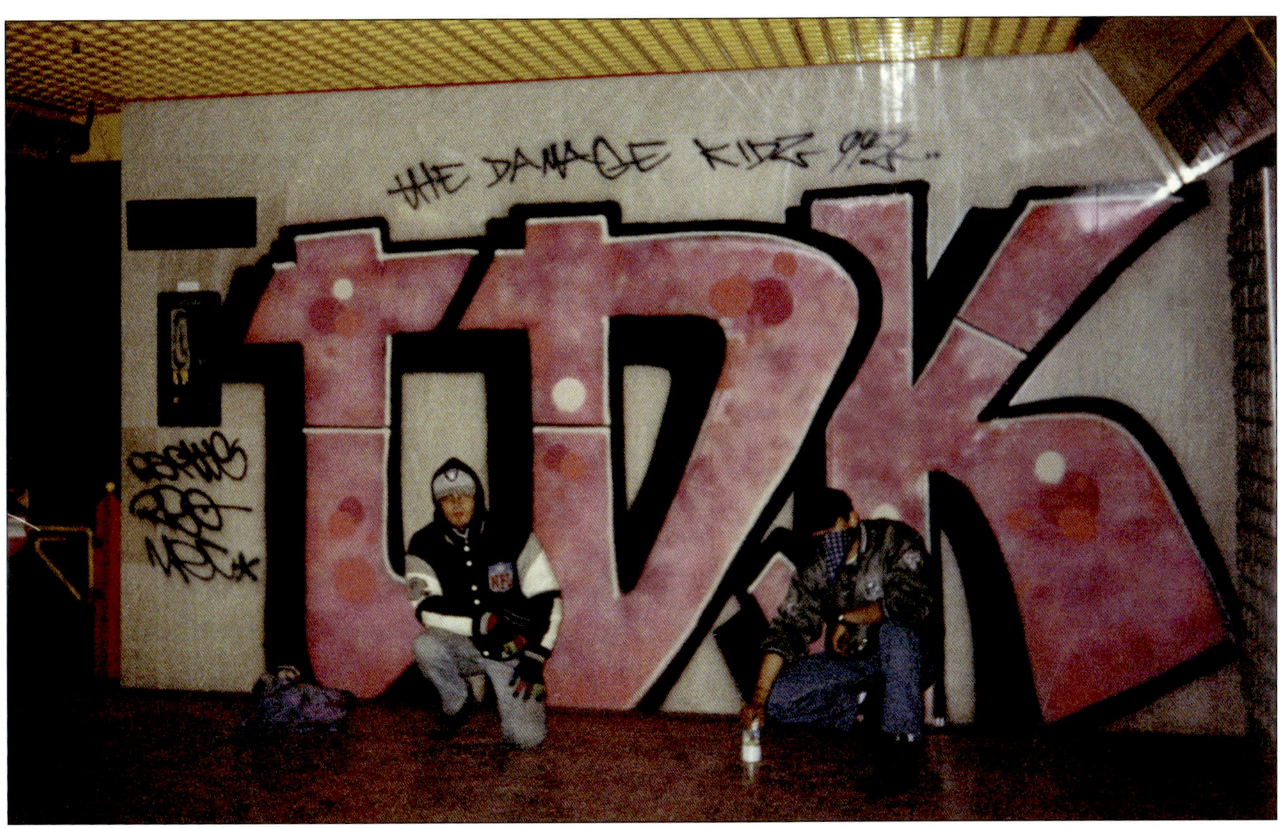

MM3 Crocetta - 1992

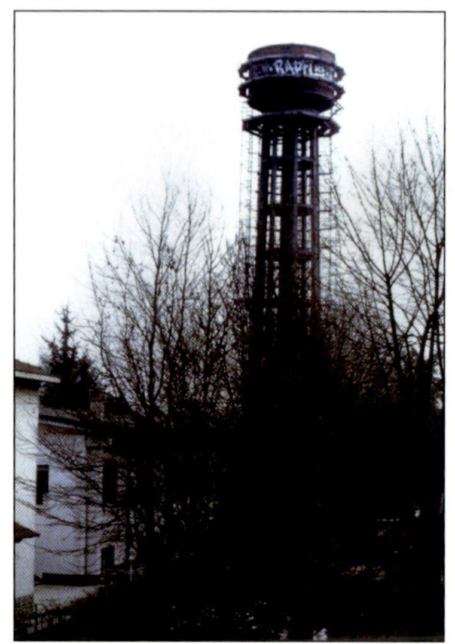

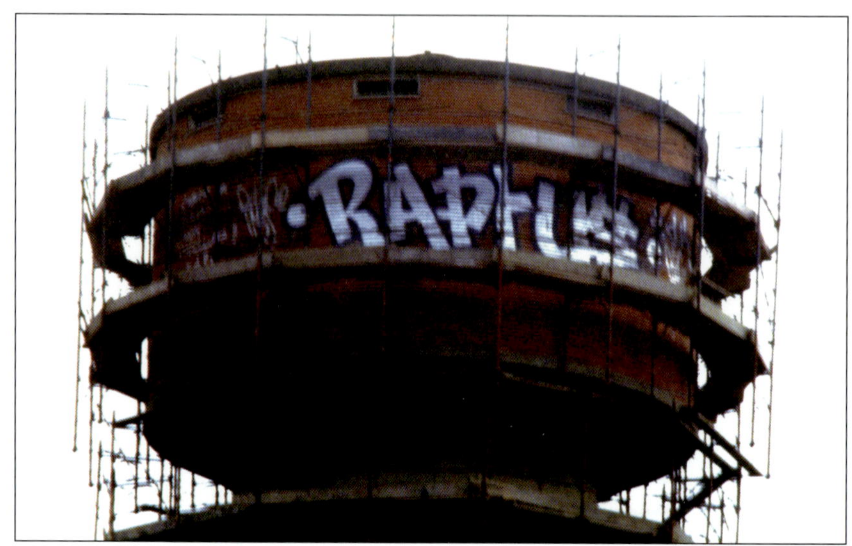

96 ft. high Water tank - 1990

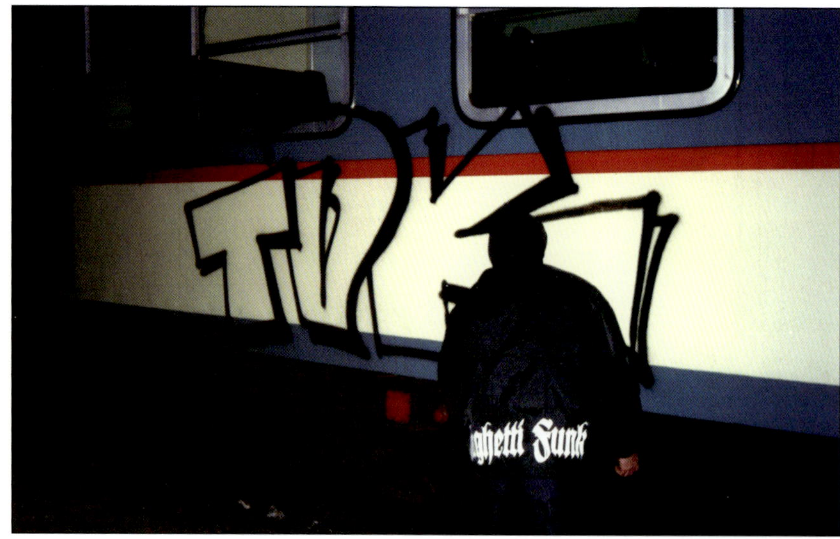

FS Train - 1993

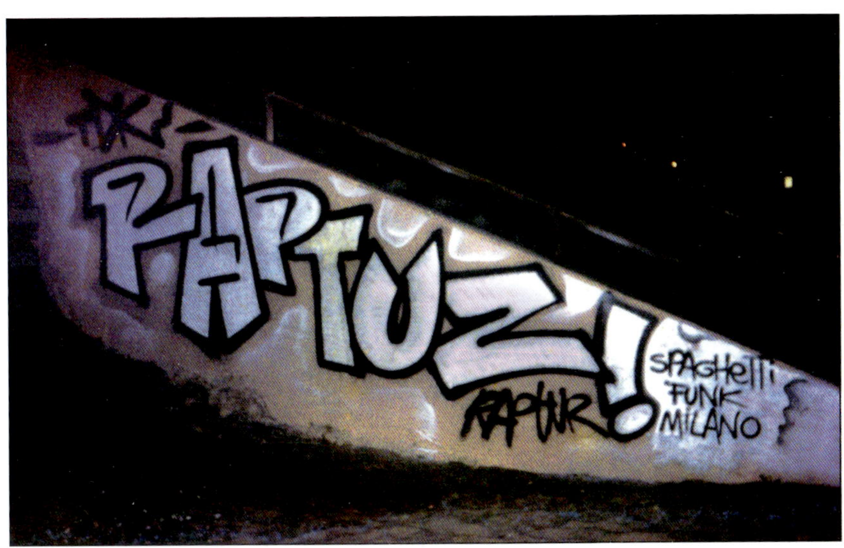

Hungtington Beach, CA boardwalk - 1994

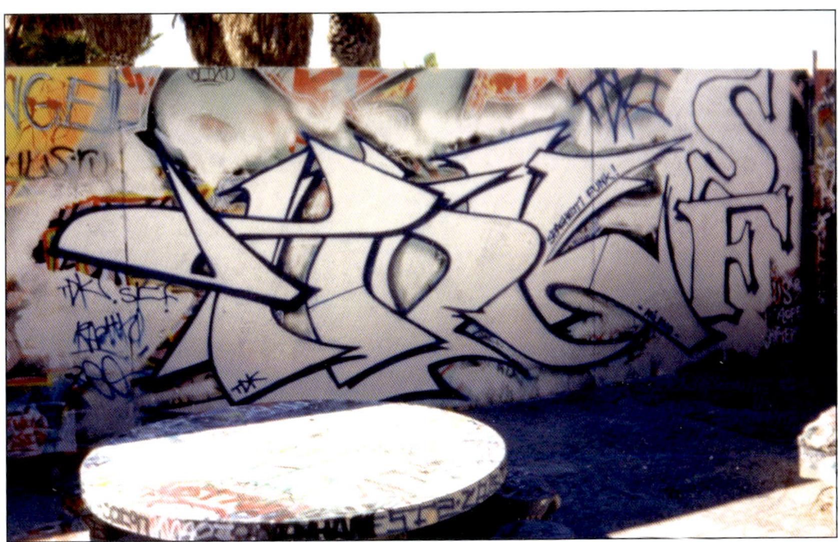

Venice Beach, CA - 1995

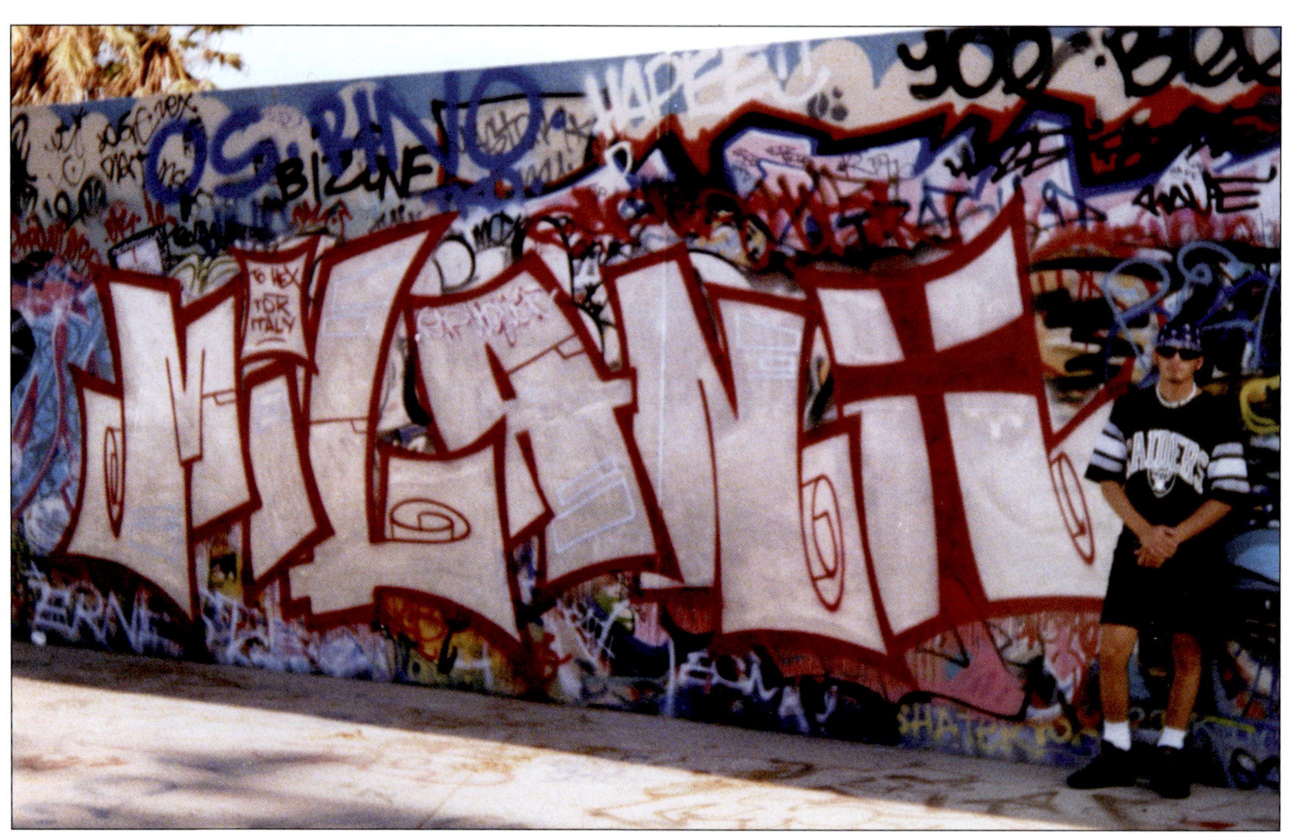

Venice Beach, CA - 1991

ORANGE POLICE DEPARTMENT
ARREST REPORT

PAGE 1 OF

DR# R99-01-0741

OCJ - BOOKING NO.	ARREST DATE	ARREST TIME	ARREST NO.	EVENT NO.
	01-17-99	2320		

ARREST LOCATION	RD#	OFFENSE LOCATION	RD#
CHAPMAN / HEWES	44N	— SAME —	44N

LAST NAME	FIRST NAME	MIDDLE NAME	D.O.B.
MURATORE	LUIGI	MARIA	04-30-68

AKA:	P.O.B.
"RAPTUS"	ITALY

ADDRESS:	CITY	STATE	ZIP CODE	TELEPHONE#
				(714) 960 - 3990

SEX:	RACE	HAIR	EYES	HGT	WGT	D.L.# /STATE	CII#
M	C	BLK	BRN	5-05	165	— NONE —	

OCCUPATION	CLOTHING WORN
ARTIST	BLU JNS / YELLOW T-SHIRT

IN CUSTODY PROPERTY

	YES	NO		YES	NO	DESCRIPTION
[ ] Wallet	✓		[ ] Rings		✓	
[ ] Purse		✓	[ ] Chains		✓	
[ ] Key	1		[ ] Watch		✓	
[ ] Checkbook		✓	[ ] Jewelry		✓	
[ ] Shoes	2		[ ] Miscellaneous			BLK BELT

[ ] Currency:	$ 50.00
[ ] Coins:	$ 0

Bulk Property Disposition:

RELEASED TO MURATORE

ARRESTEE'S SIGNATURE	SEARCH OFFICER	RELEASING OFFICER
(signature)	SCHAFR 1080	SCHAFR 1080

Arrest report, Orange CA - 1999

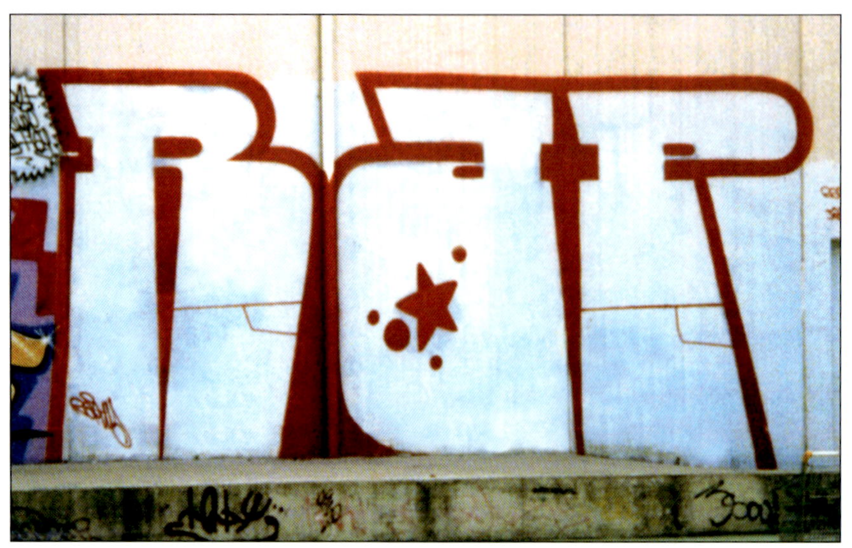

Rodano (MI) - 1991

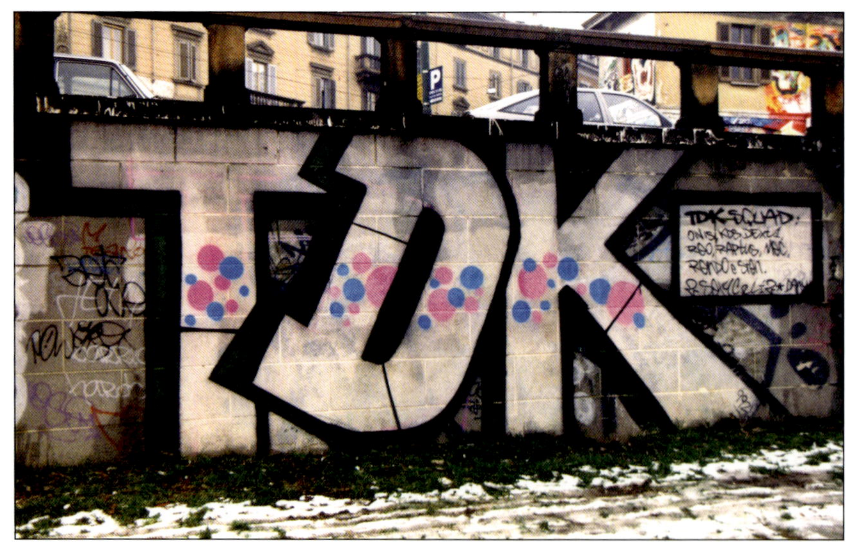

Milan, darsena - 1992

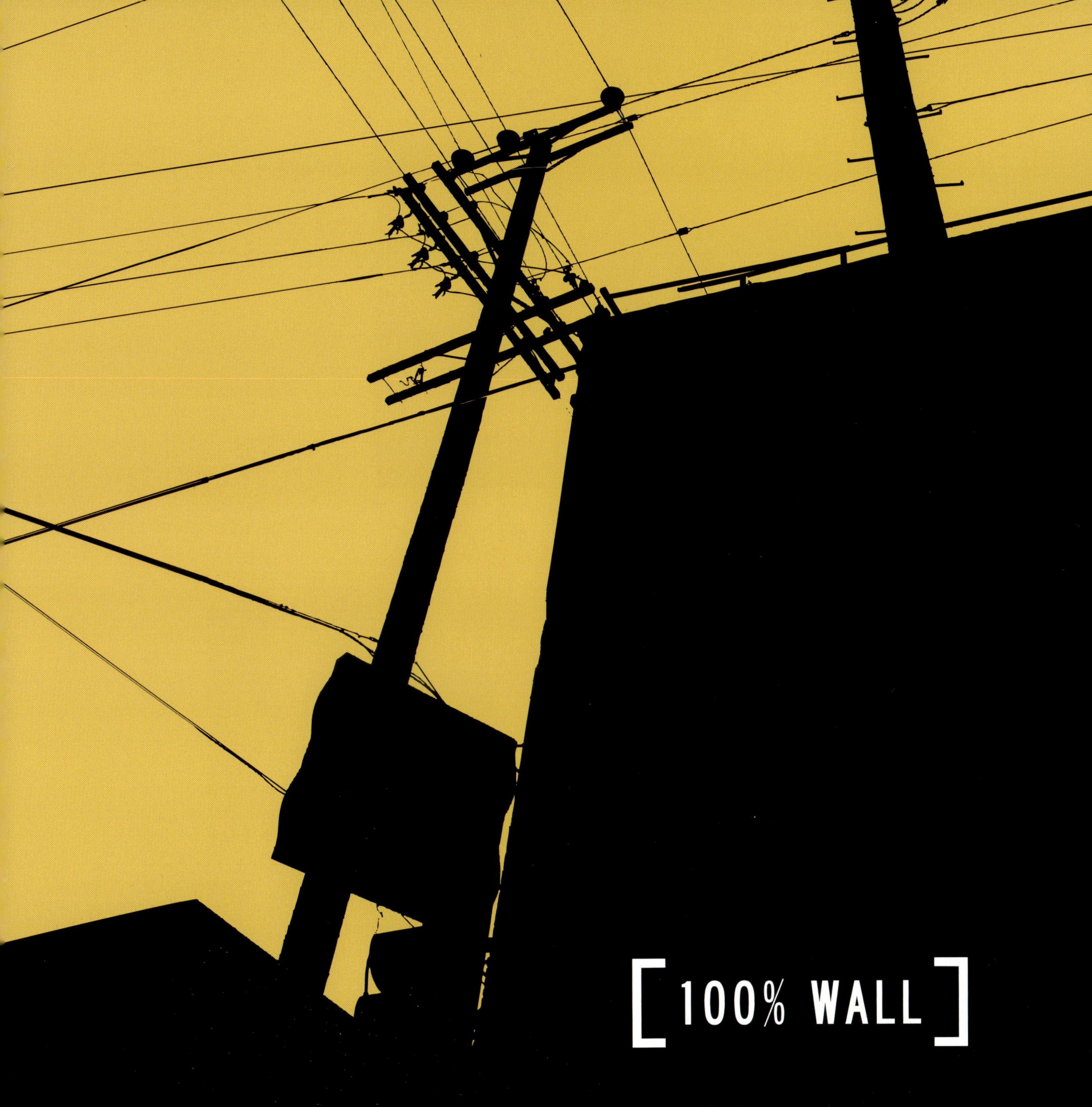

[100% WALL]

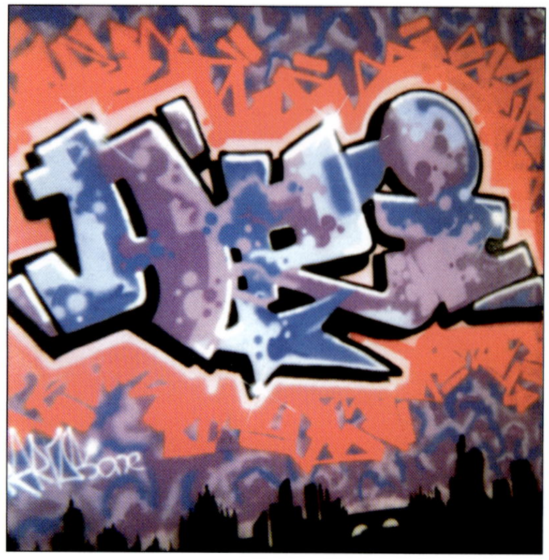

Ari - 1988

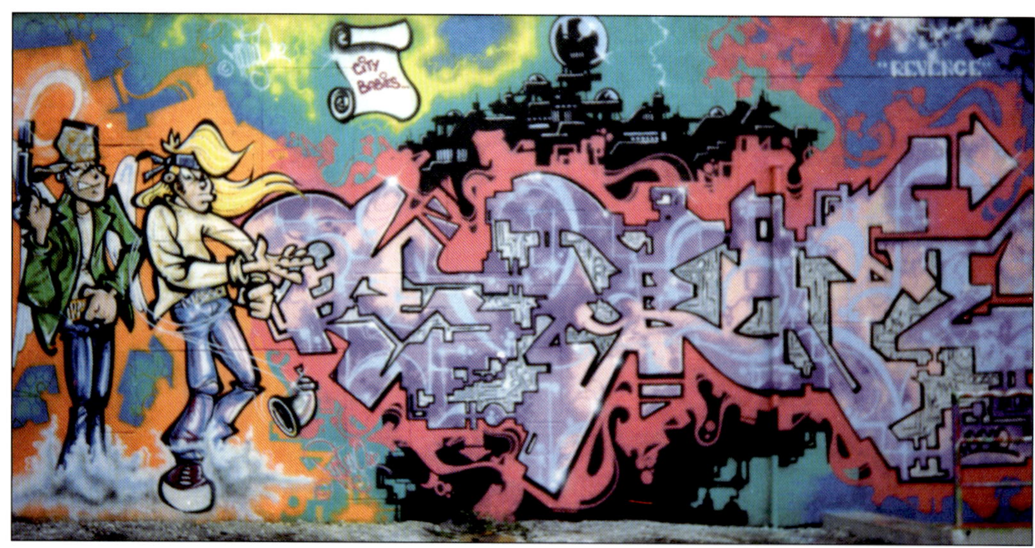

Revenge with Asso - 1989

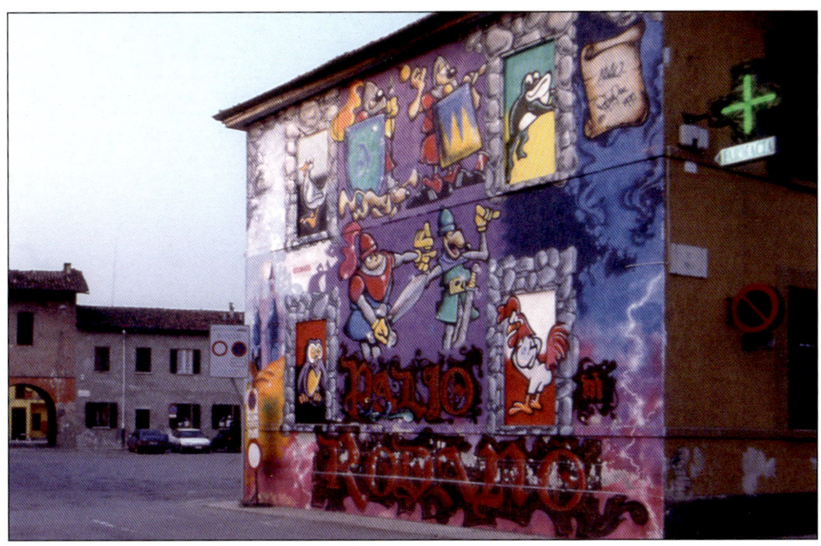

Palio di Rodano - 1990

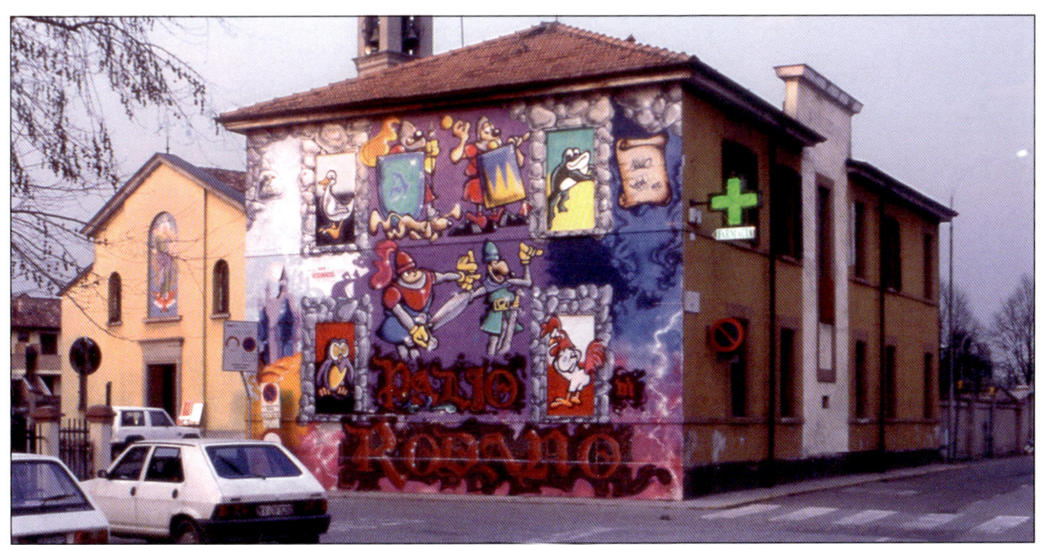

Palio di Rodano - 1990

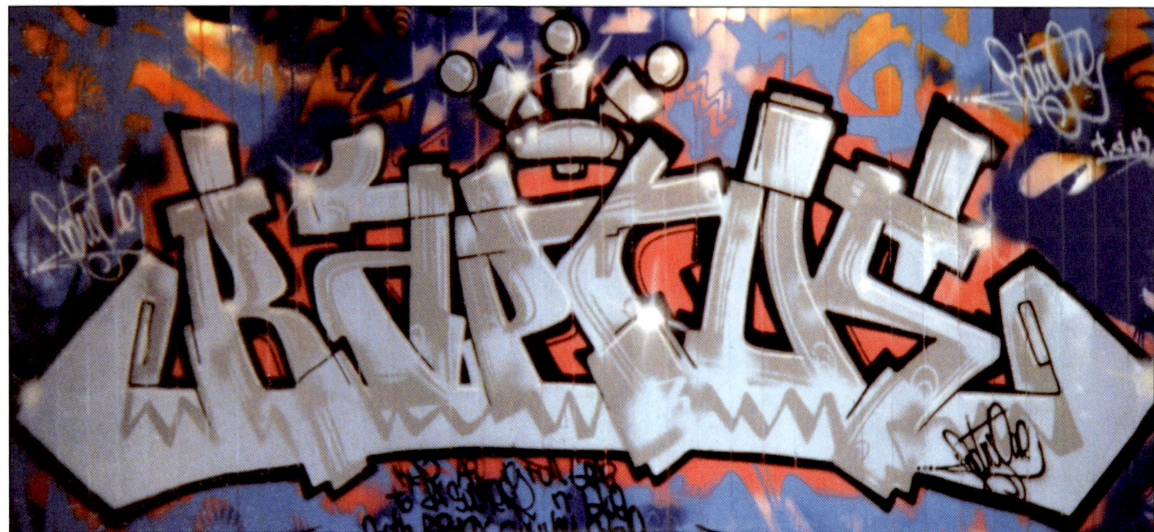

Raptus - 1990

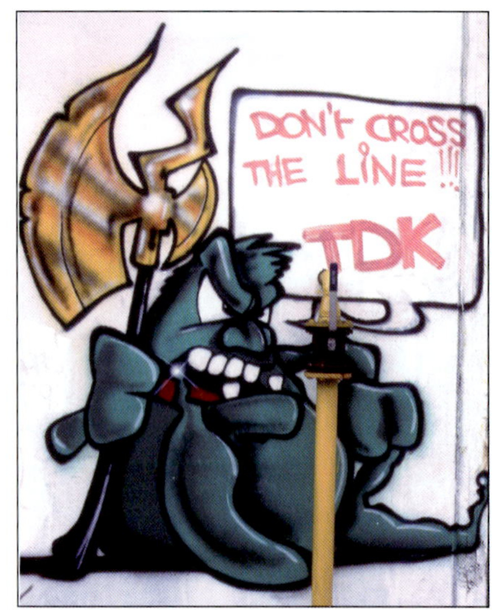

Character - 1990

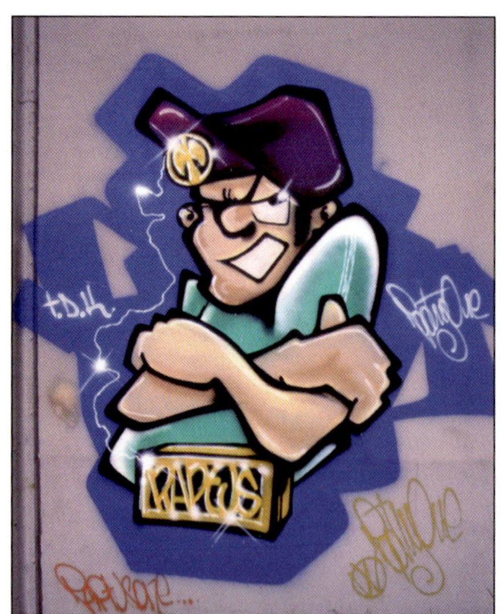

Character - 1990

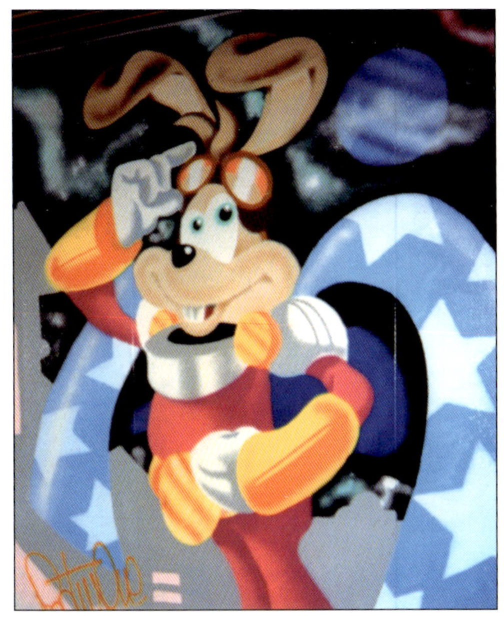

Character - 1990

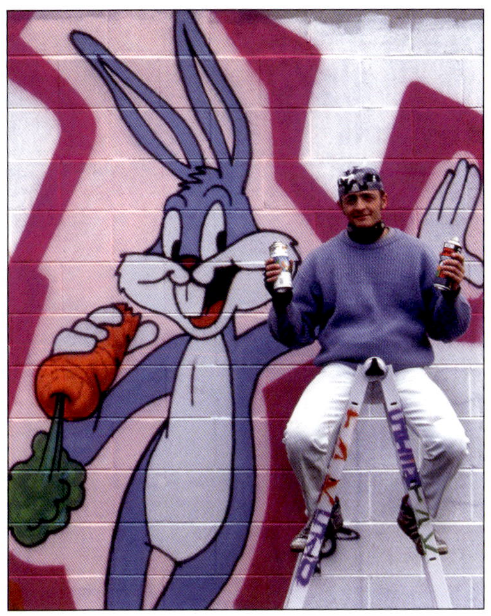

Character - 1990

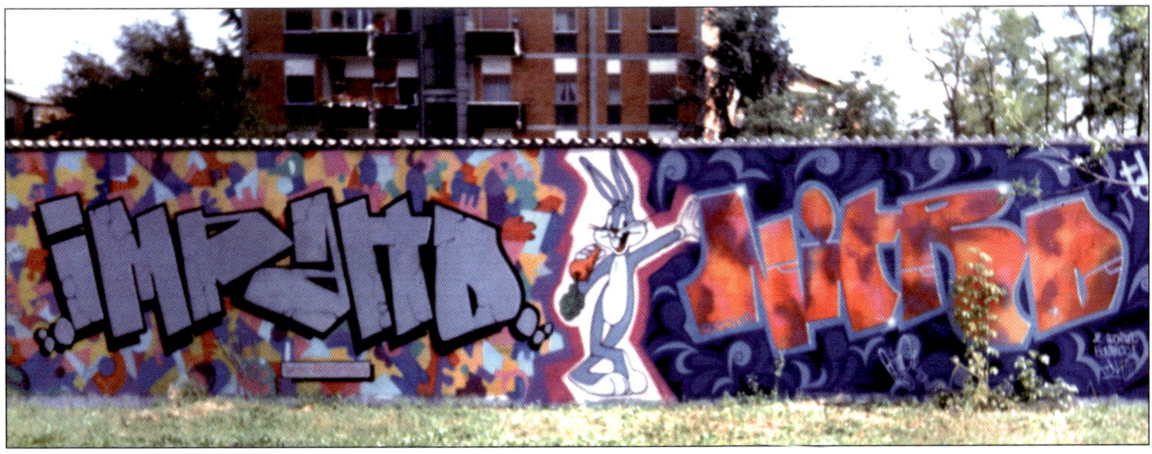

Impatto nitro - 1990

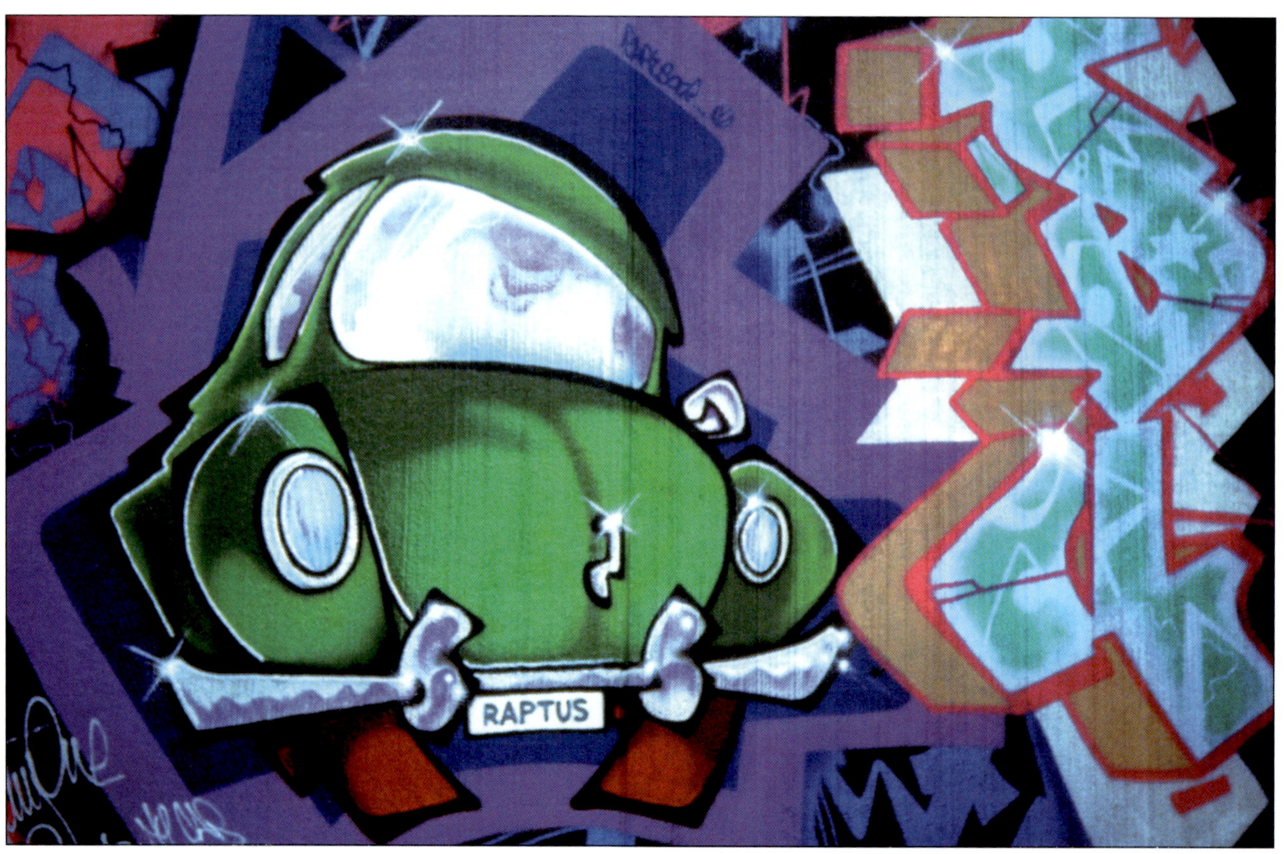

Raptuz beetle - 1990

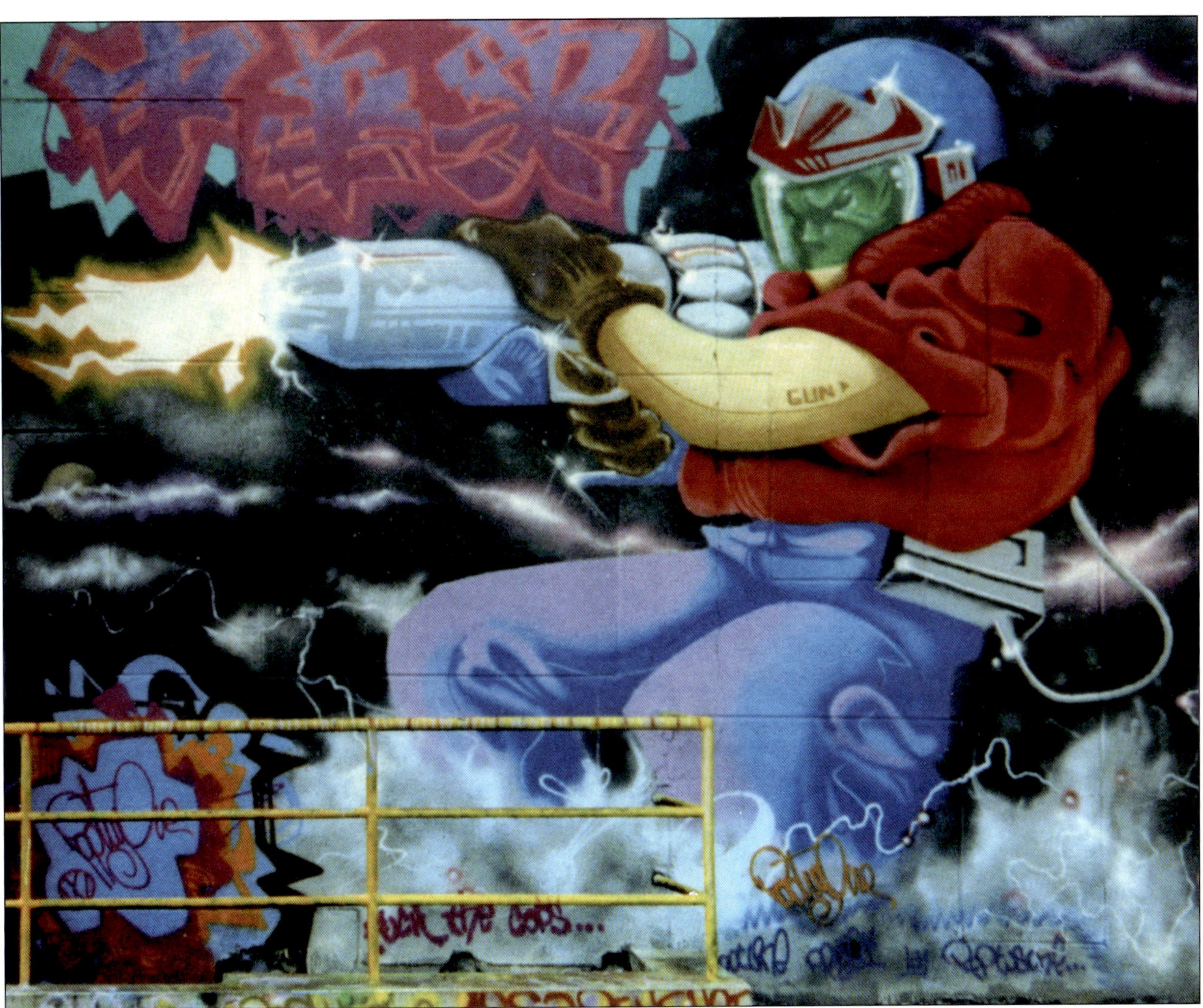

Character - 1990

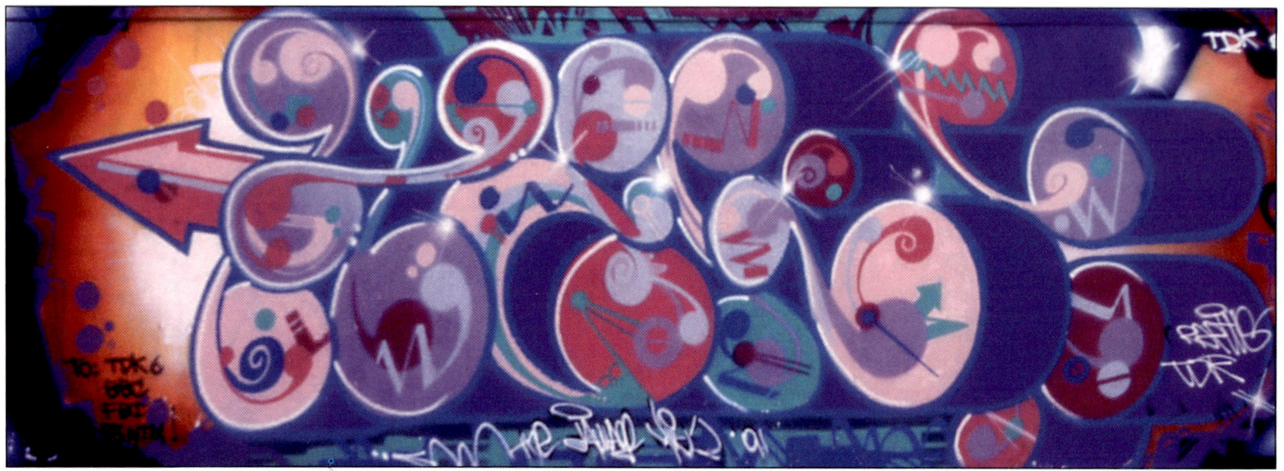

TDK - 1991

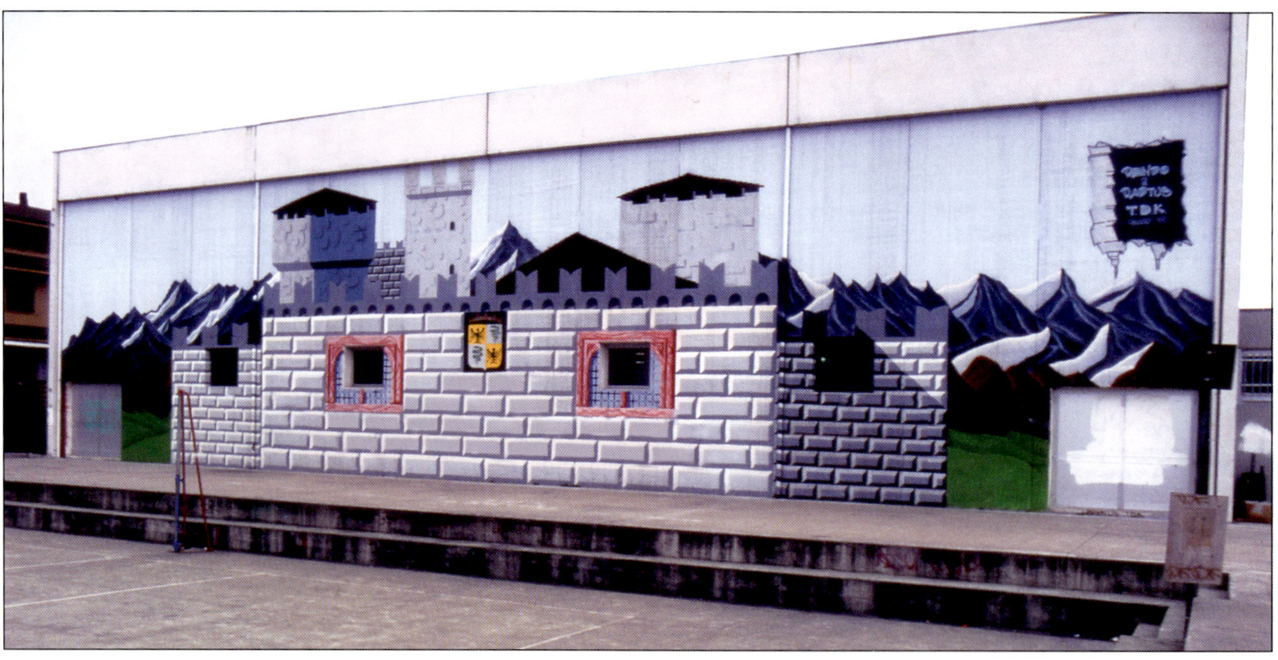

Palio di Rodano with Rendo - 1991

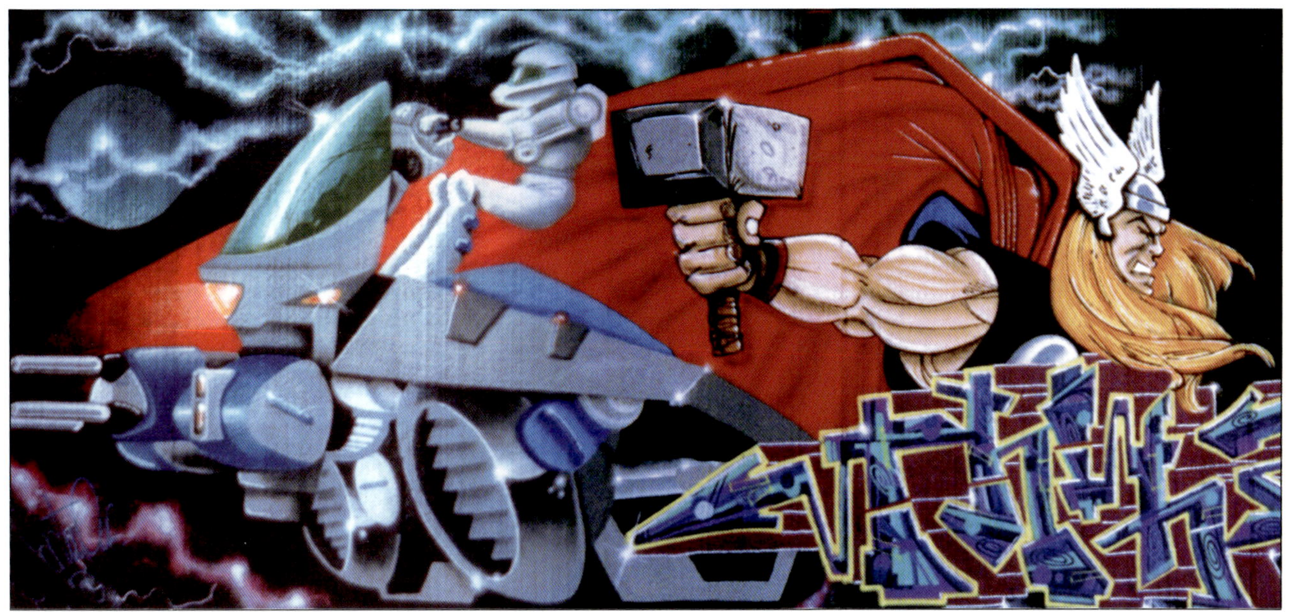

Space thunder - 1991

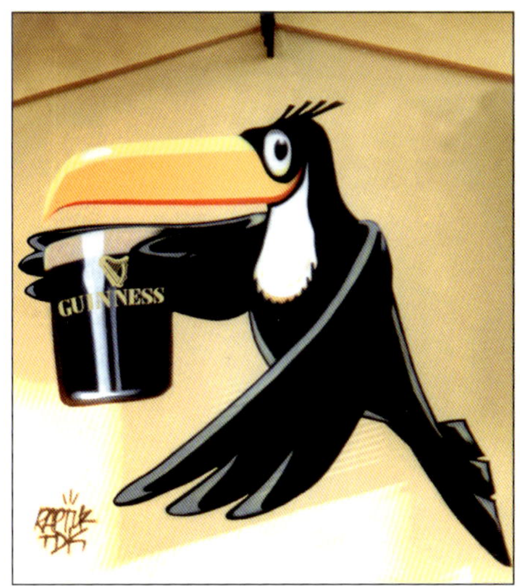

Character - 1991

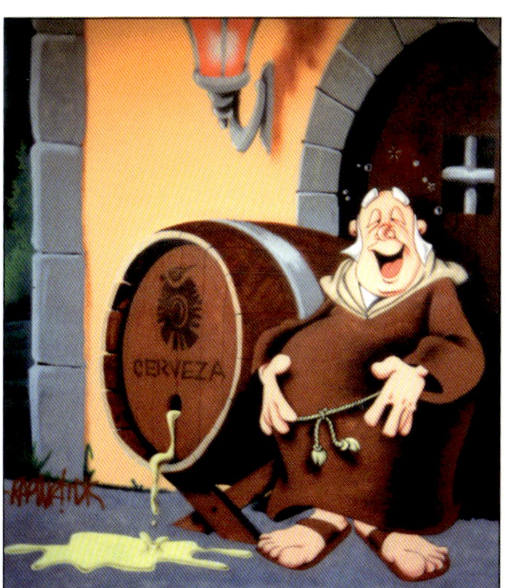

Character - 1991

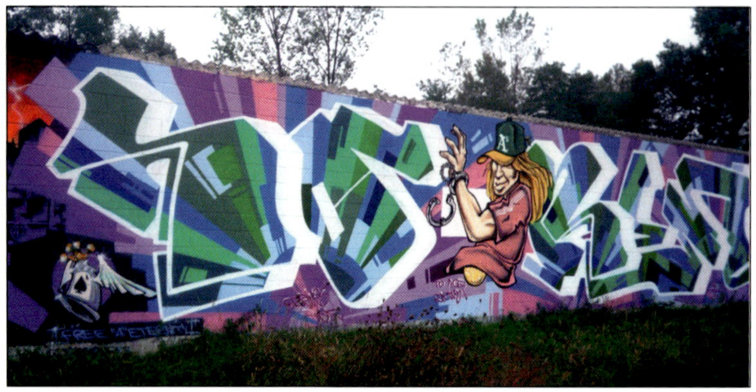

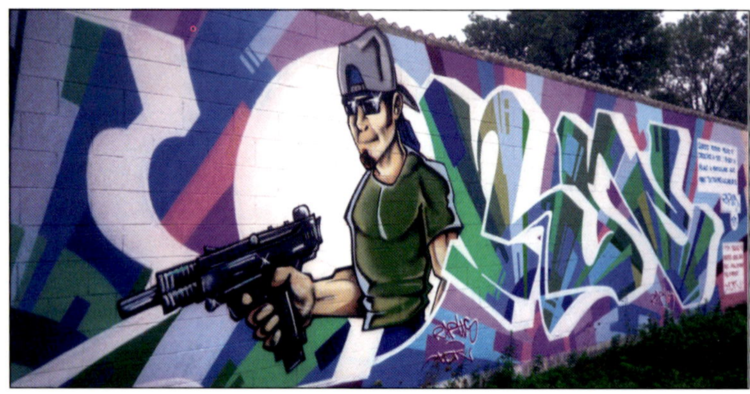

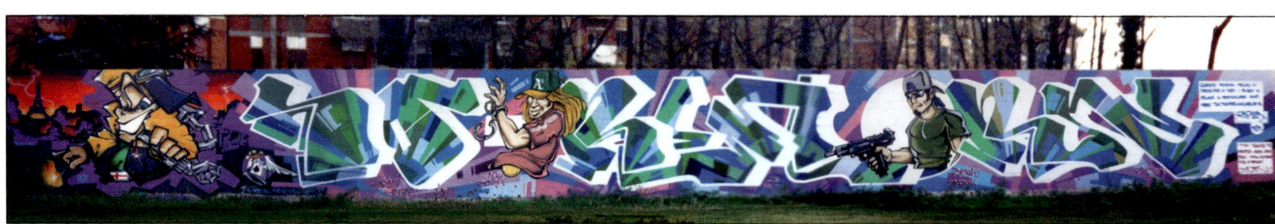

No Remorse - 1991

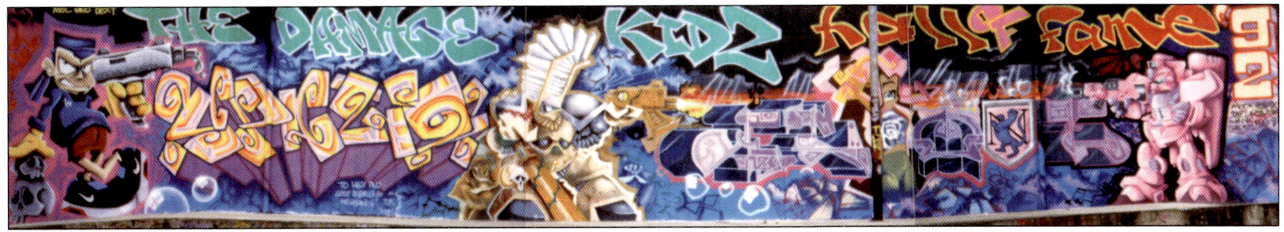

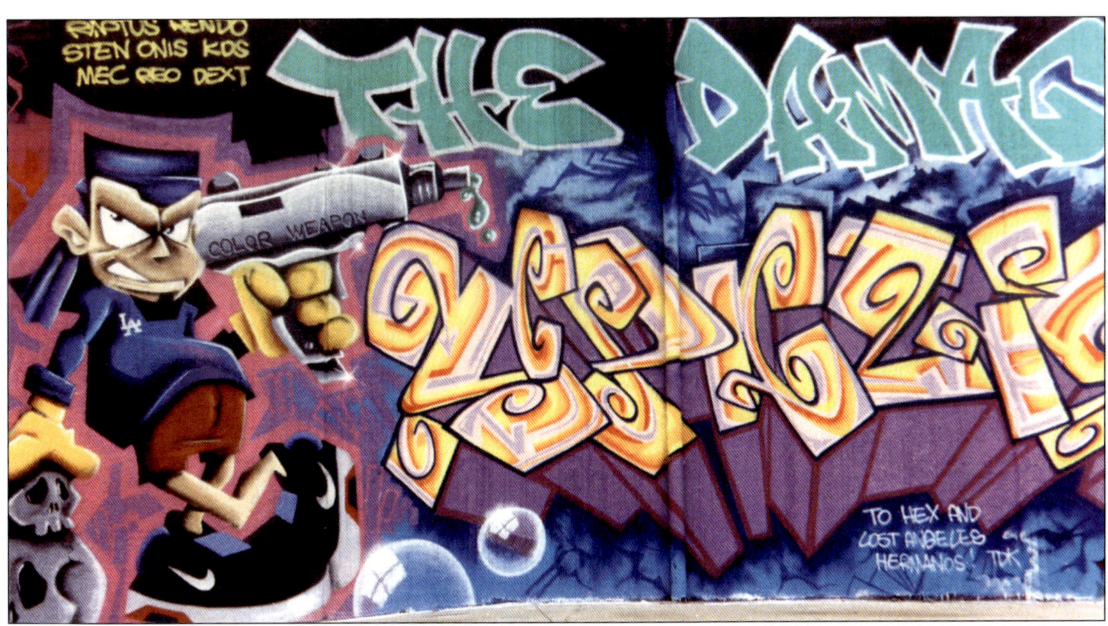

Spazio d'azione - 1992

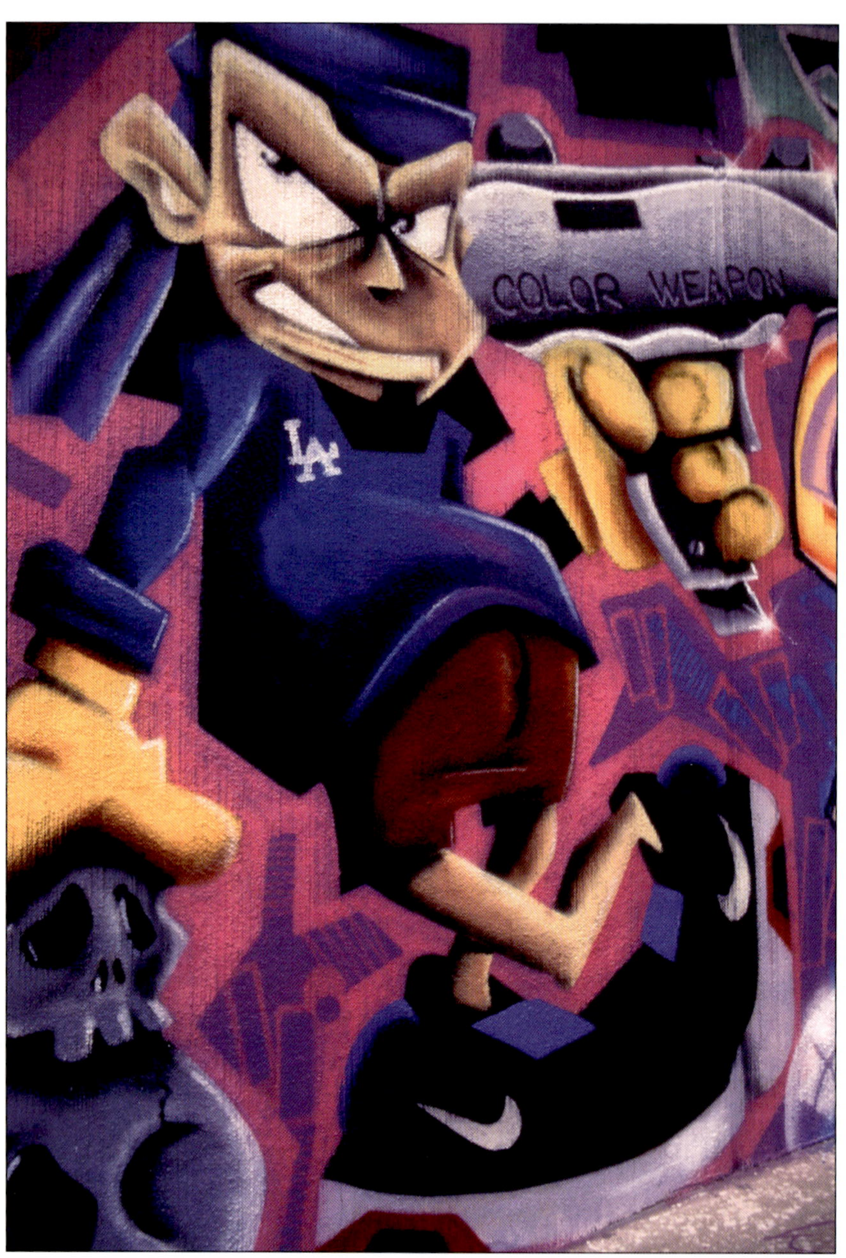

Color weapon - 1992

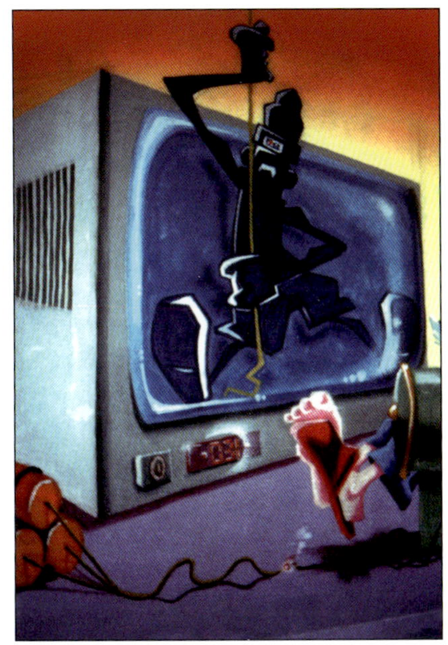

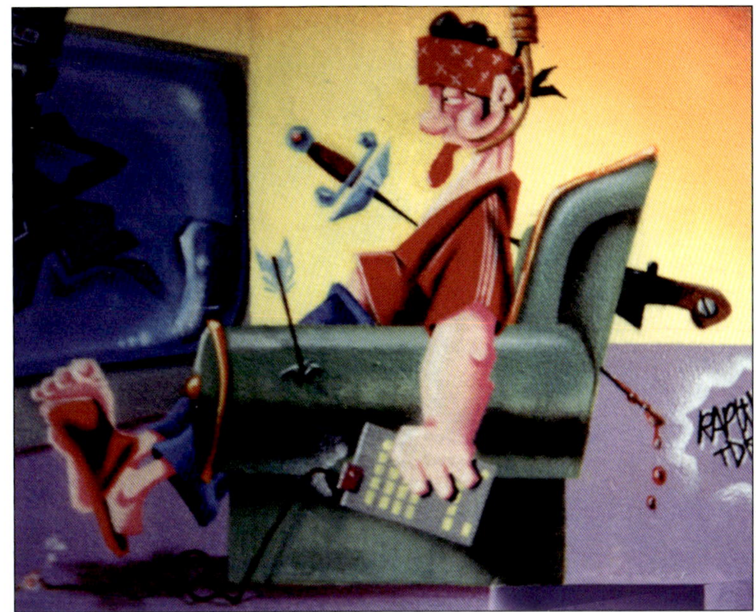

TV killer - 1993

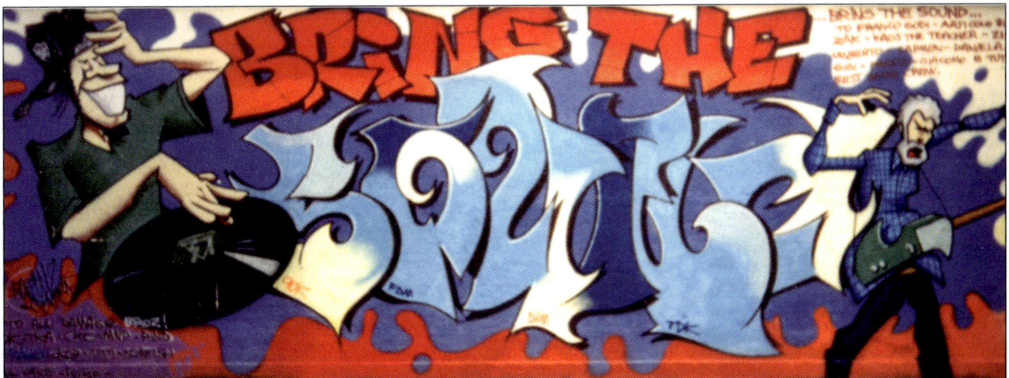

Bring the sound - 1993

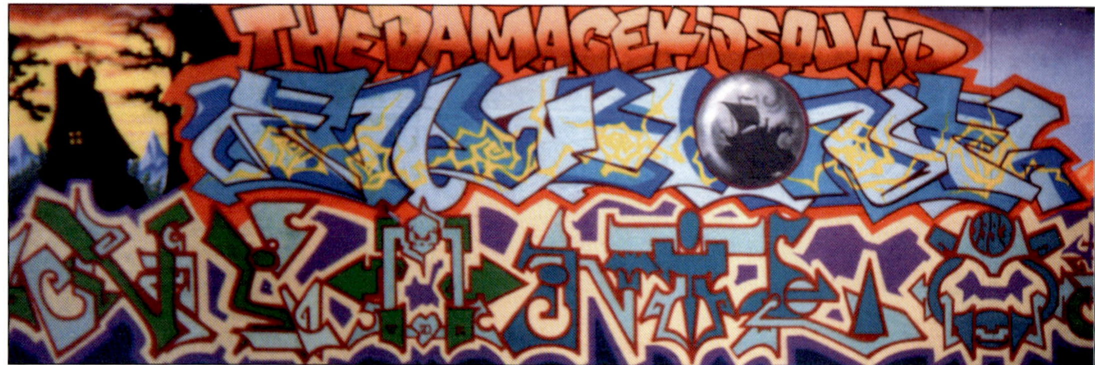

Evoluzione with Rendo - 1993

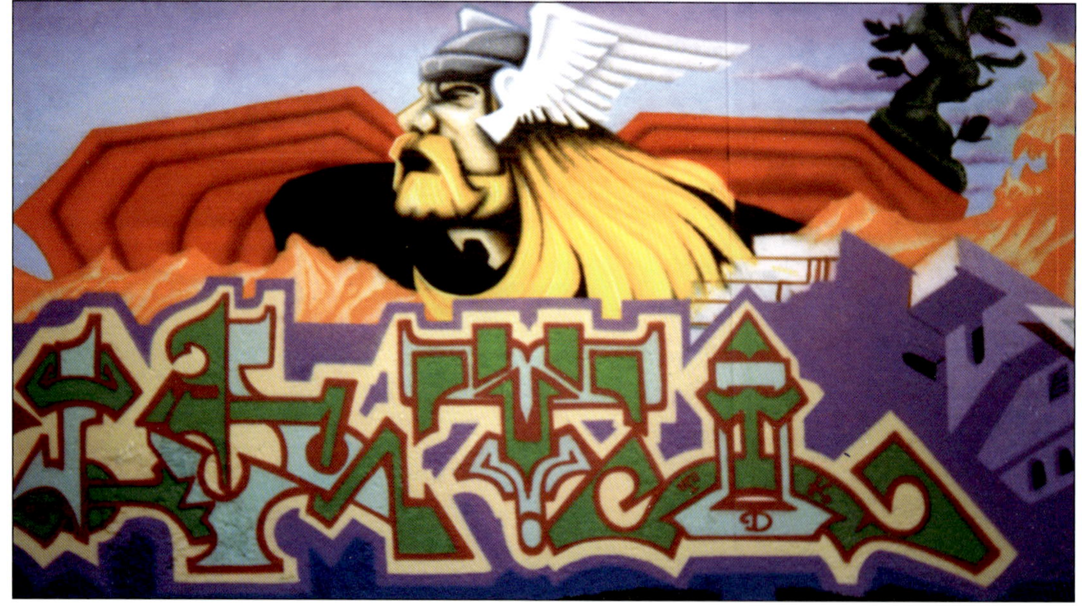

Evoluzione with Rendo - 1993

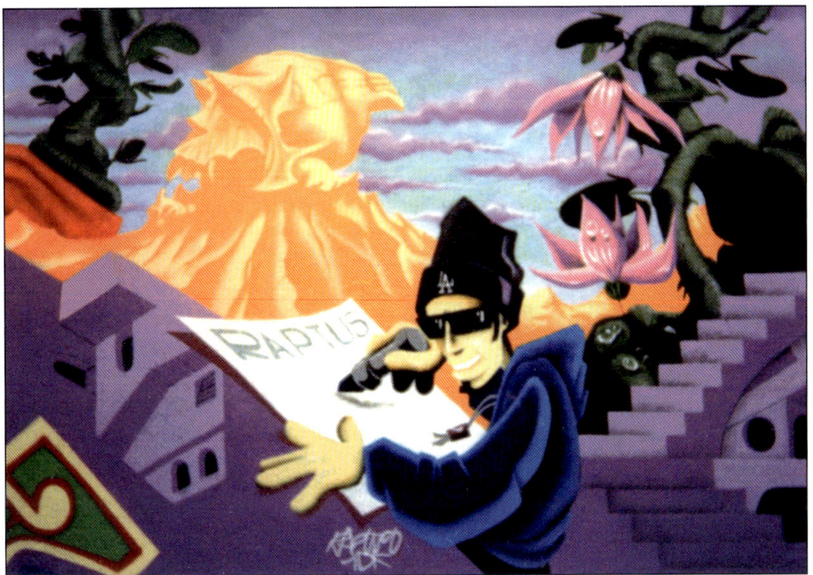

Evoluzione - 1993

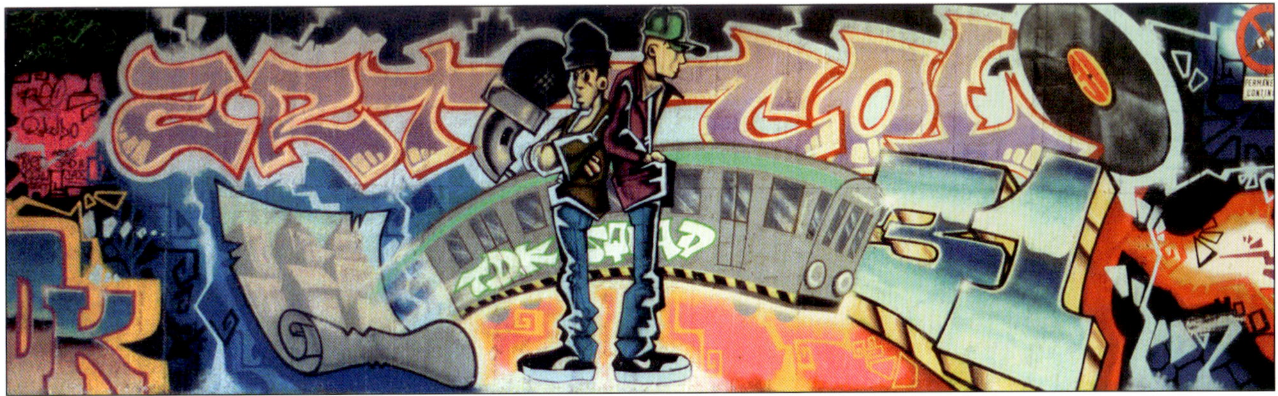

Articolo 31 with TDK crew - 1994

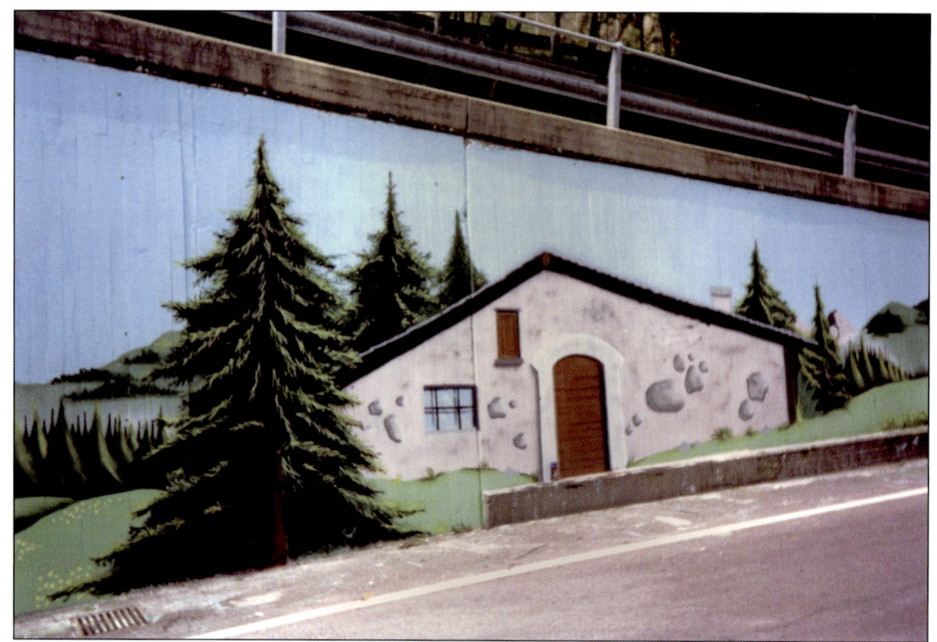

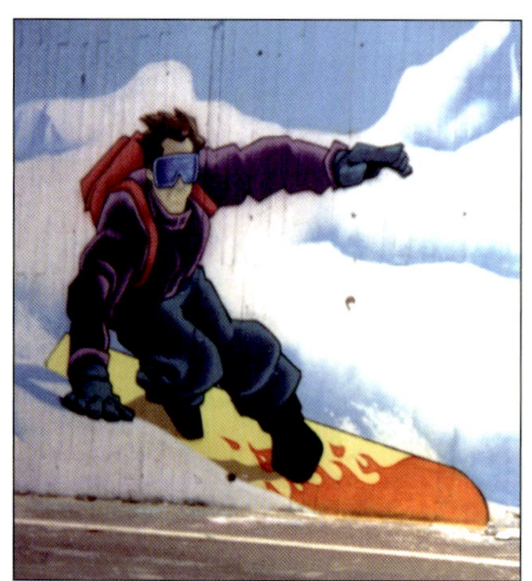

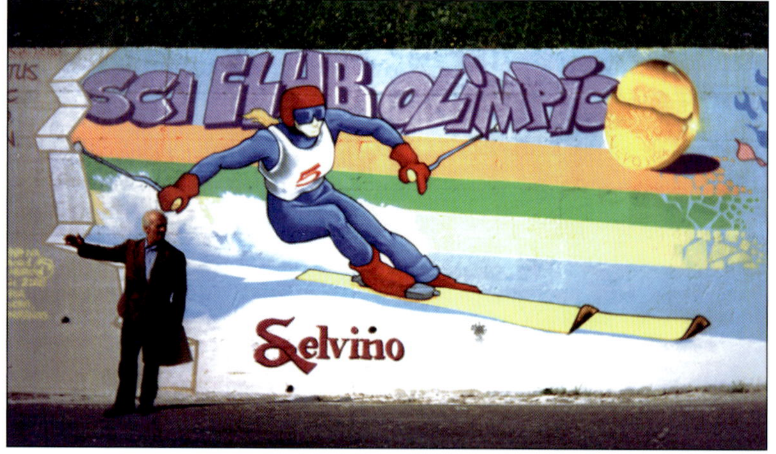

78° "Giro d'Italia" - 1994

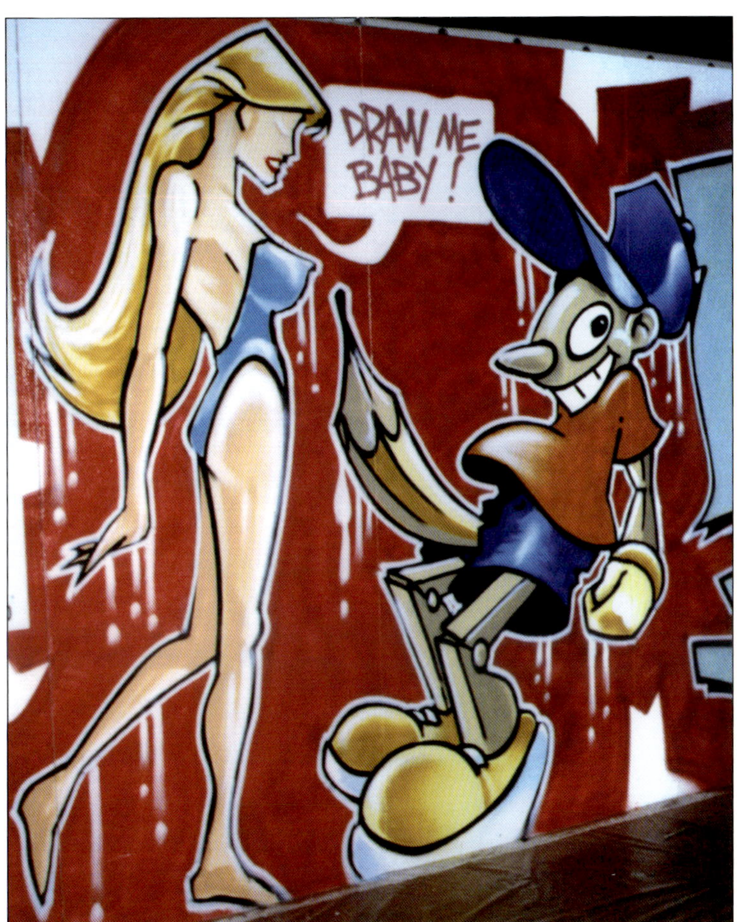

Draw me - 1995

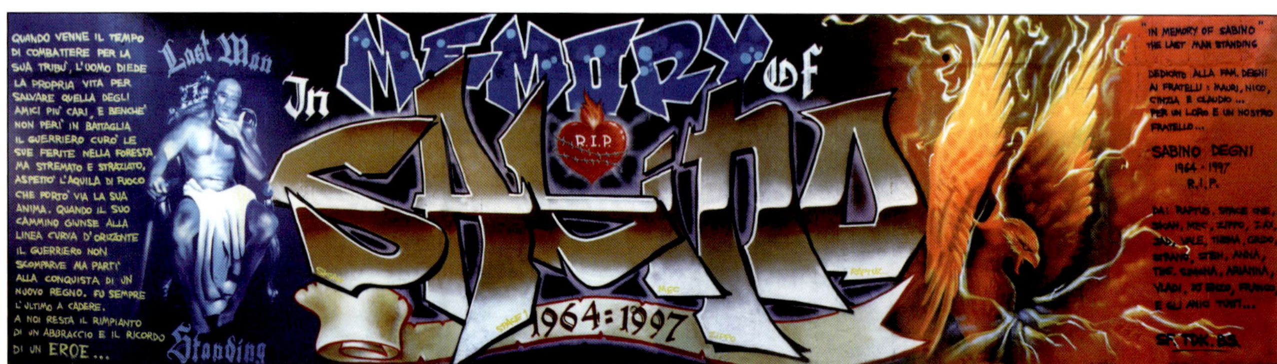

In memory of Sabino with Skah - 1997

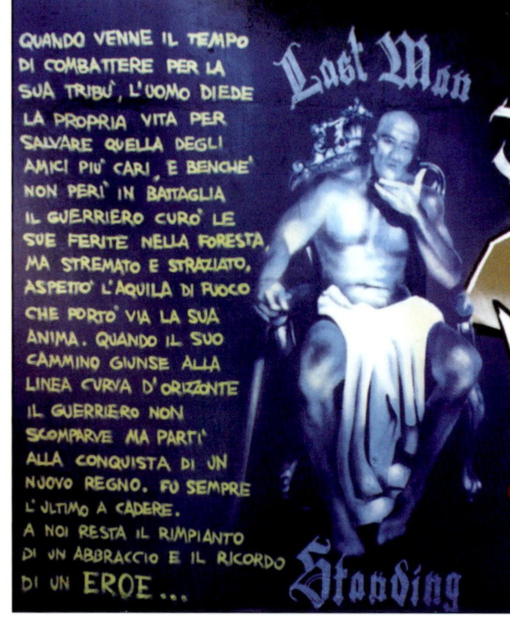

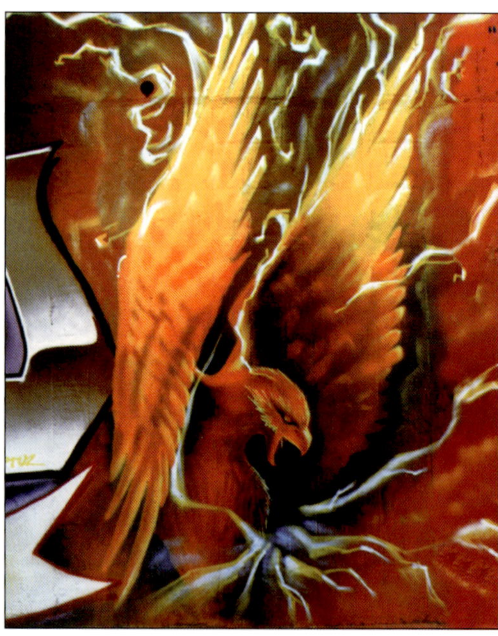

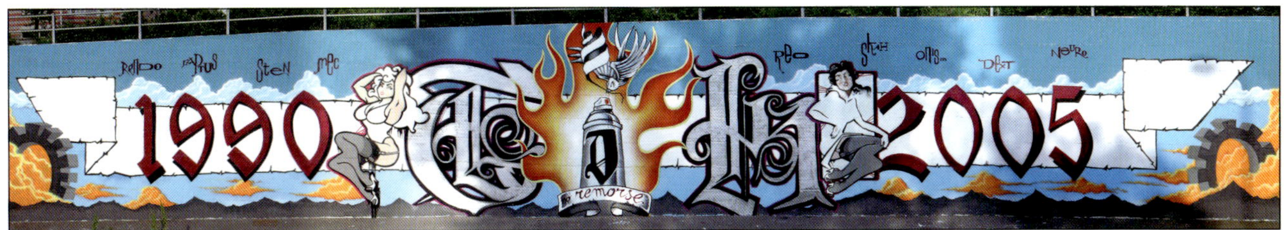

TDK 15th. anniversary with TDK crew - 2005

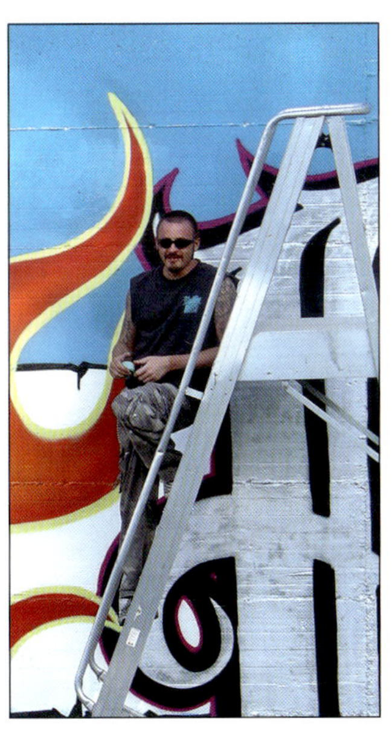

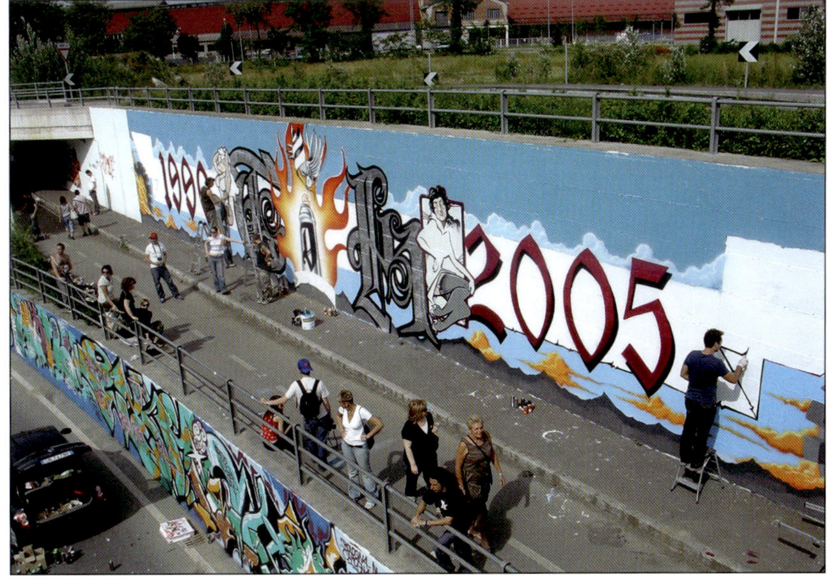

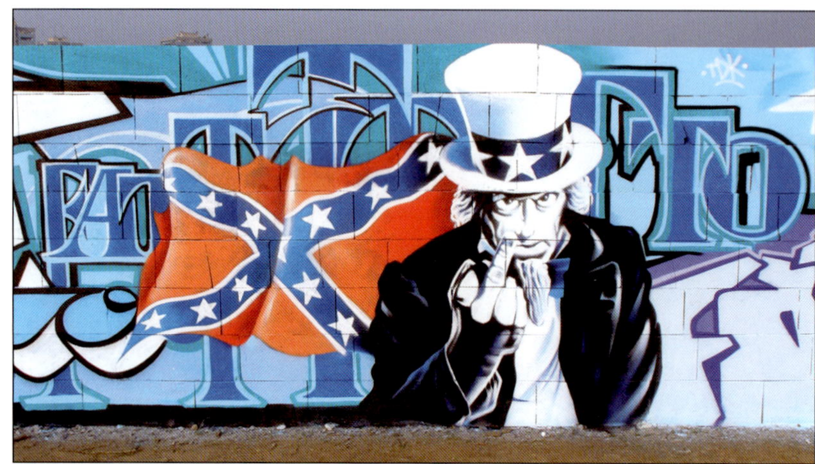

Uncle Sam - 2006

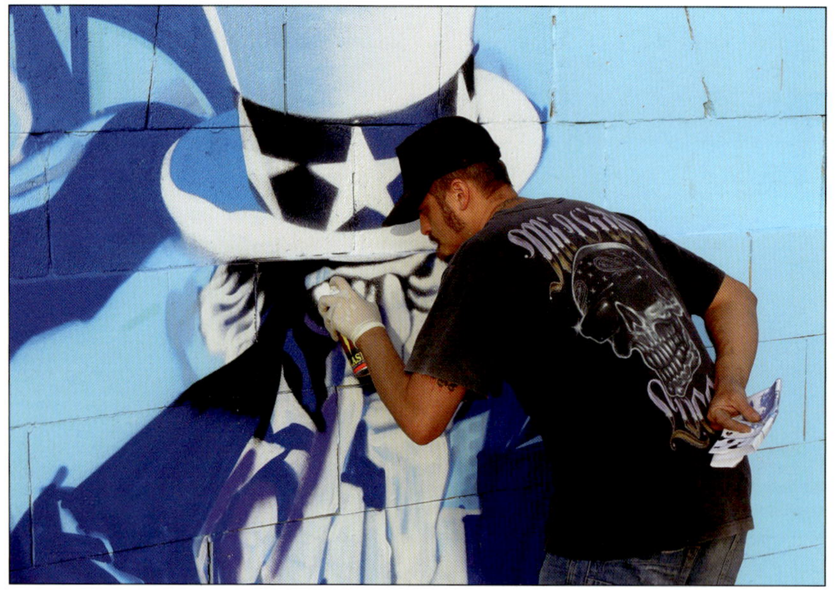

Uncle Sam work in progress - 2006

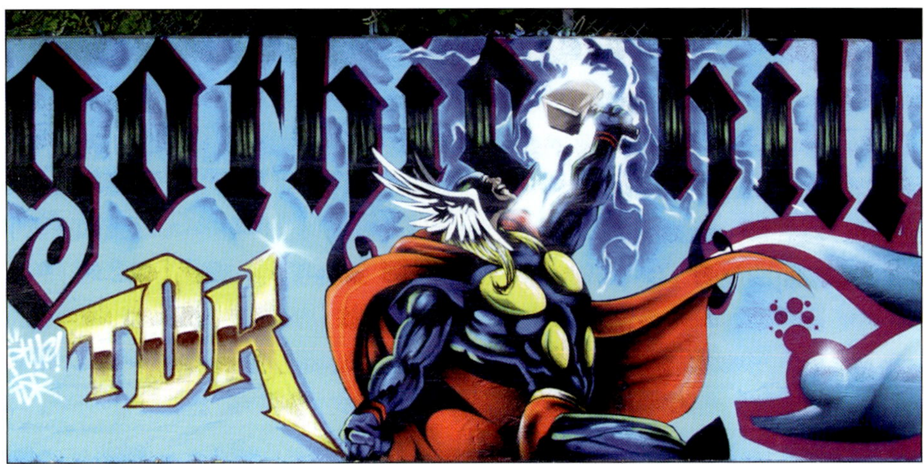

Gothic hill - 2006

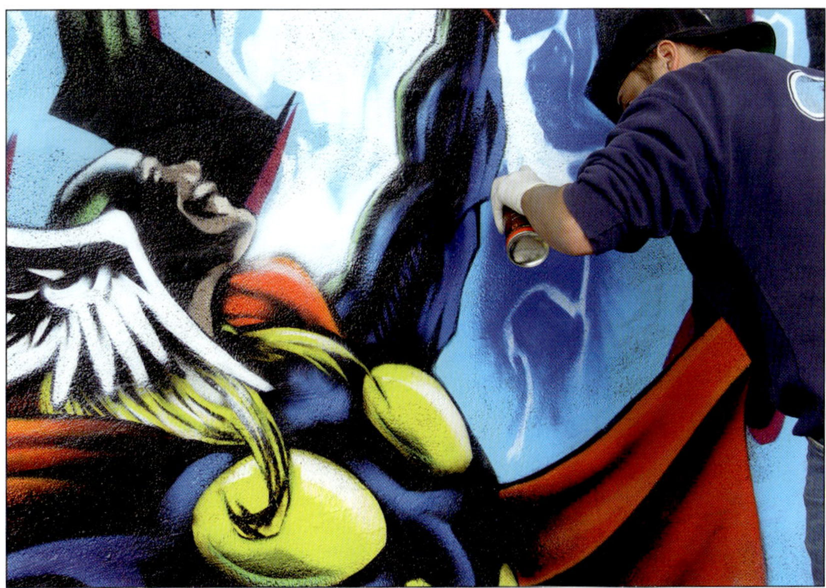

Gothic hill work in progress - 2006

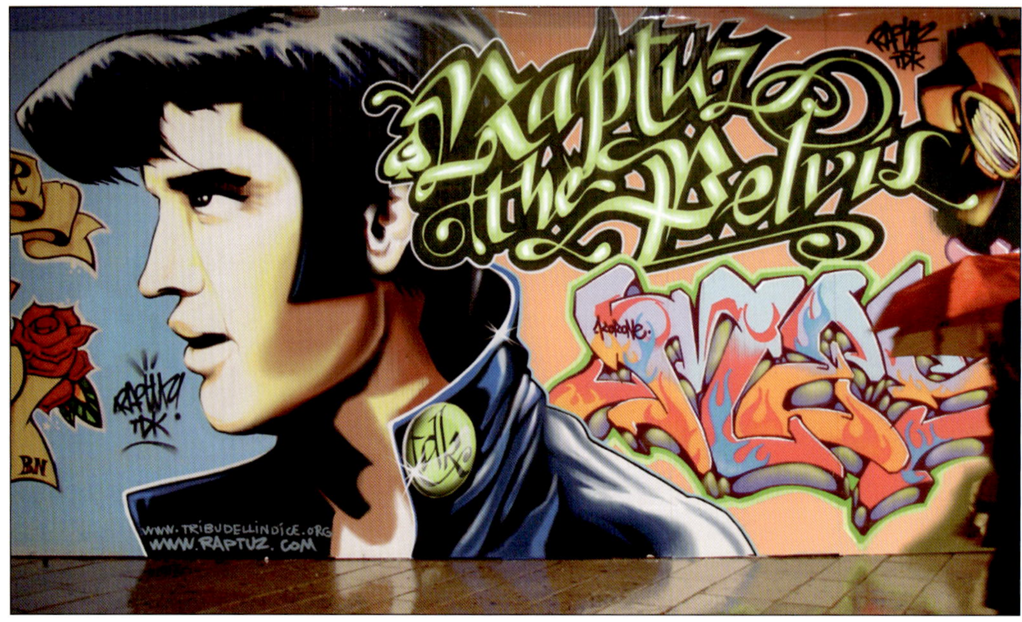

Raptuz the pelvis - 2006

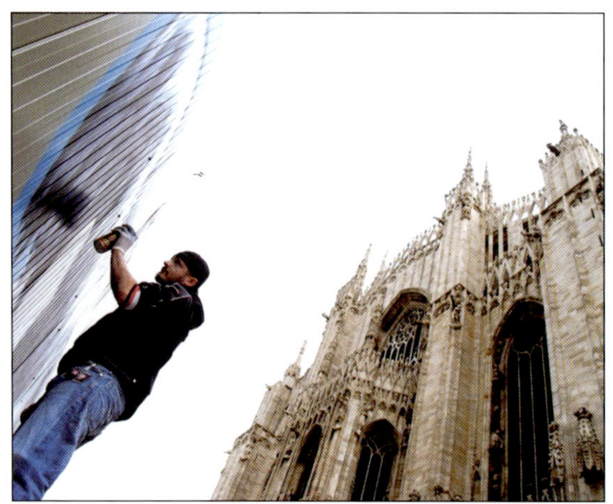

Milan Duomo writing session - 2006

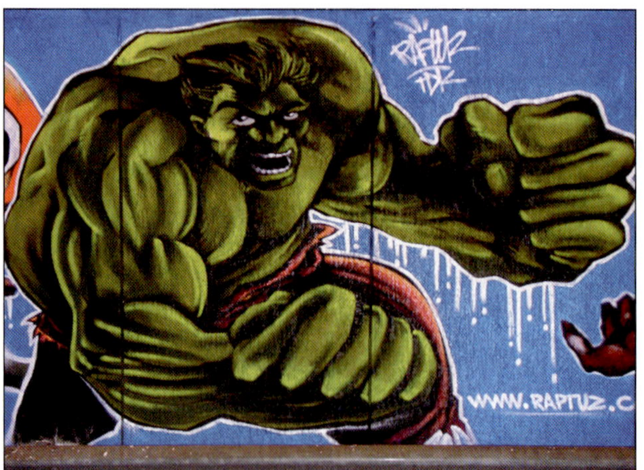

Hulk - 2006

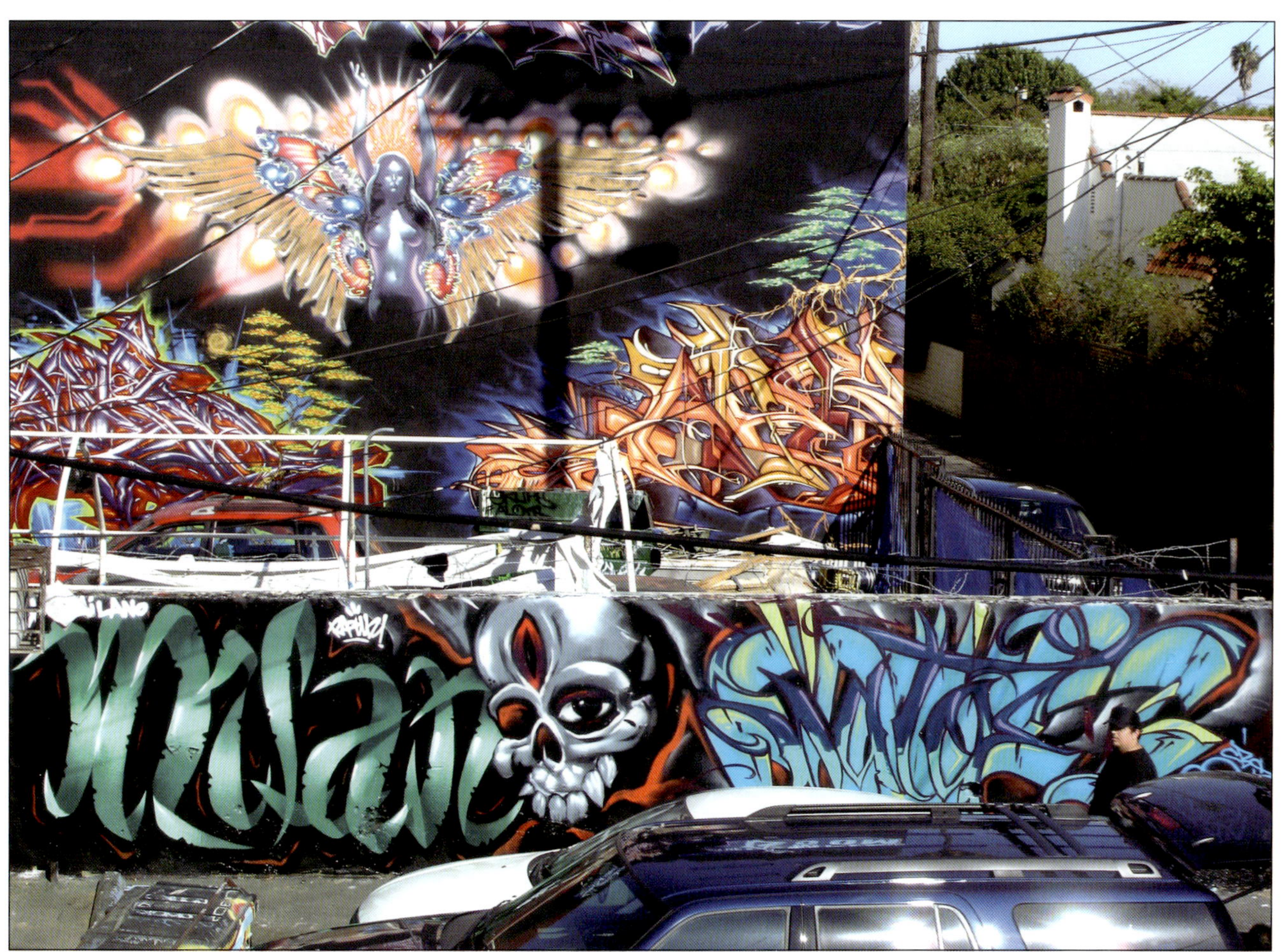

Milano with CBS crew Hollywood - 2006

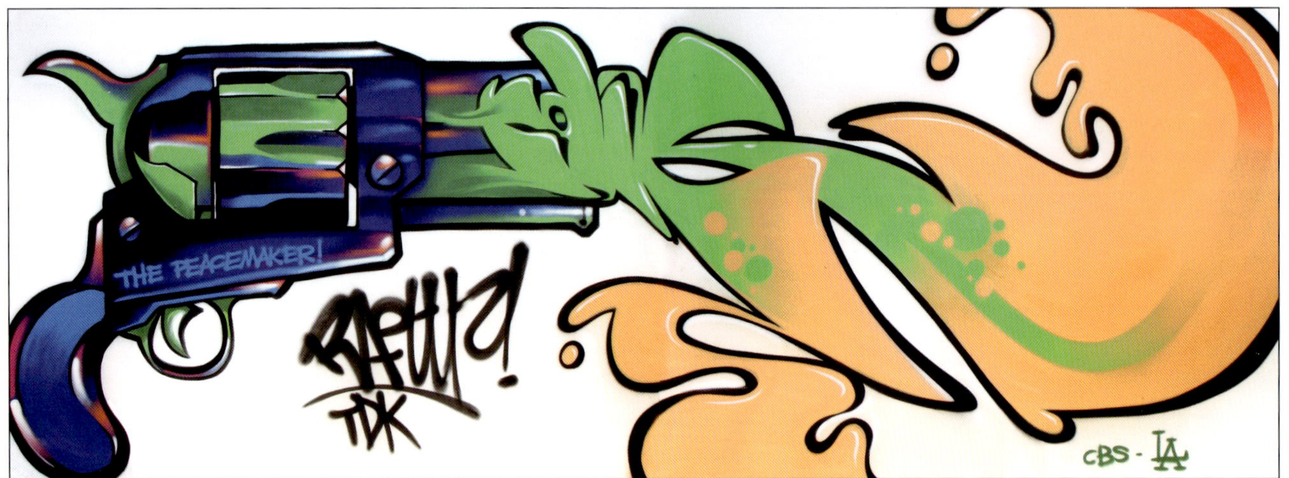

Peacemaker - 2007

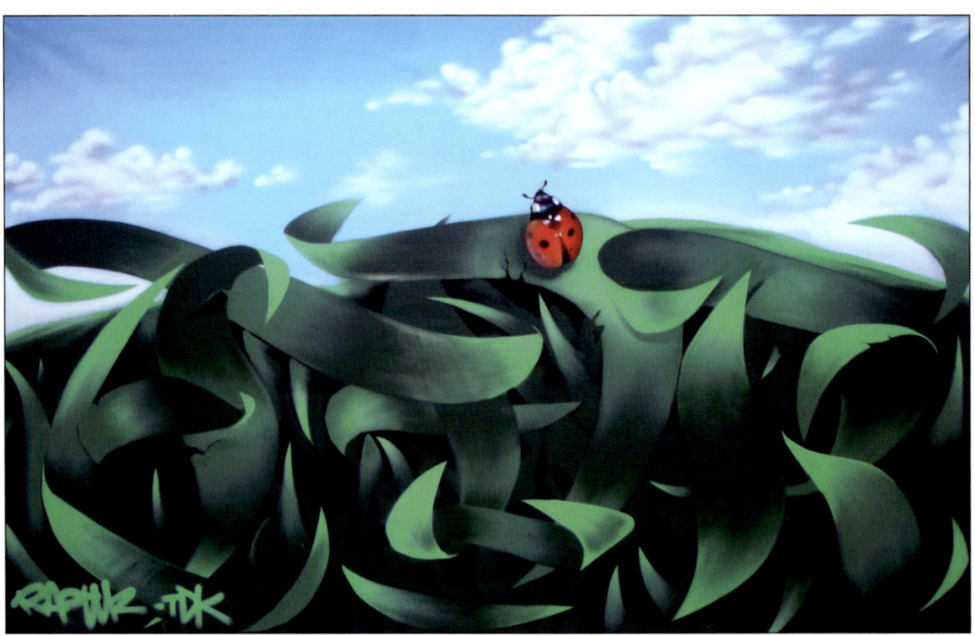

TDK - 2007

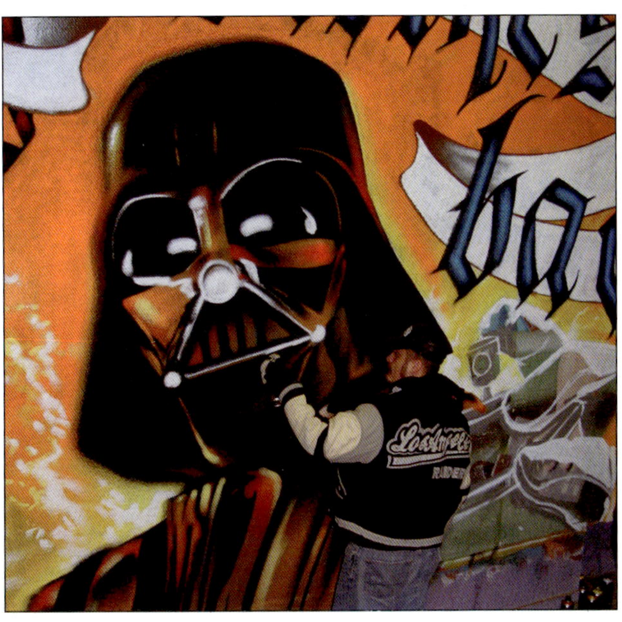

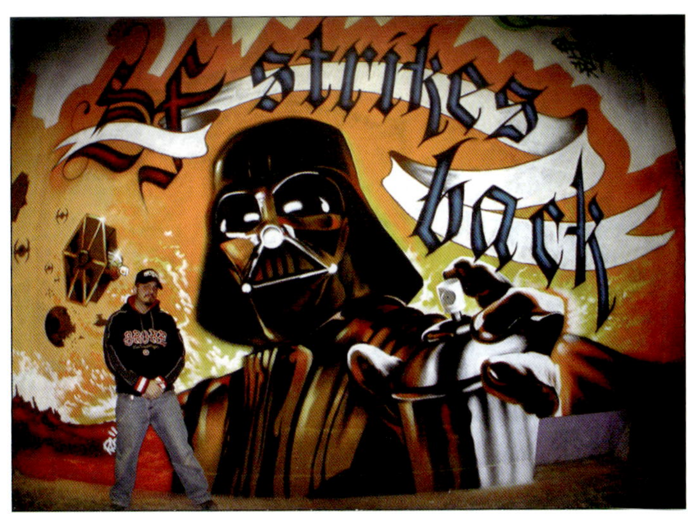

SF strikes back - 2007

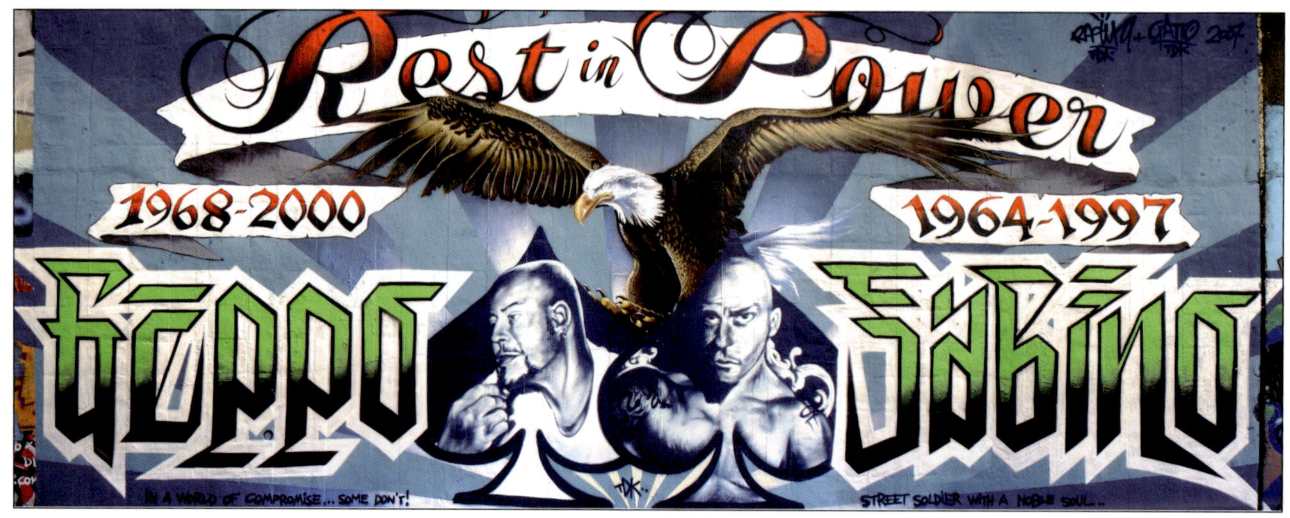

In memory of Geppo & Sabino with Max Gatto - 2007

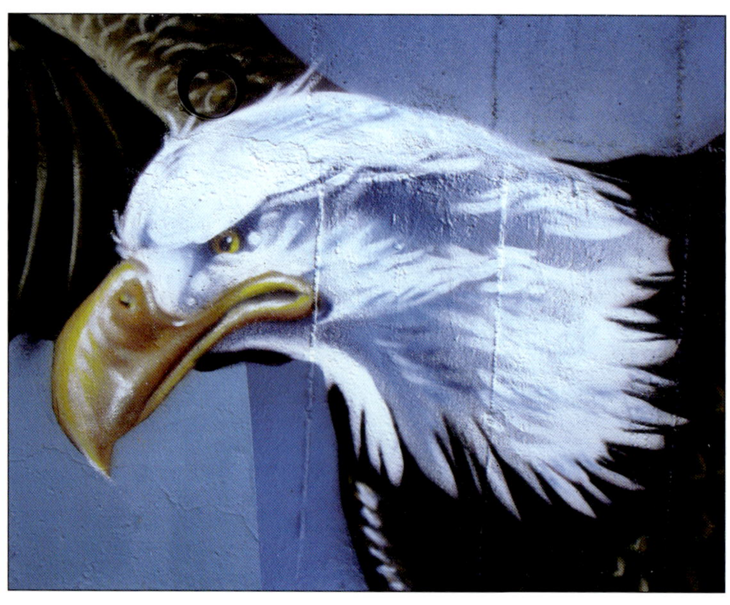

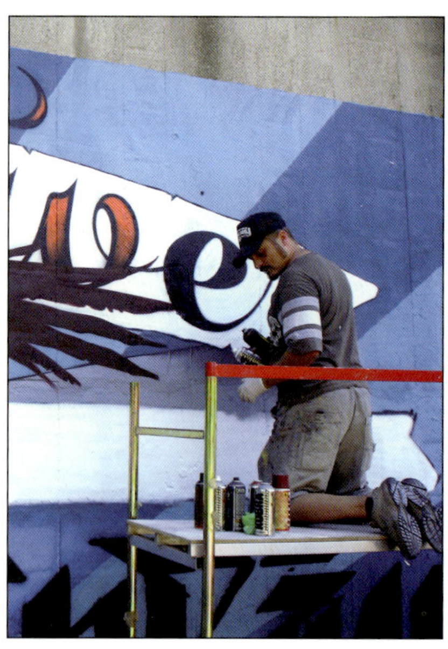

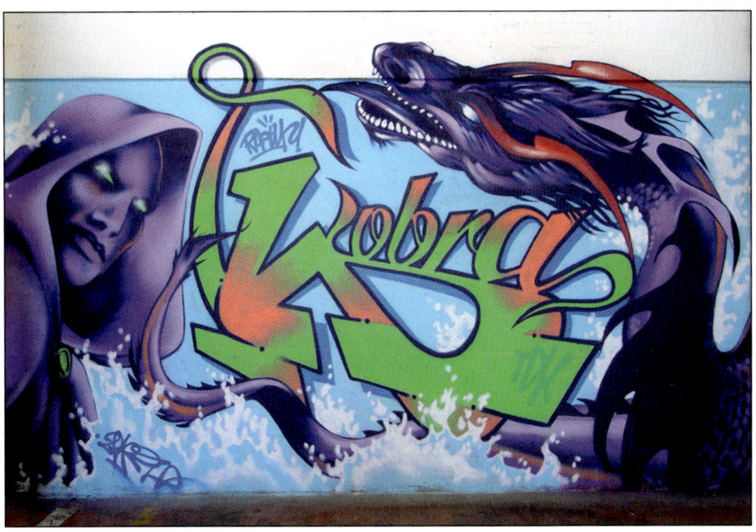

Kobra spraycan factory with Zero - 2007

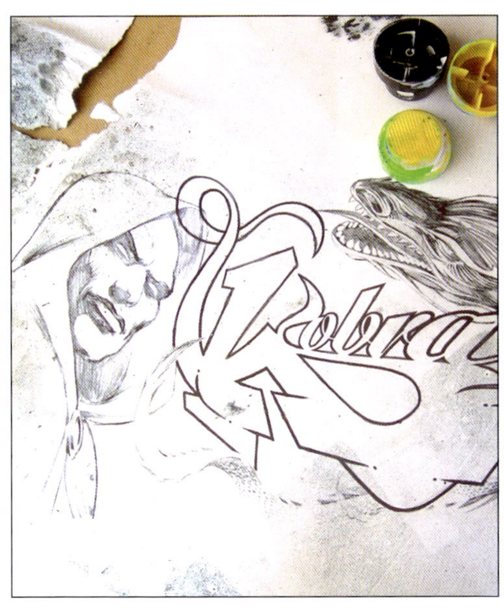

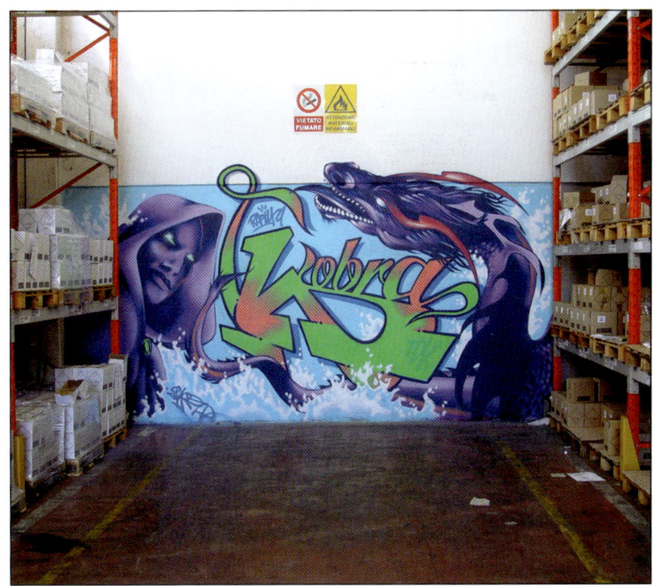

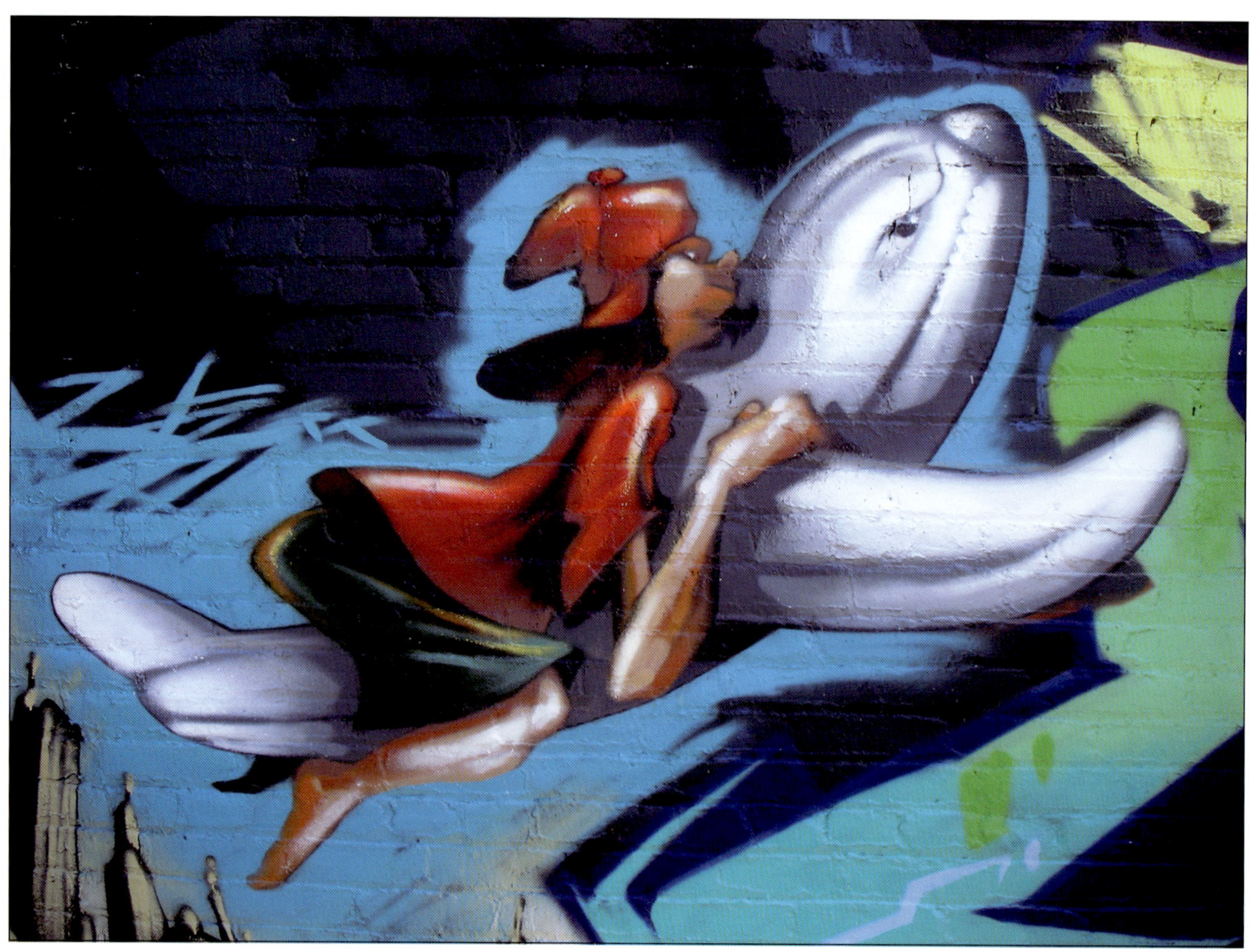

Character Downtown LA - 2007

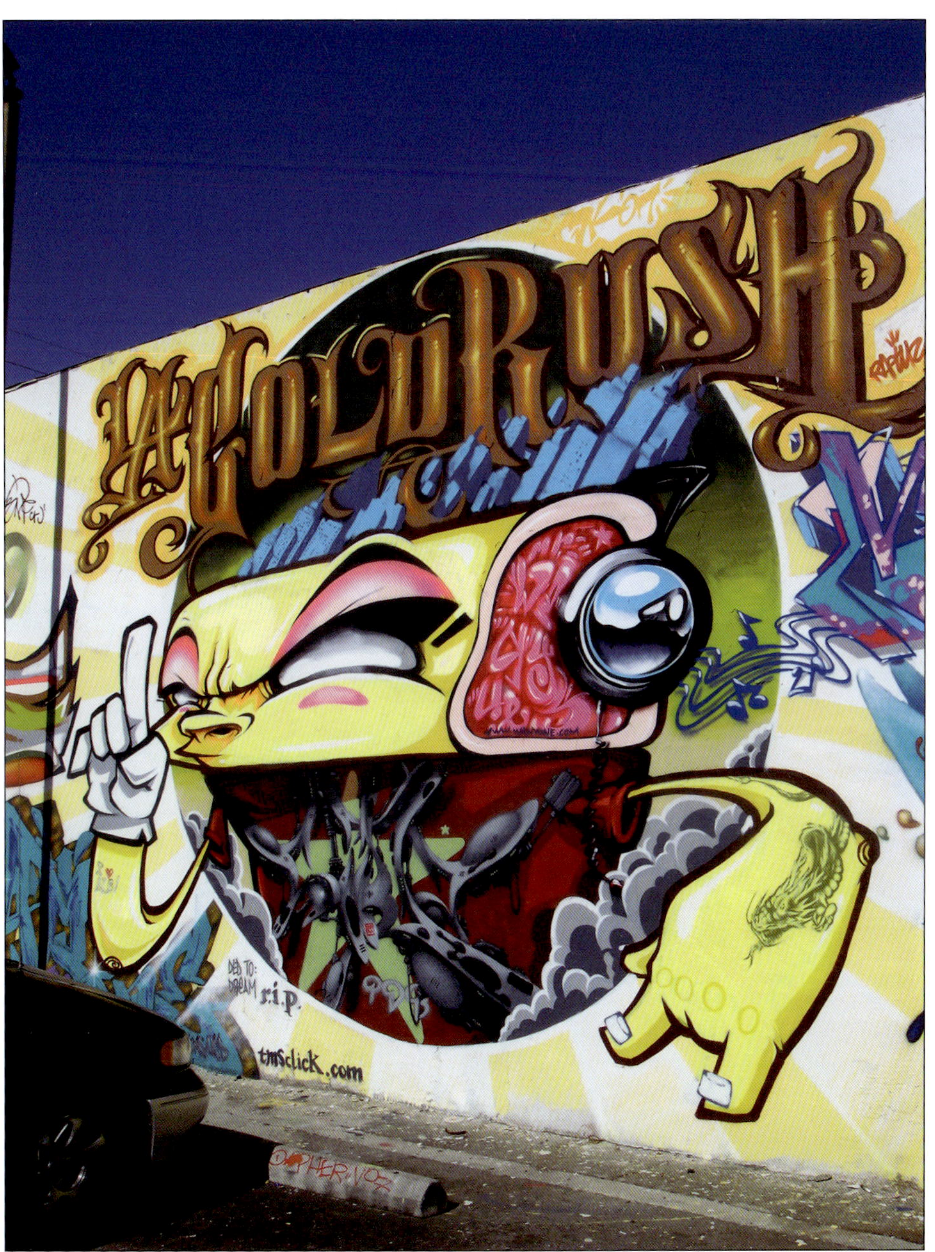

LA-Goldrush with Mr.Wany & Sirtwo East LA - 2007

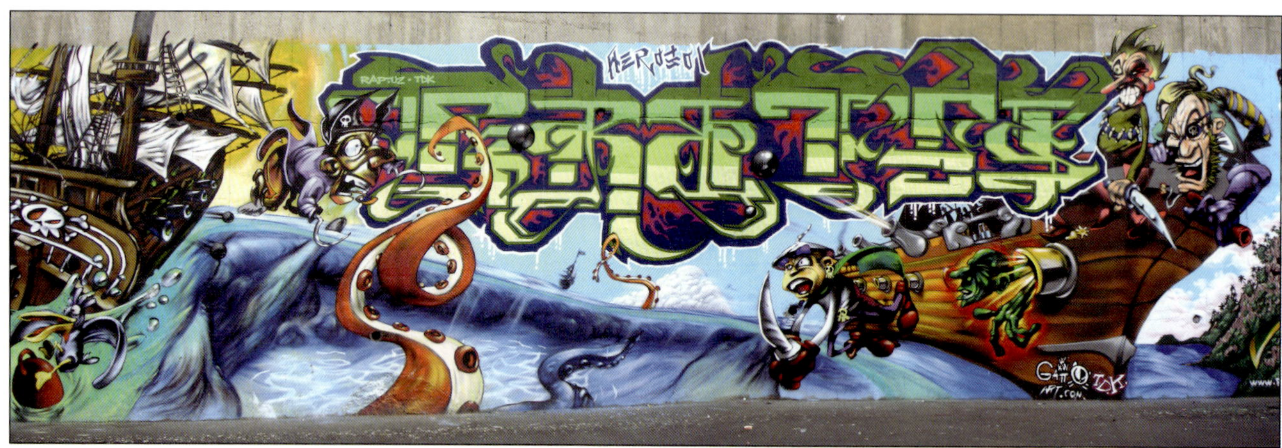

Aerosol pirates with Max Gatto - 2007

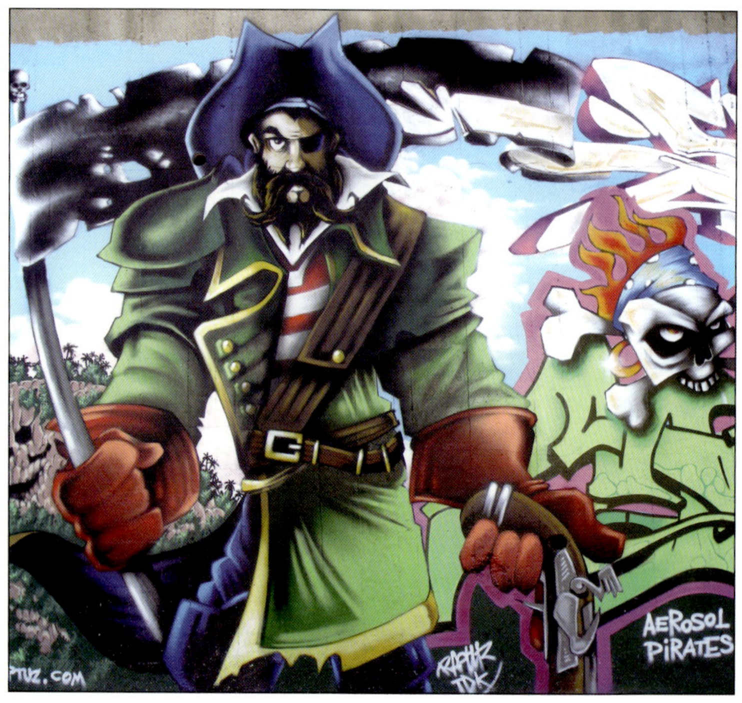

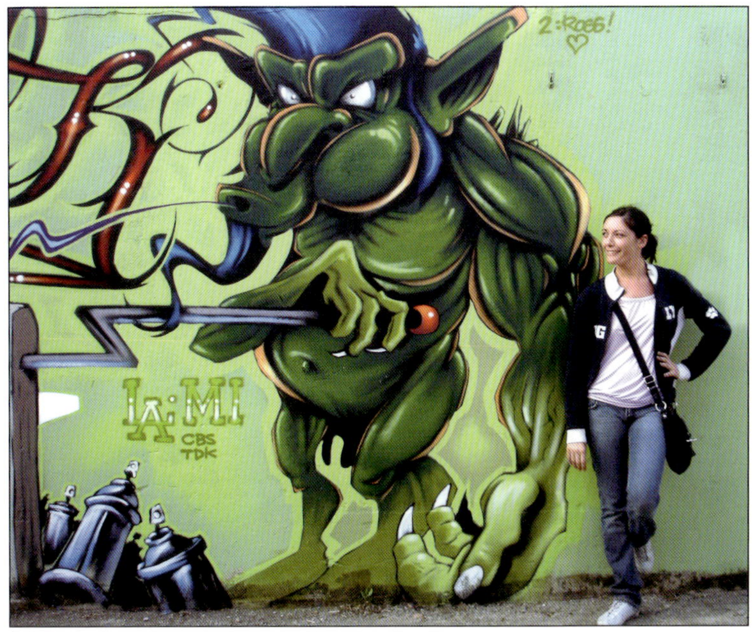

Troll - 2007

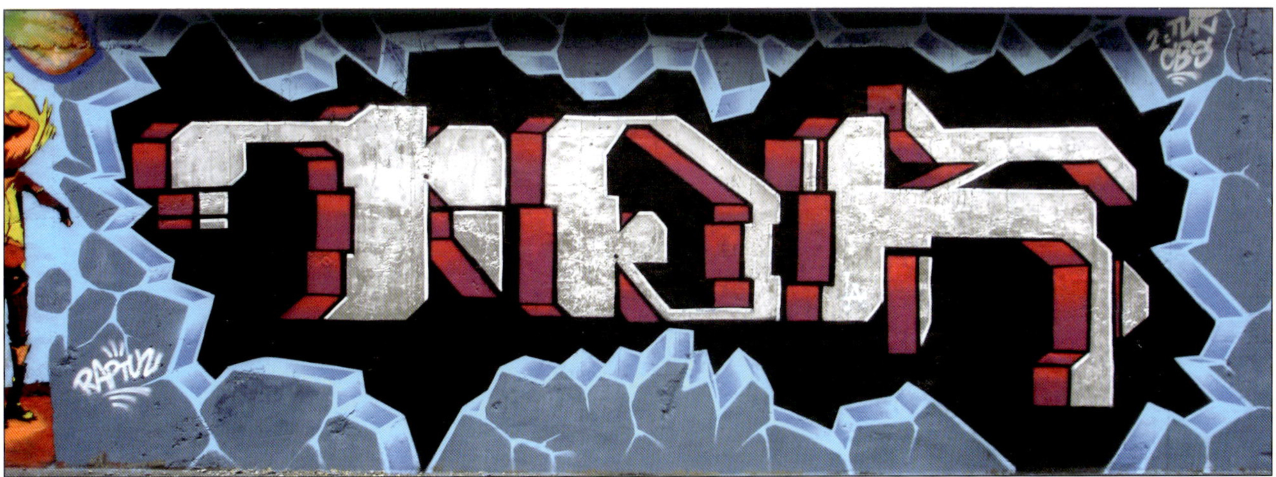

TDK - 2007

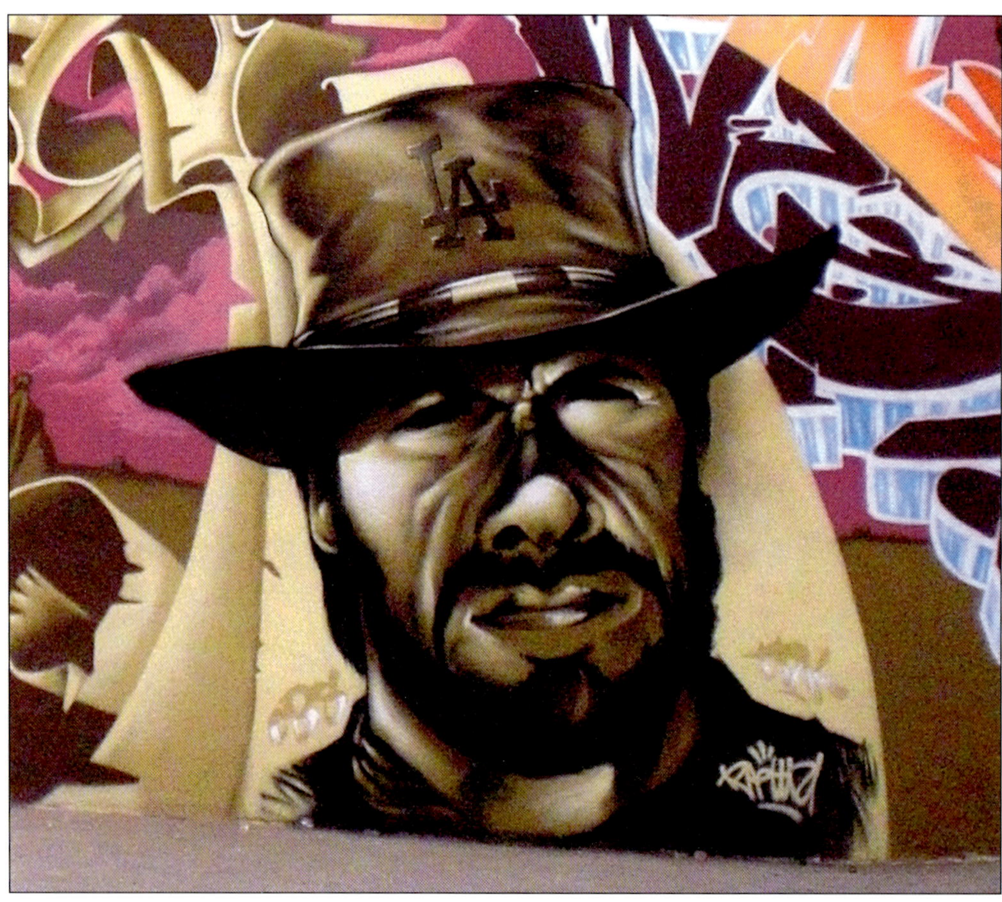

Italian cowboy Hollywood - 2007

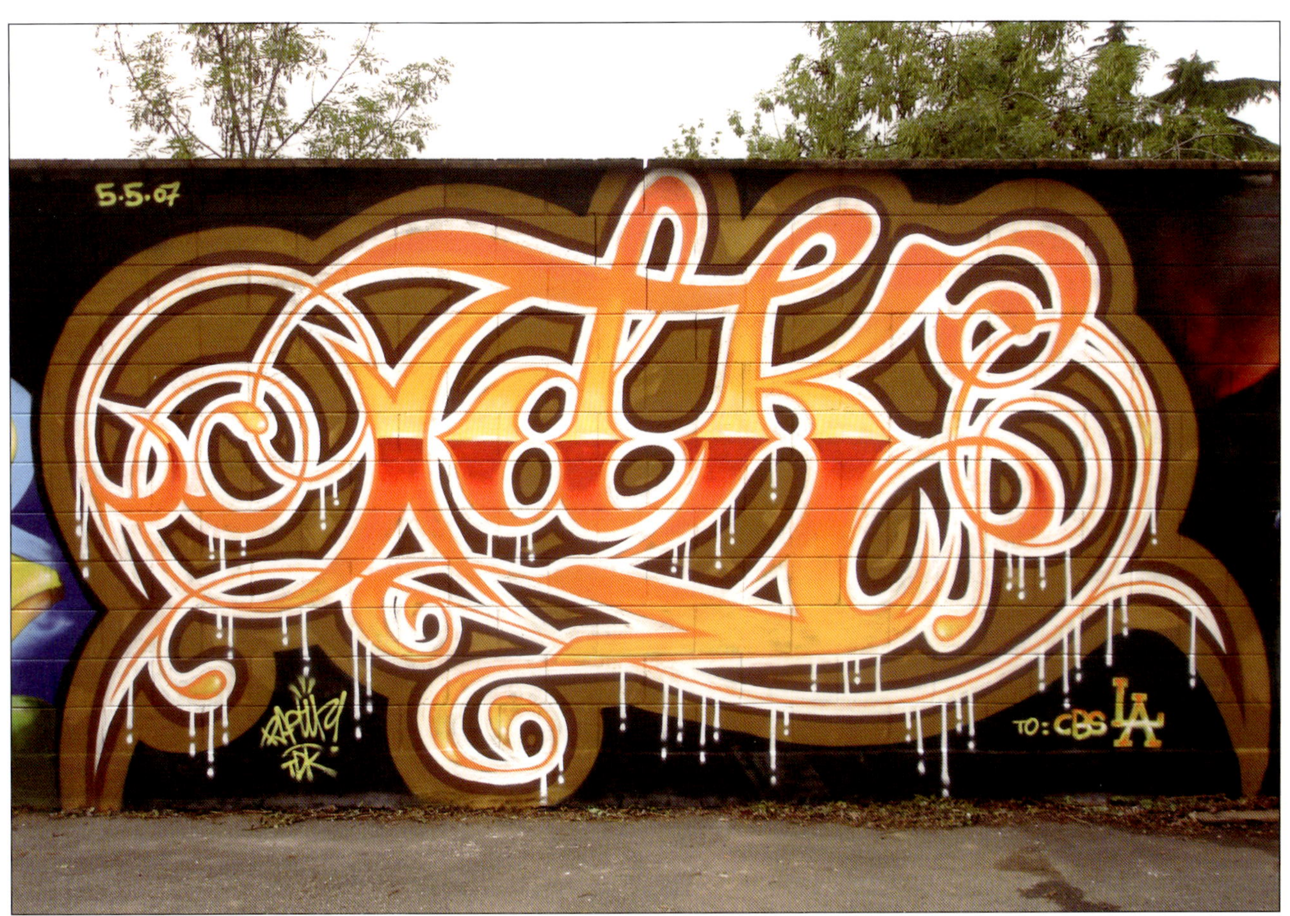

TDK - 2007

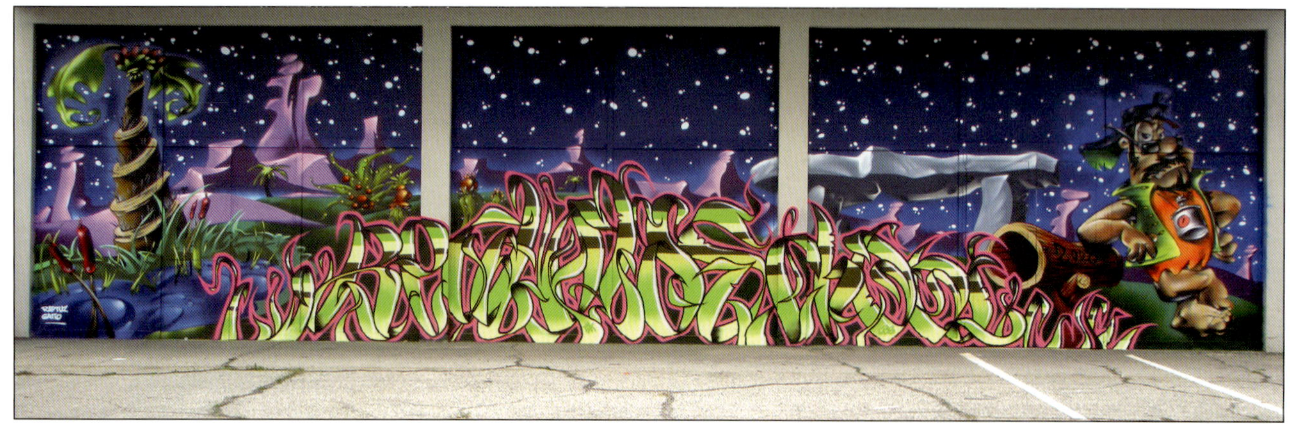

Real old school with Max Gatto - 2008

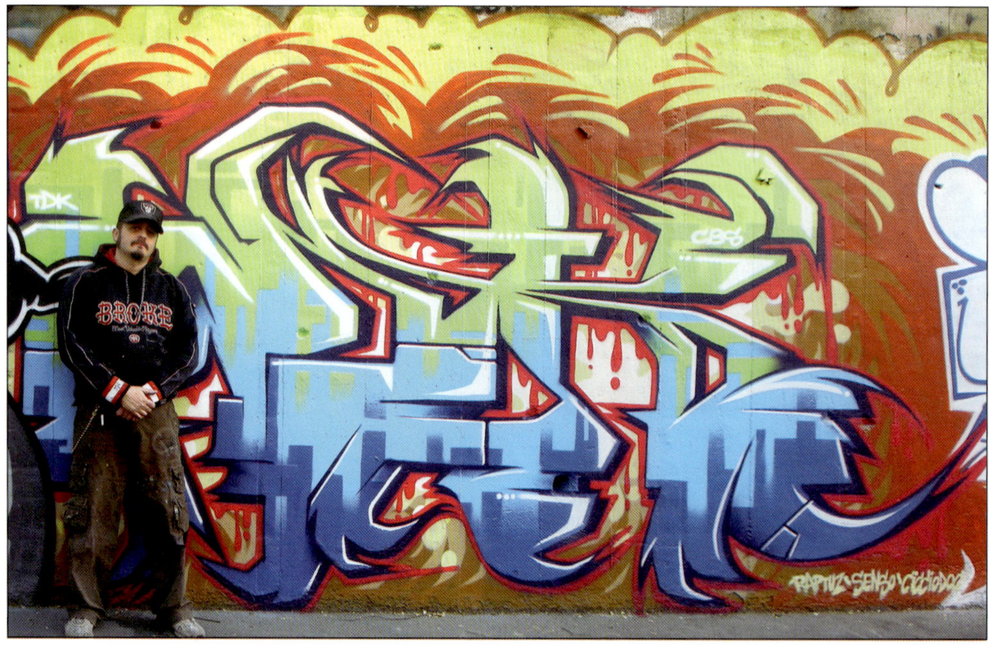

TDK - 2008

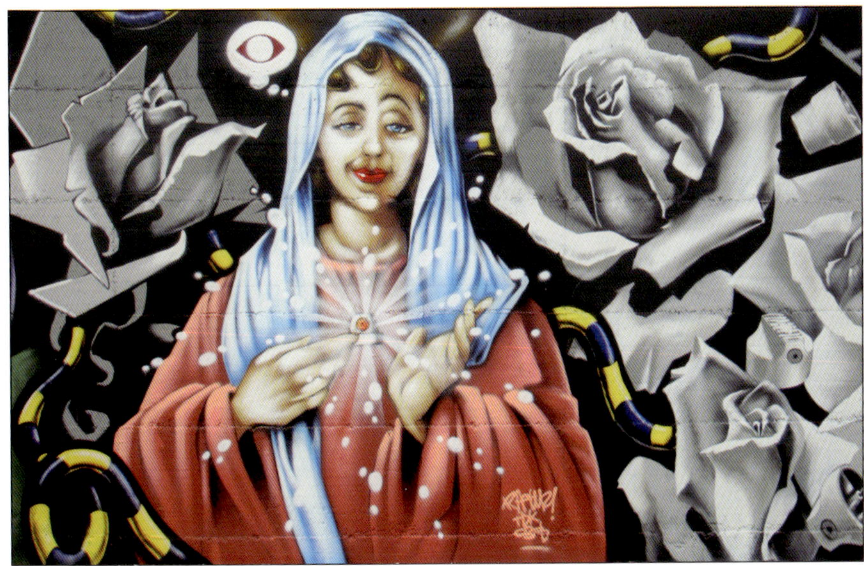

Drunk Madonna - 2009

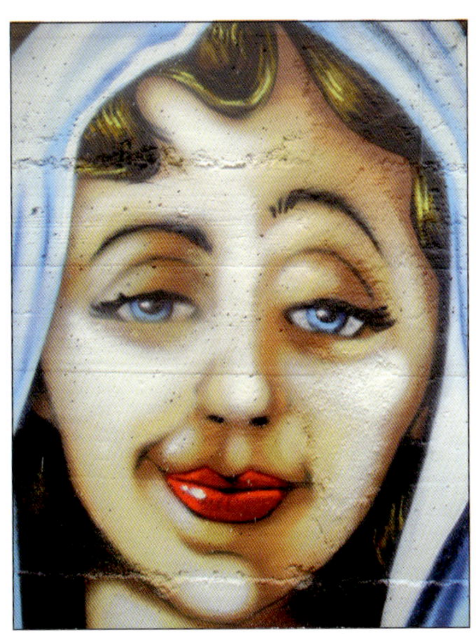

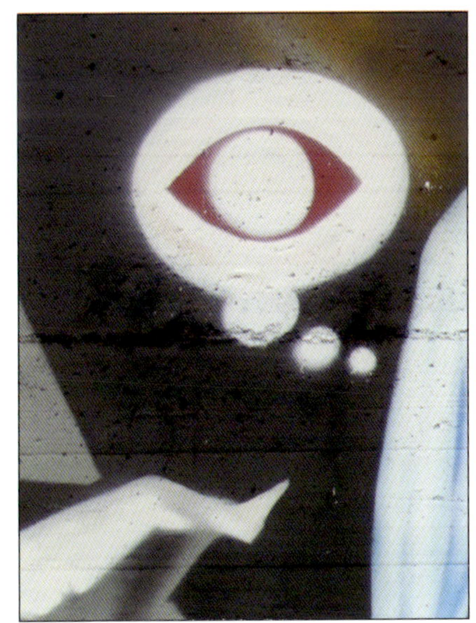

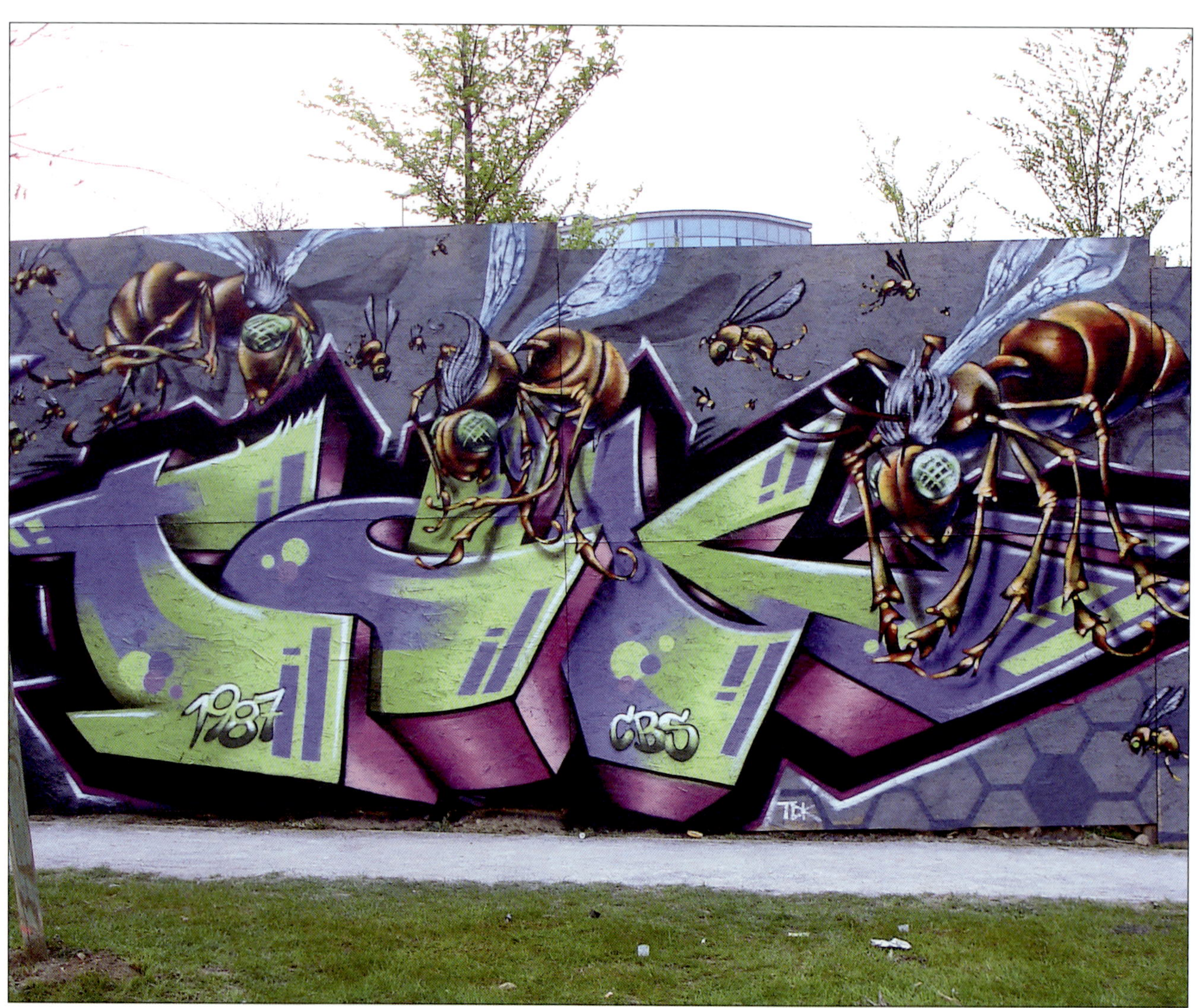

TDK with Max Gatto - 2009

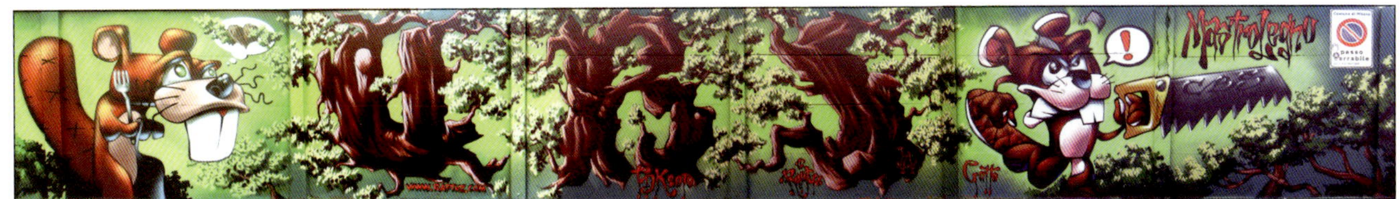

CBS with Max Gatto & Zero - 2010

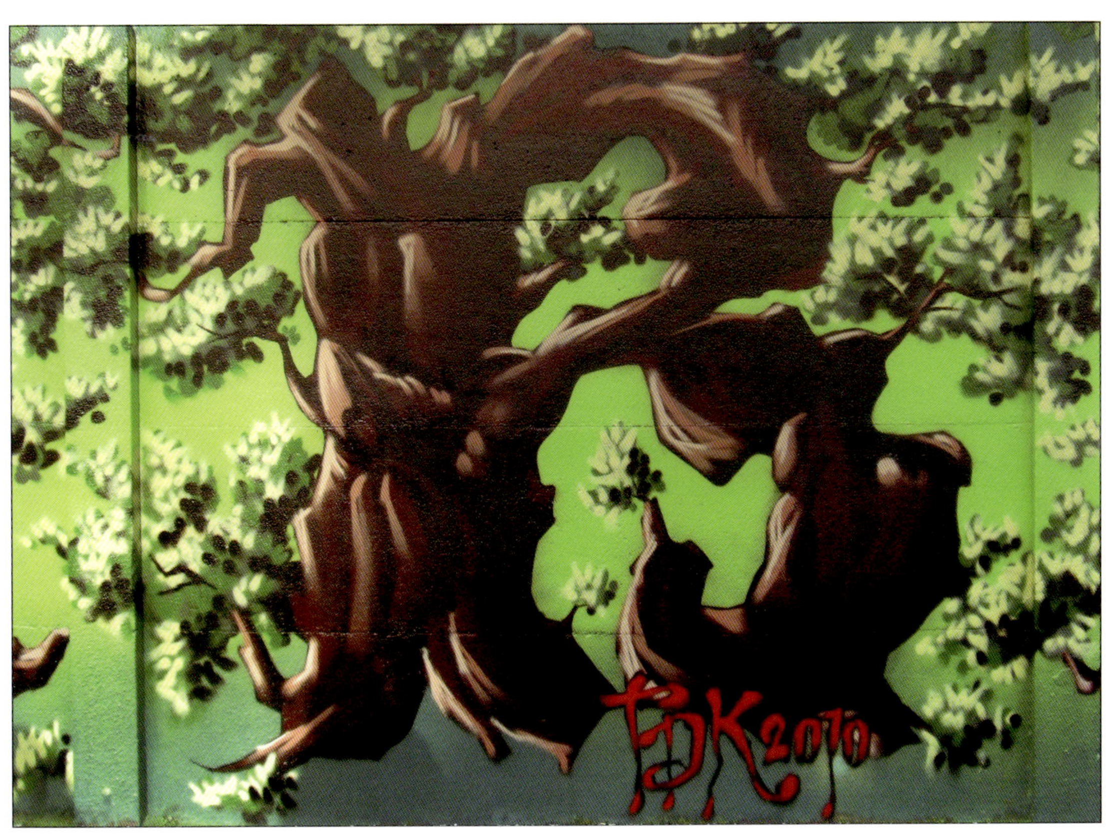

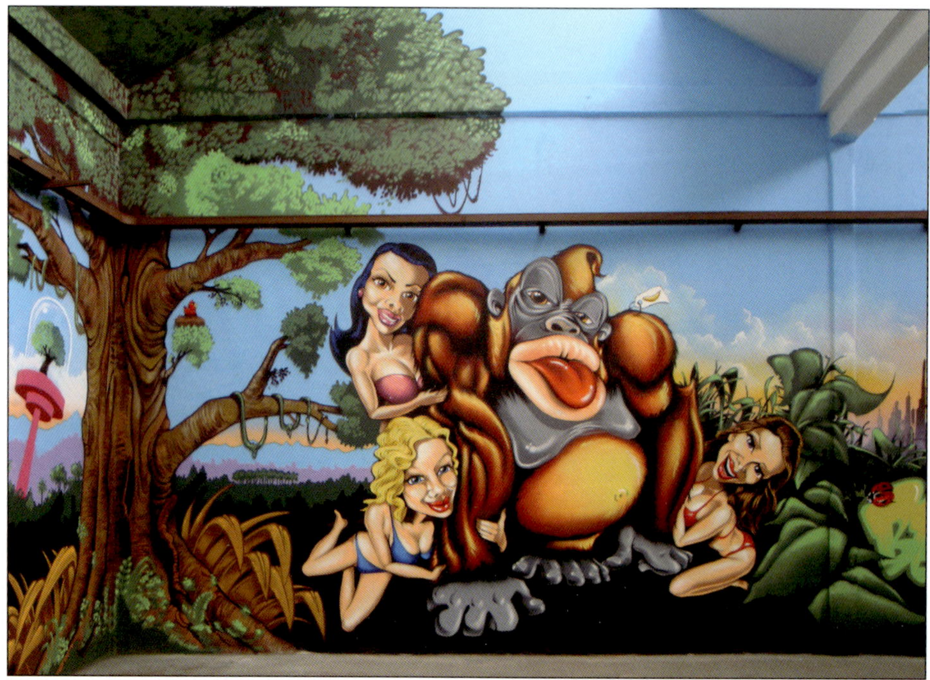

Orangotown - 2010

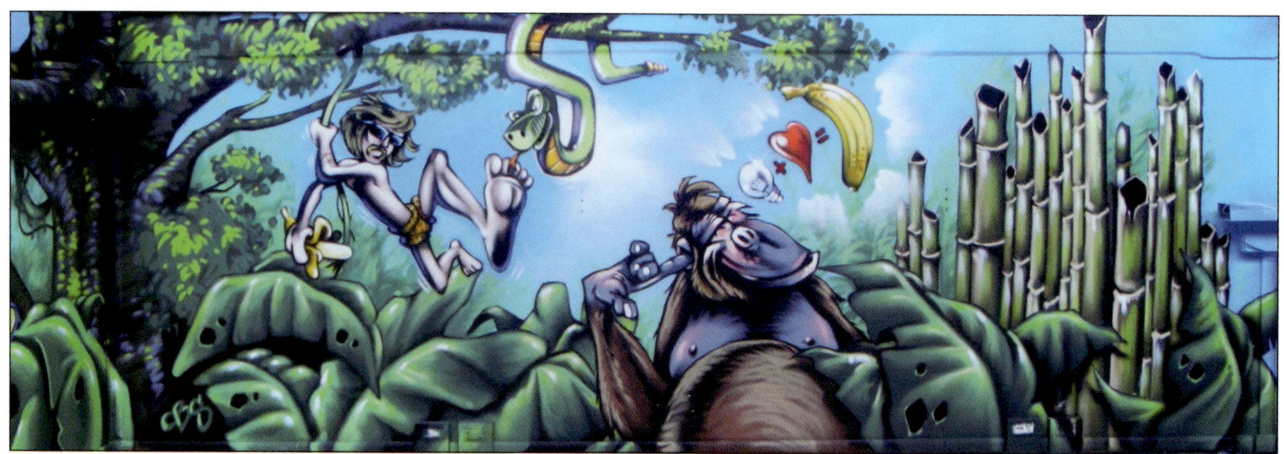

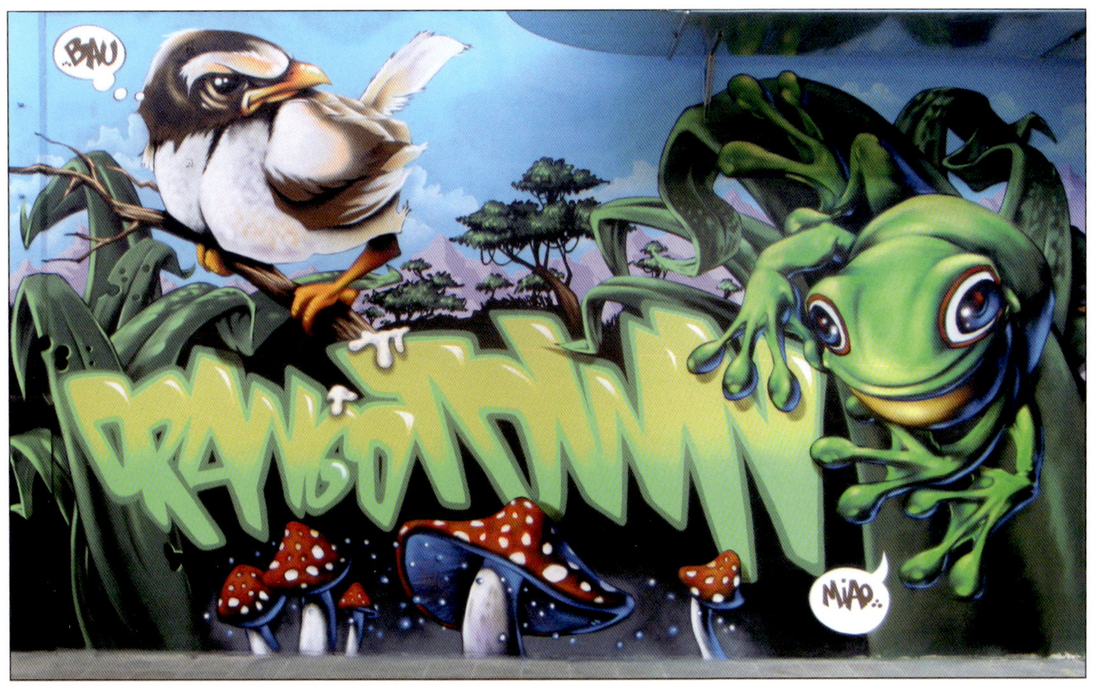

Orangotown - 2010

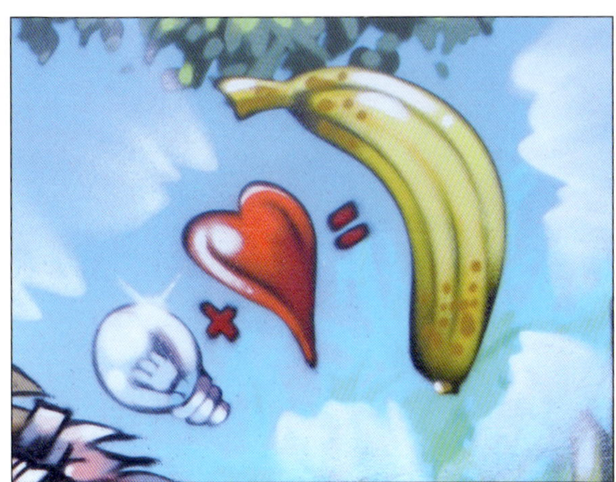

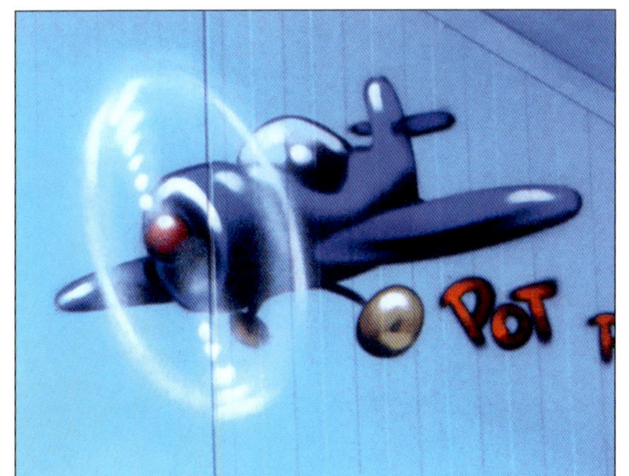

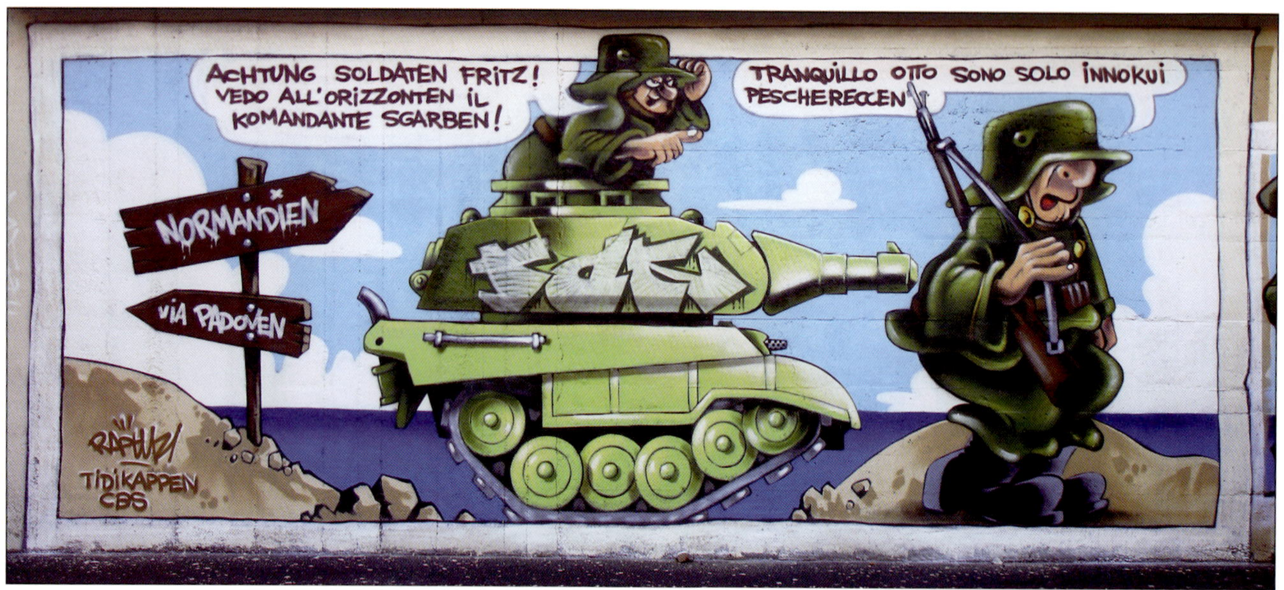

Sturmtruppen - 2010

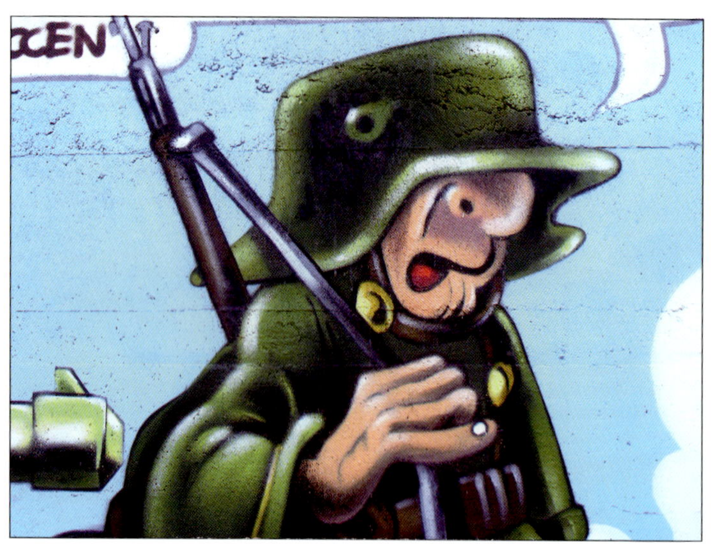

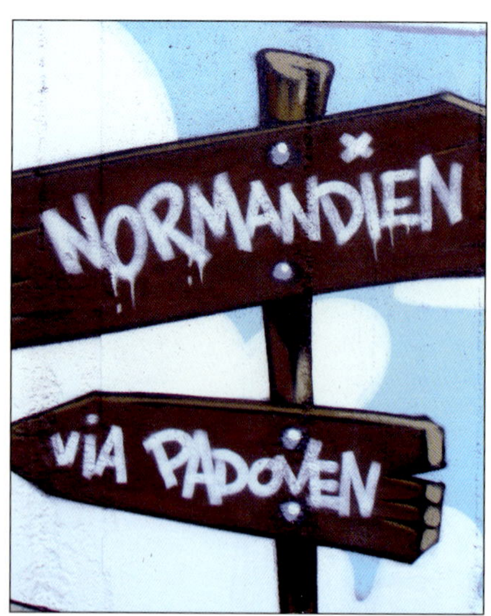

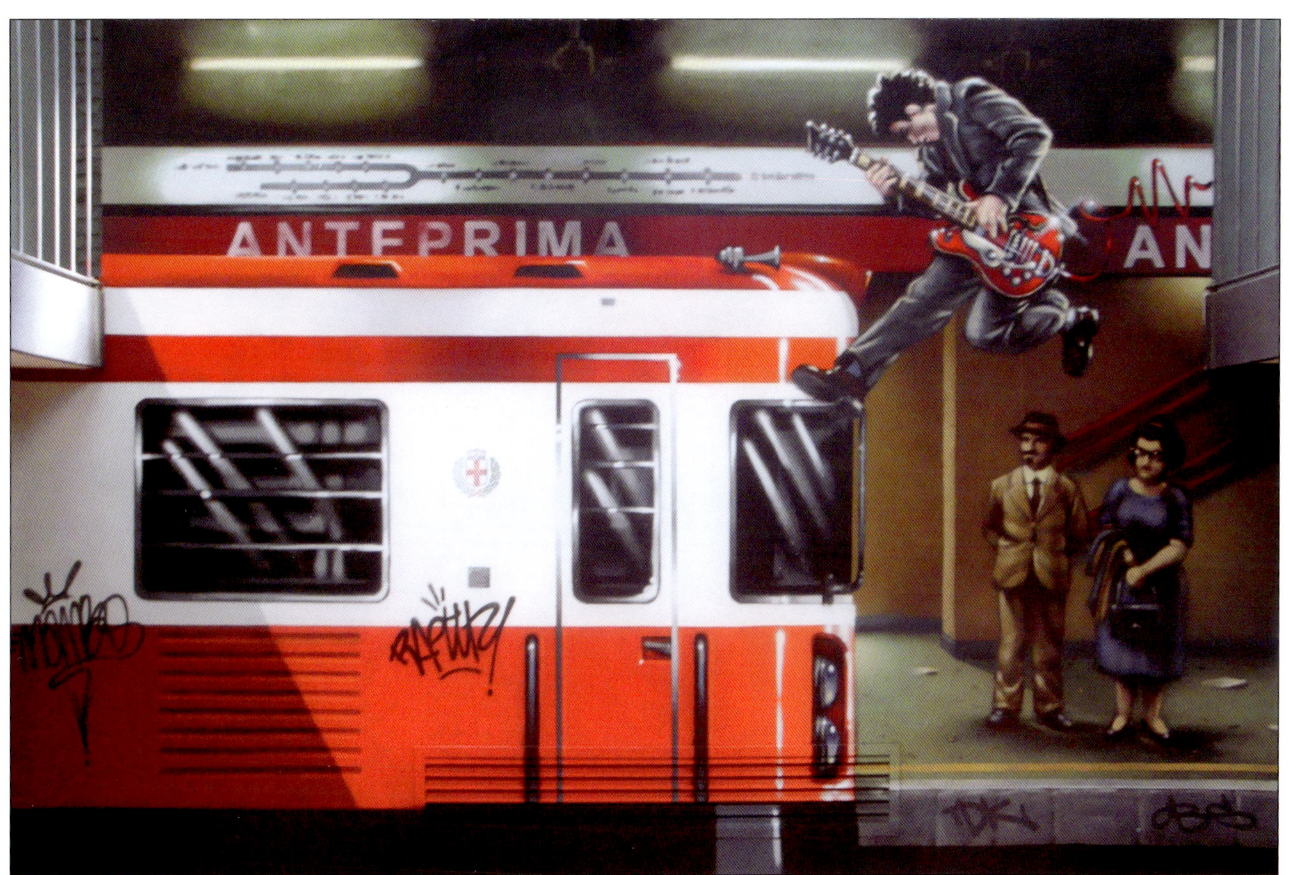

Anteprima station with Mambo - 2010

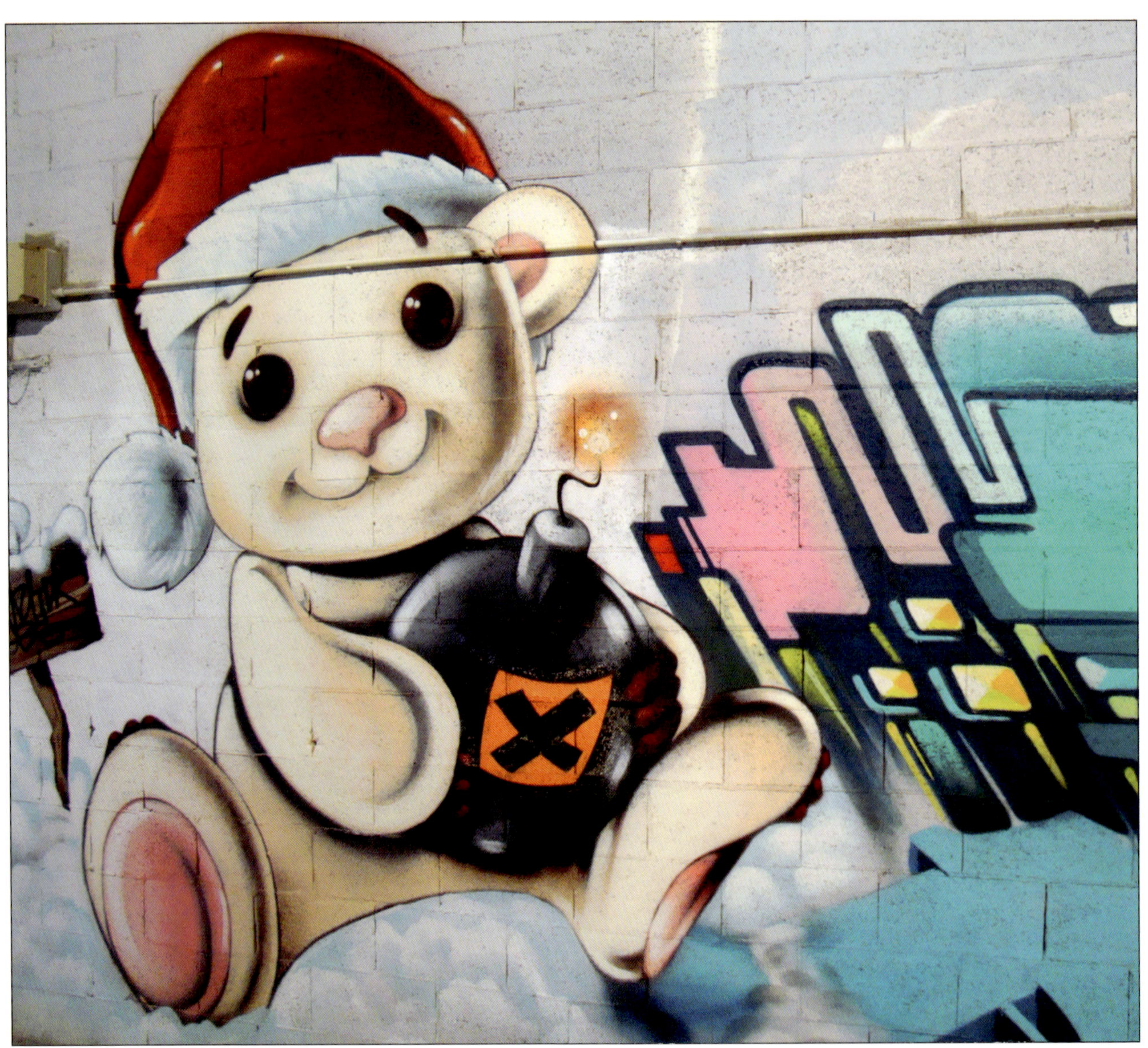

Puppet cromatica - 2010

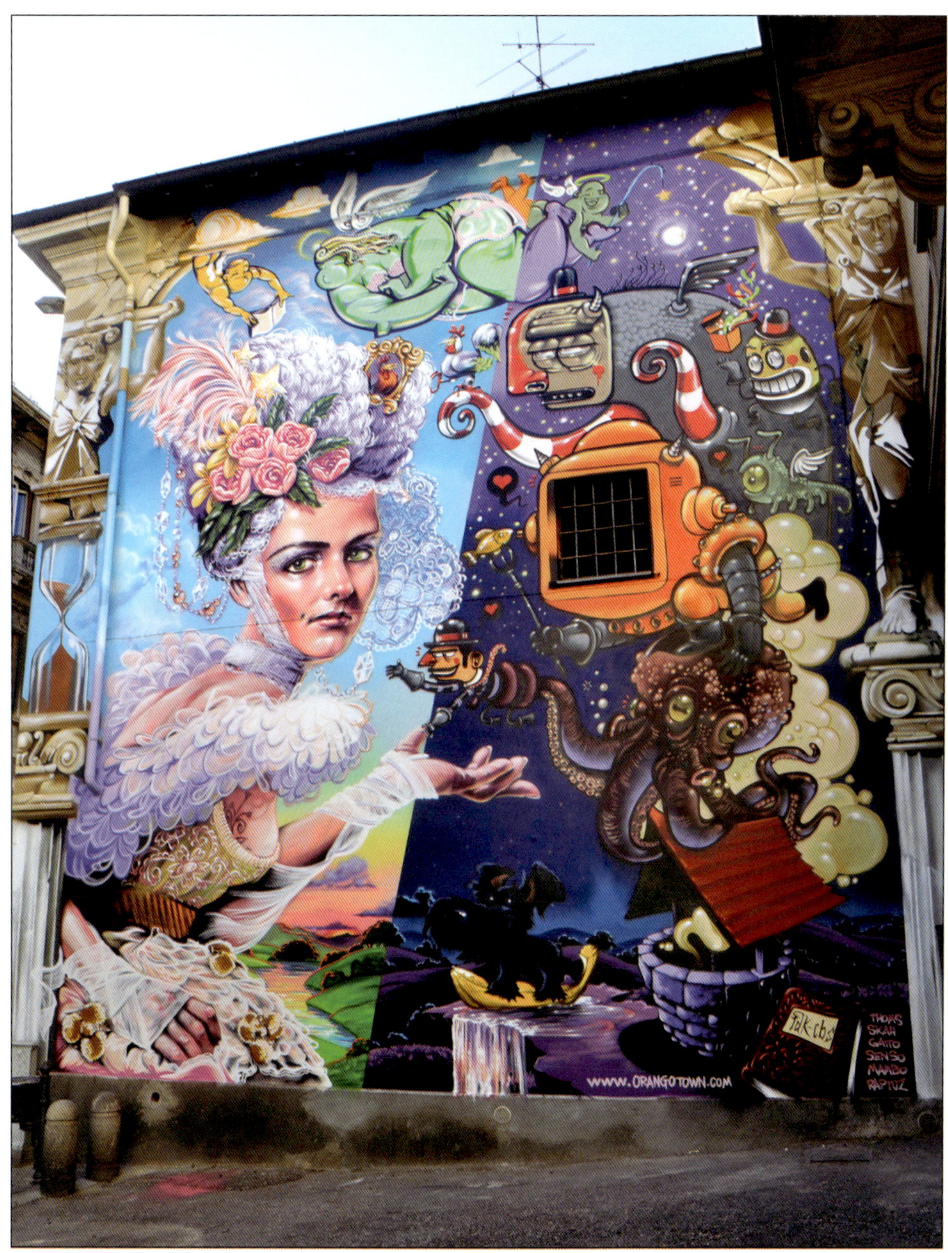

Gallarate in wanderwall with TDK/CBS crew - 2010

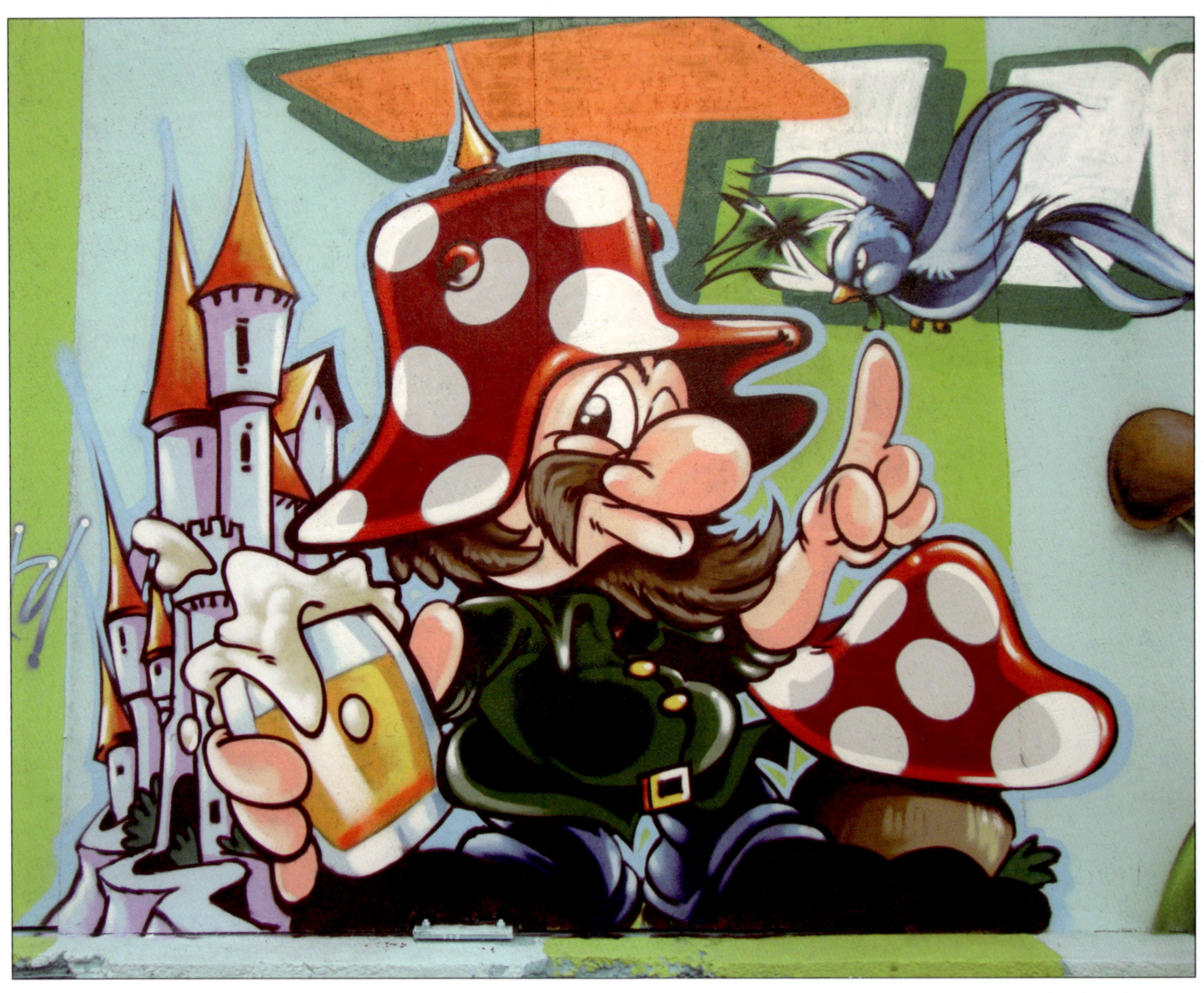

Raptuz the dworf - 2010

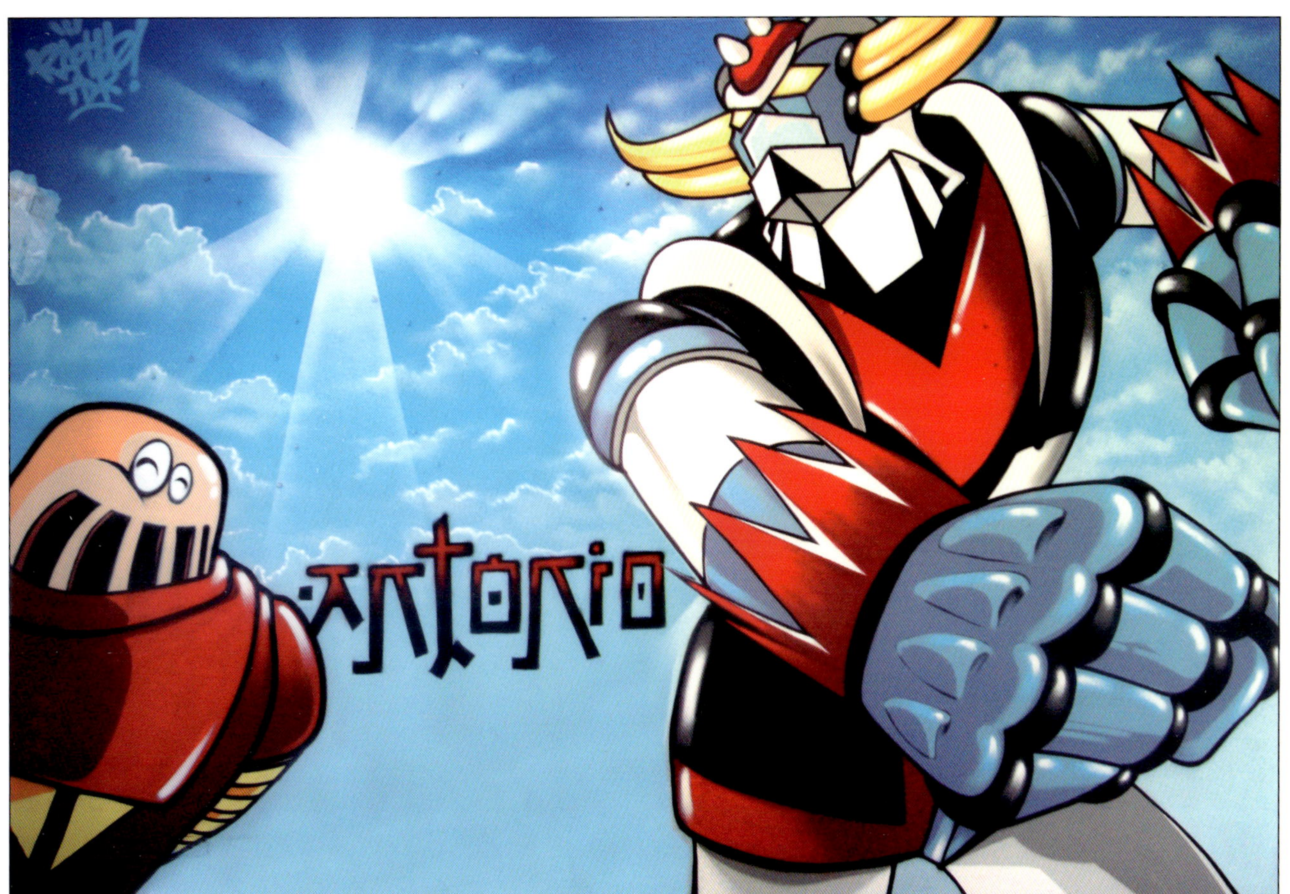

Antonio's robots - 2010

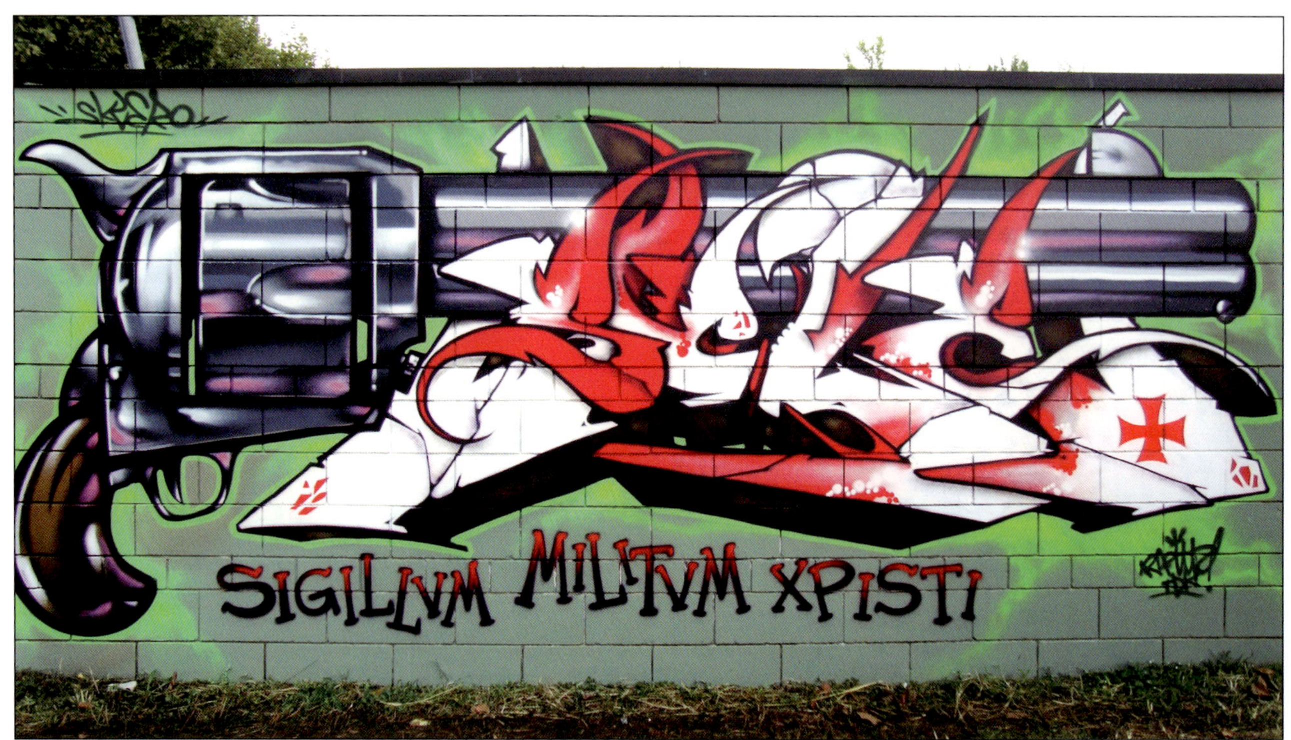

Sigillum militum xpisti with Sklero - 2010

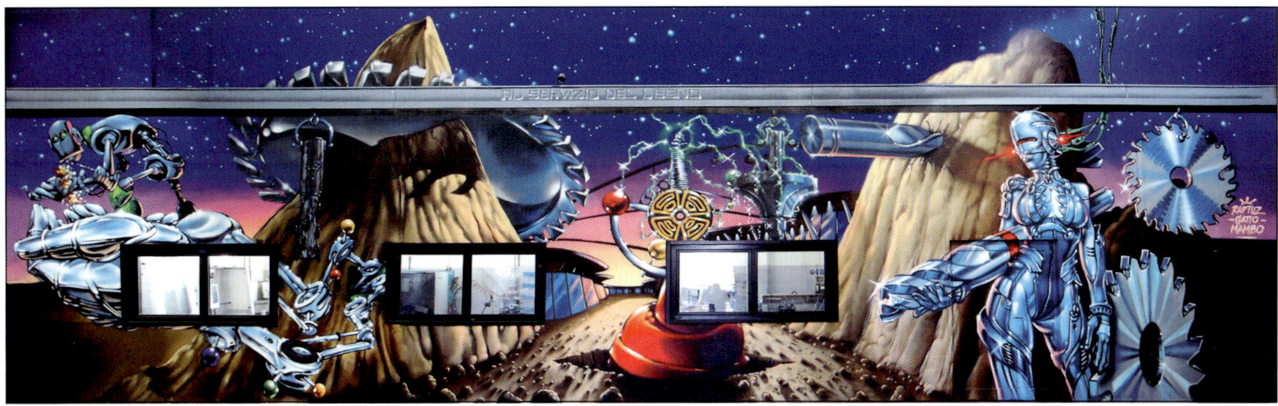

Trombini's with Max Gatto & Mambo - 2010

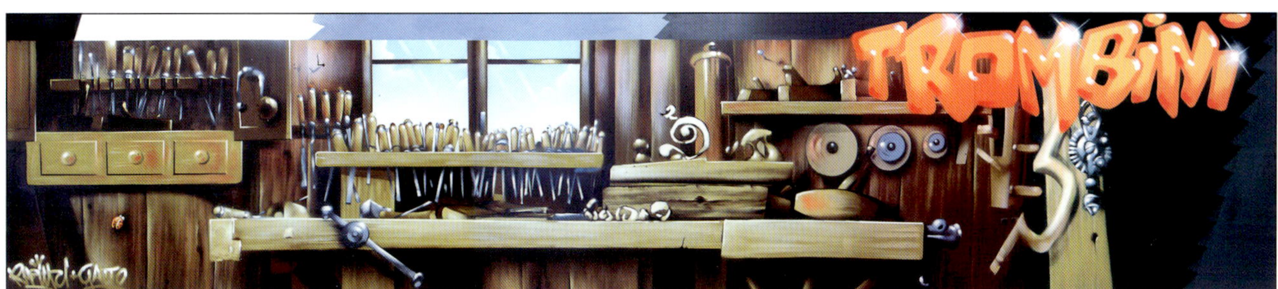

Trombini's with Max Gatto - 2010

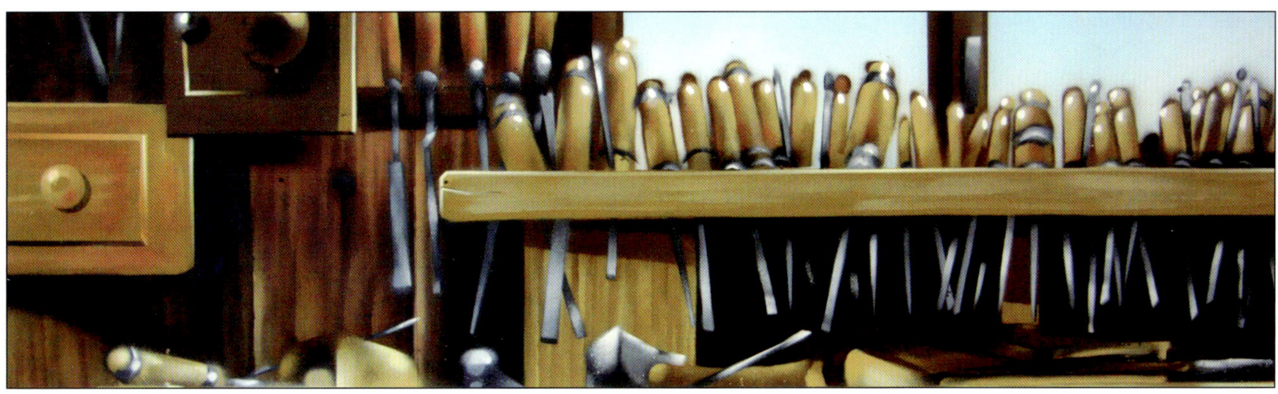

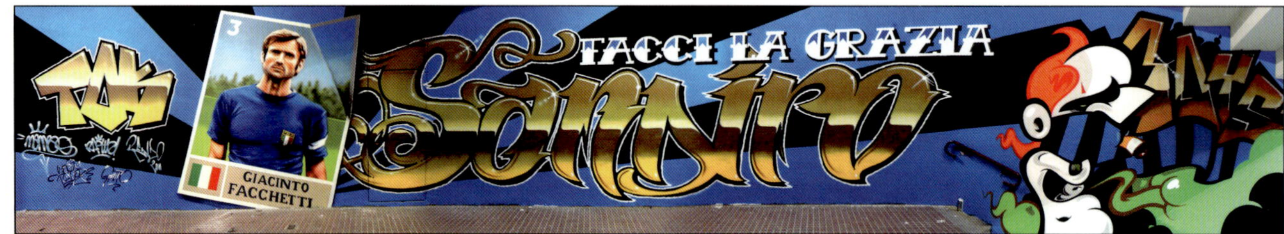

San Siro stadium wall with TDK crew - 2011

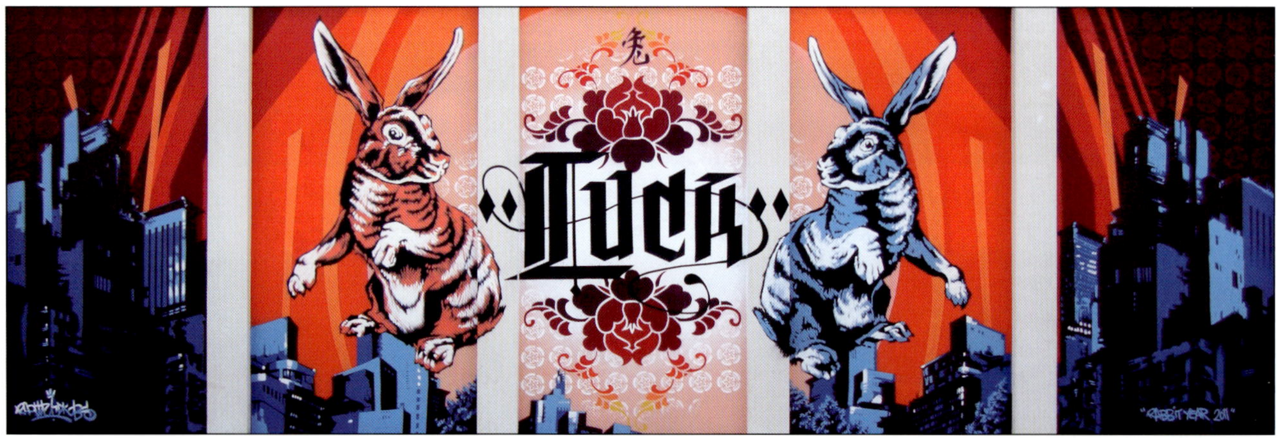

Rabbit year - 2011

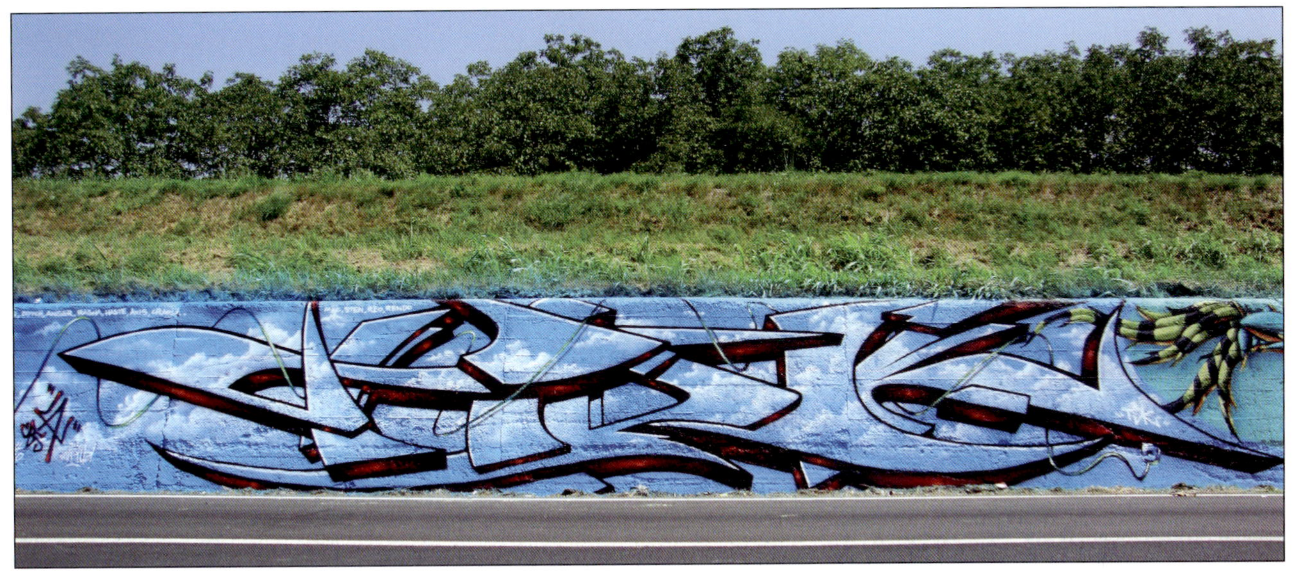

TDK - 2011

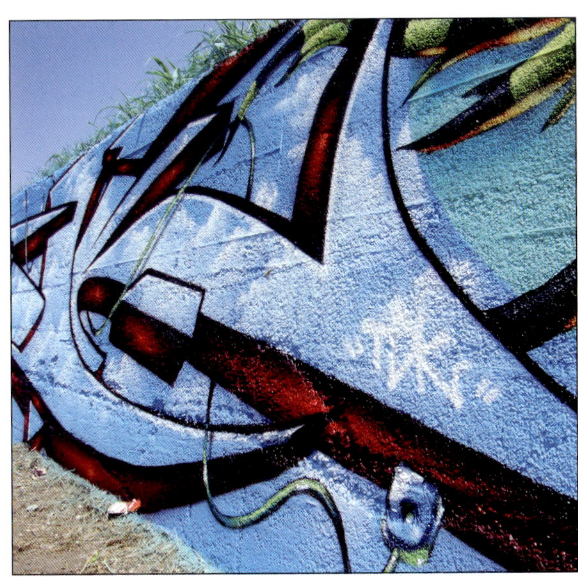

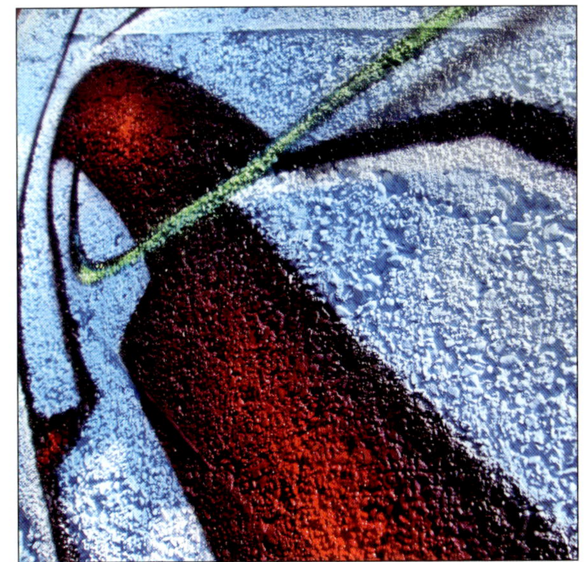

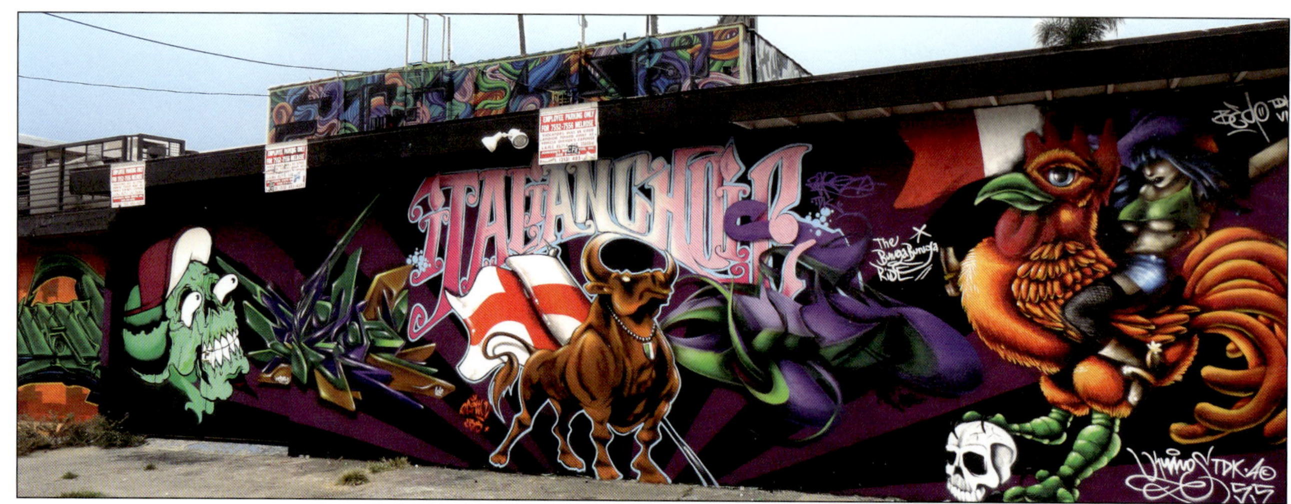

Italian choice with CBS crew Hollywood - 2011

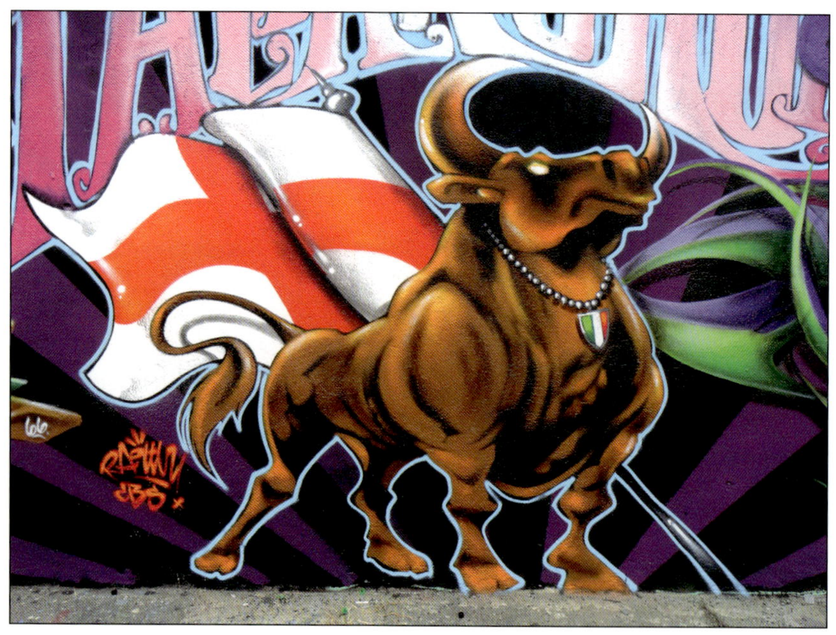

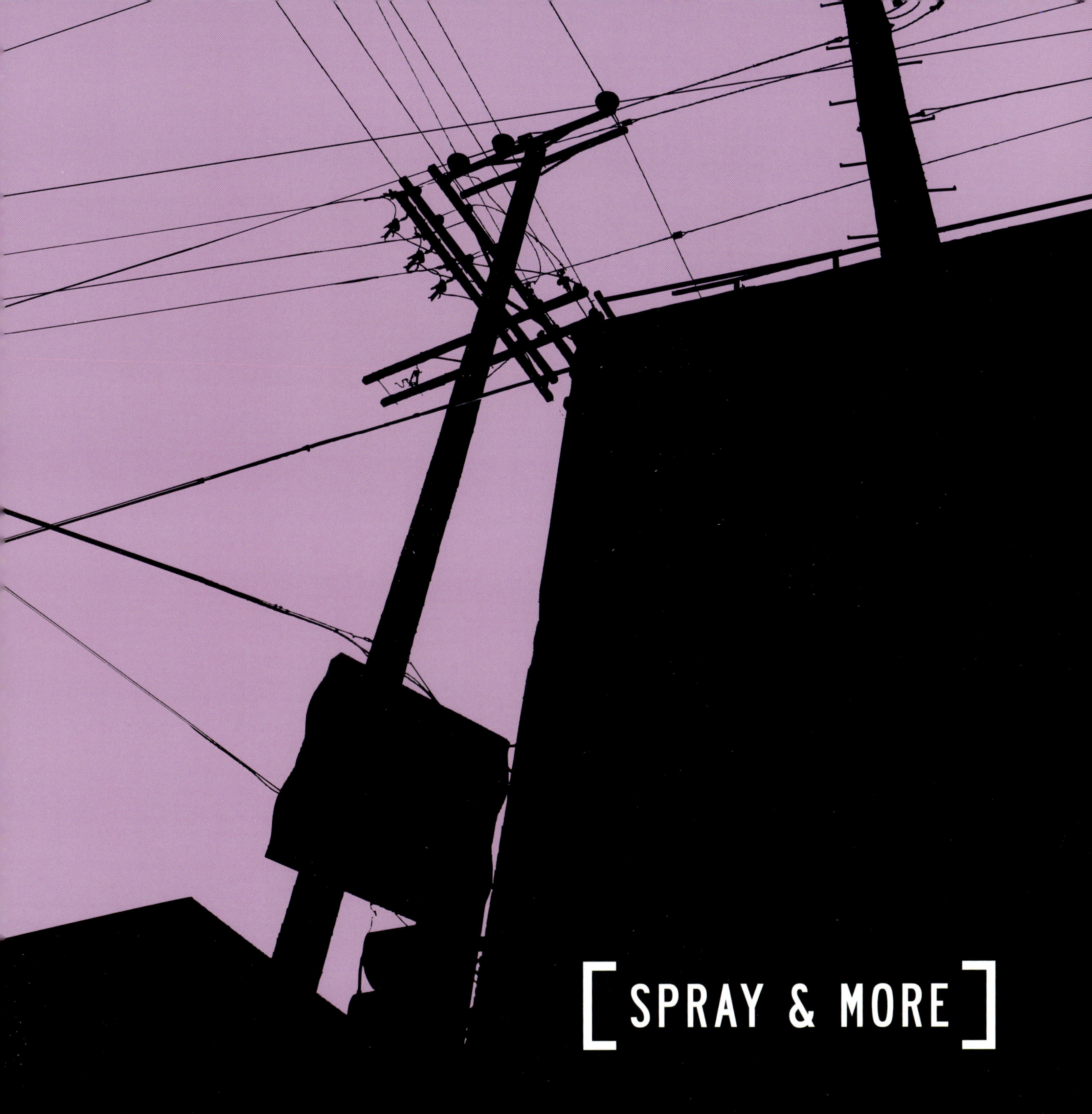
[SPRAY & MORE]

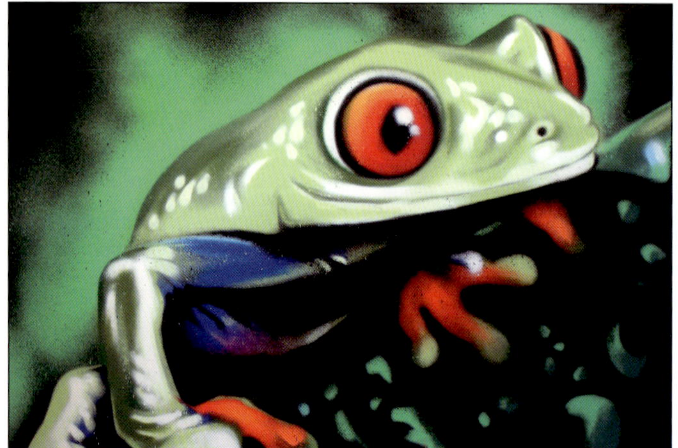

Frog II - spraycan on canvas, cm.150x100 - 2007

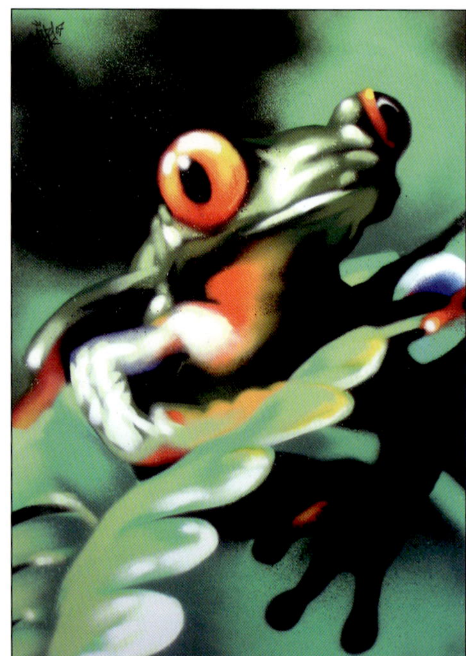

Frog - spraycan on canvas, cm.100x150 - 2007

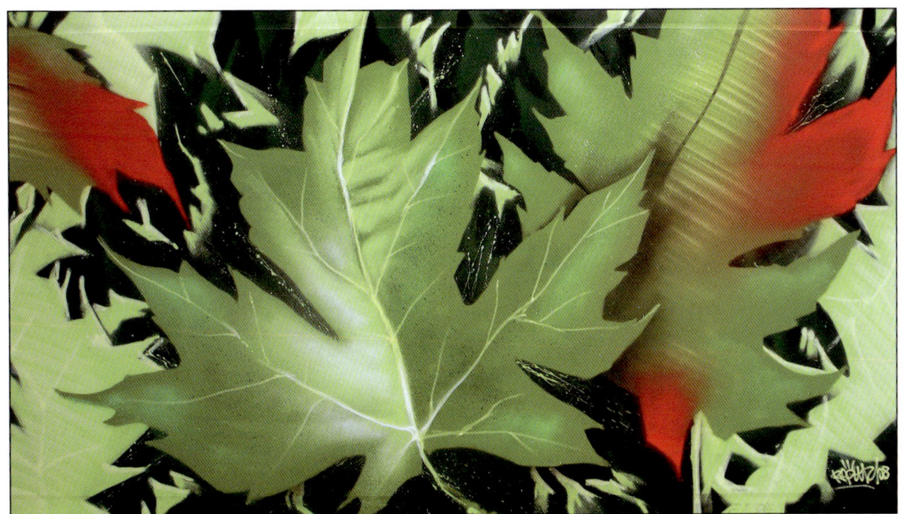

Leaves - spraycan on canvas, cm.250x120 - 2008

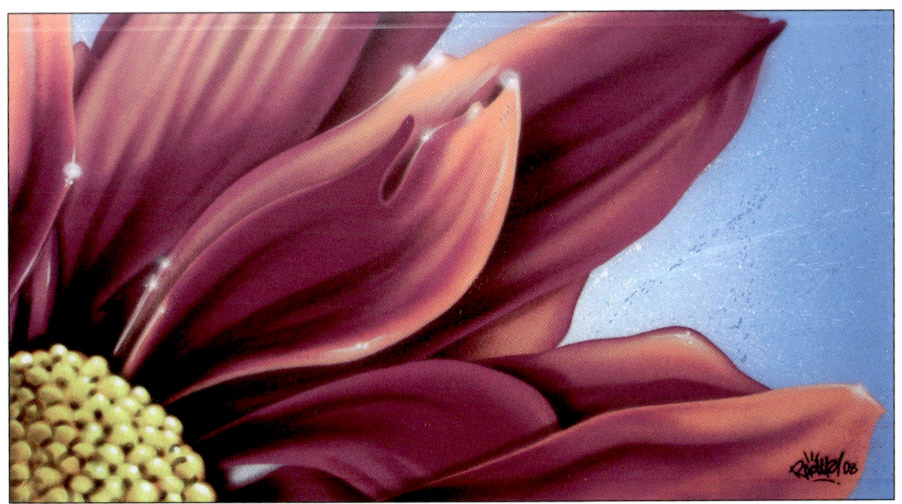

Fuchsia closeup - spraycan on canvas, cm.250x120 - 2008

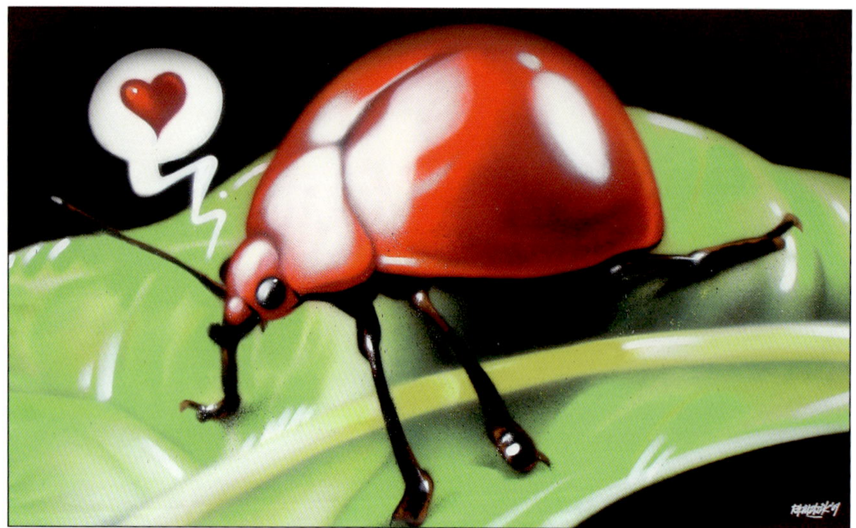

Dirty job - spraycan on canvas, cm.150x80 - 2009

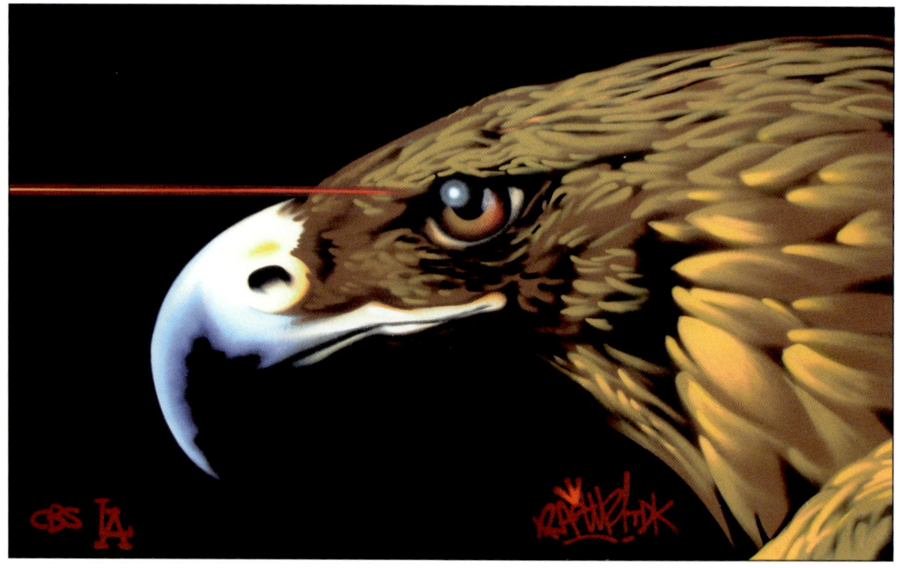

Eagle eye - spraycan on canvas, cm.300x200 - 2008

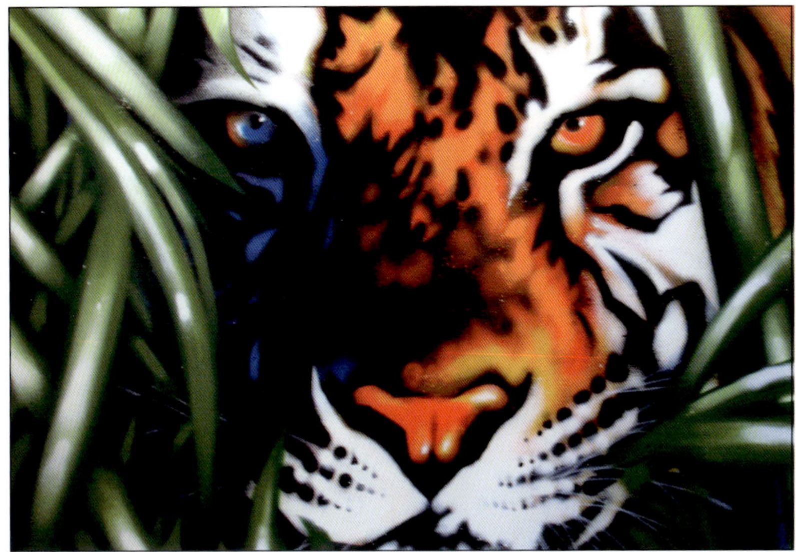

Tiger - spraycan on canvas, cm.150x100 - 2007

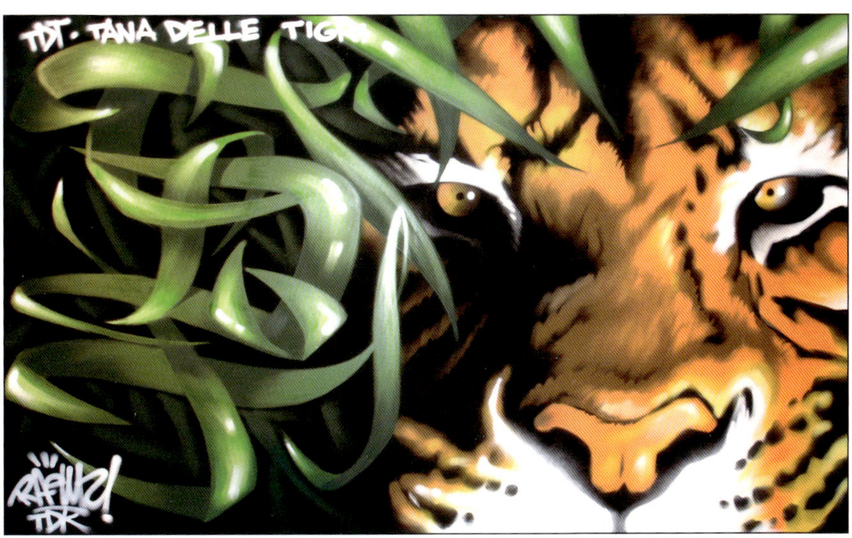

Tana delle tigri - spraycan on canvas, cm.300x200 - 2007

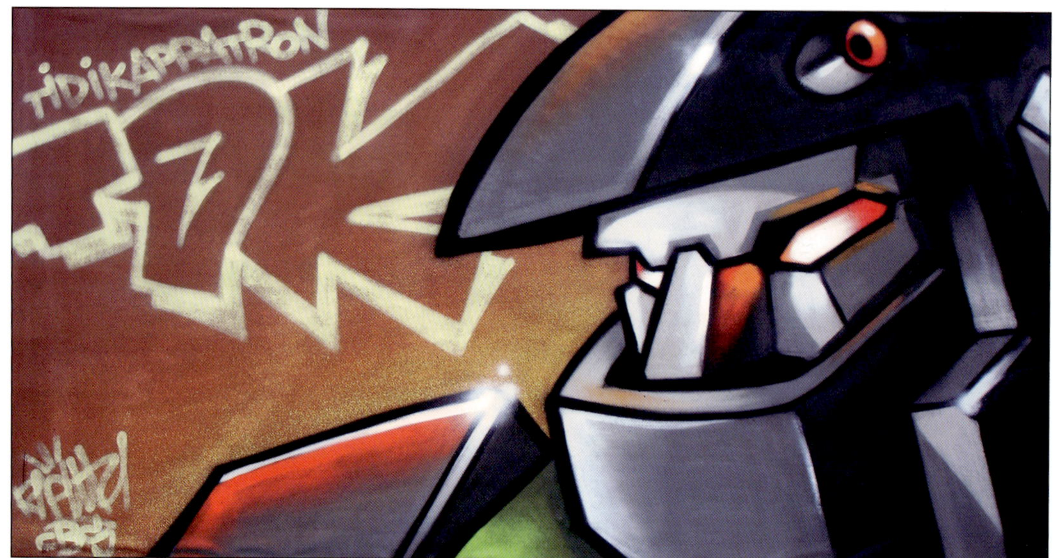

Tidikappatron - spraycan on canvas, cm.200x100 - 2009

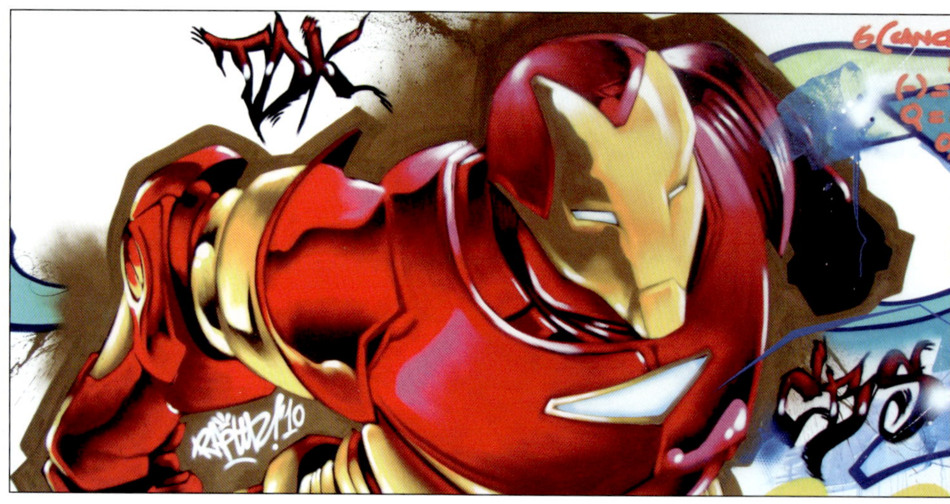

Ironman - spraycan on canvas, cm.400x200 - 2010

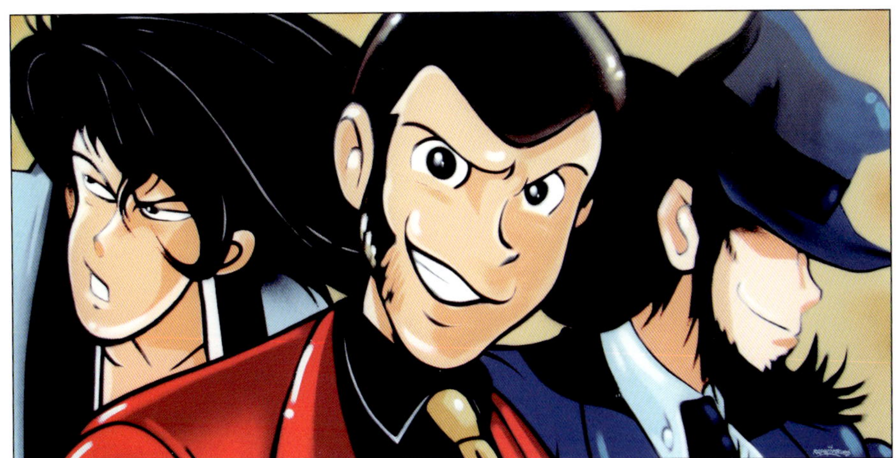

Lupin III - spraycan on canvas, cm.200x100 - 2010

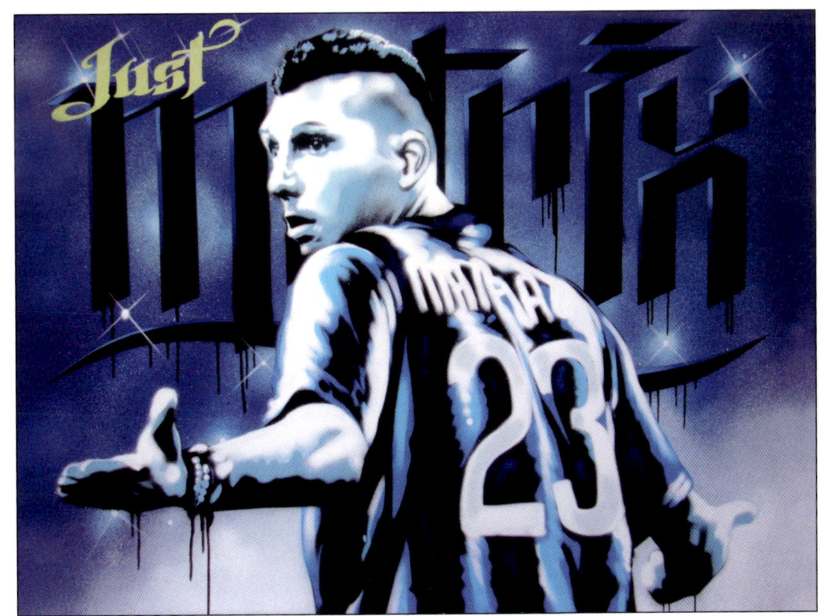

Just Matrix - spraycan on canvas, cm.200x150 - 2011

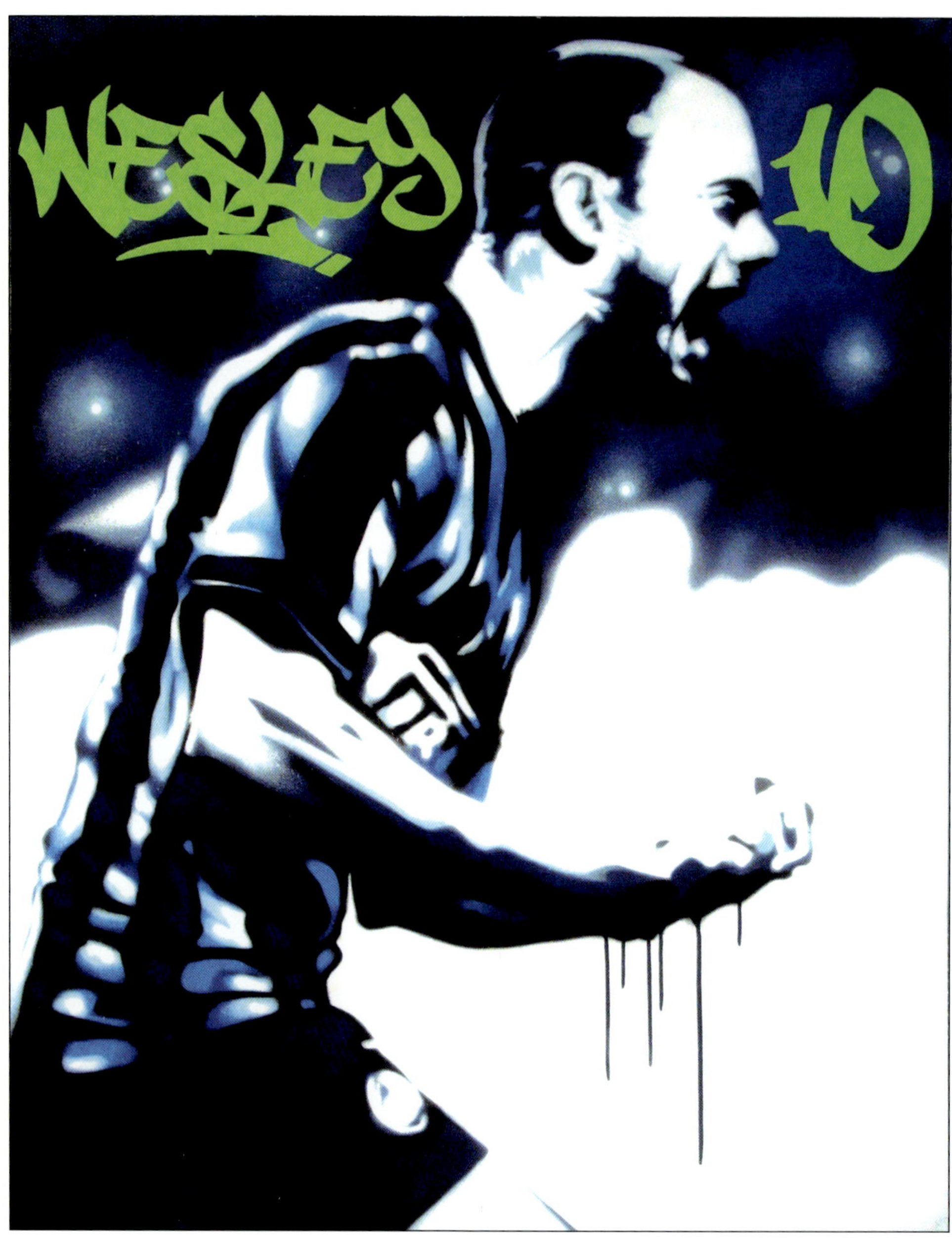

Wesley 10 - spraycan on canvas, cm.150x200 - 2010

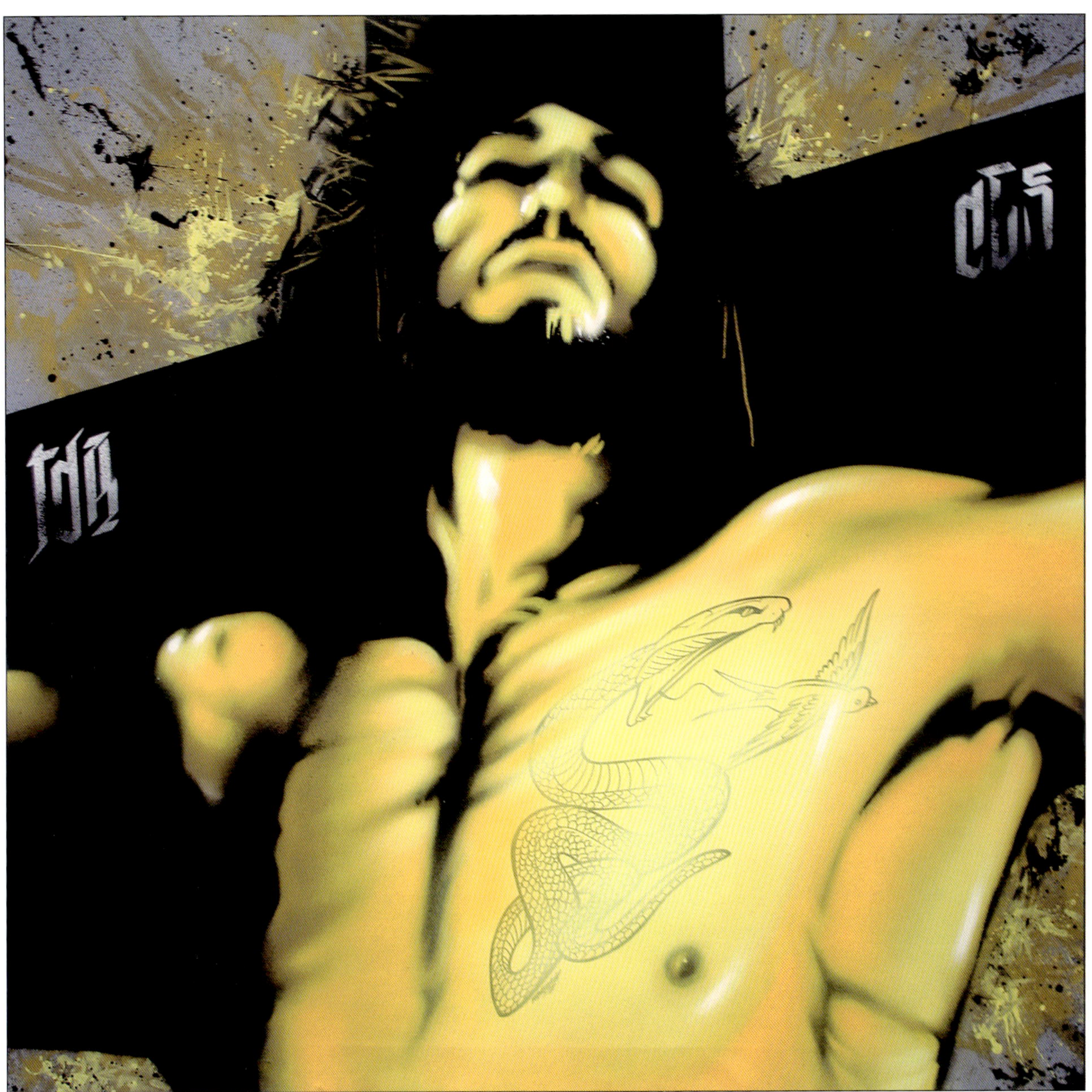

Angel of death - spraycan on canvas, cm.200x200 - 2009

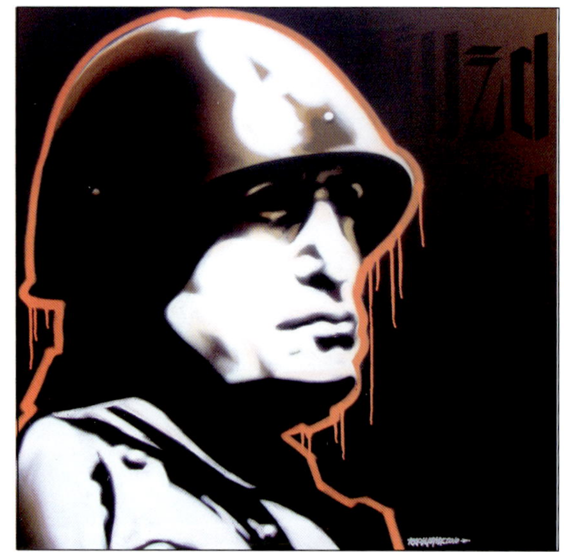

28/04/1945 - spraycan on canvas, cm.100x100 - 2010

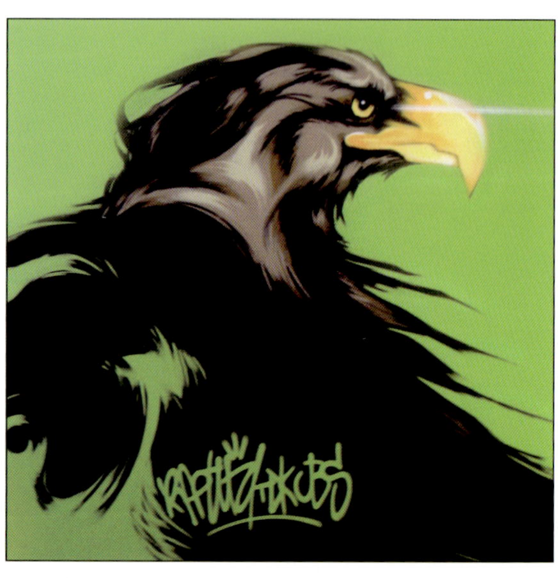

Aquila - spraycan on canvas, cm.100x100 - 2010

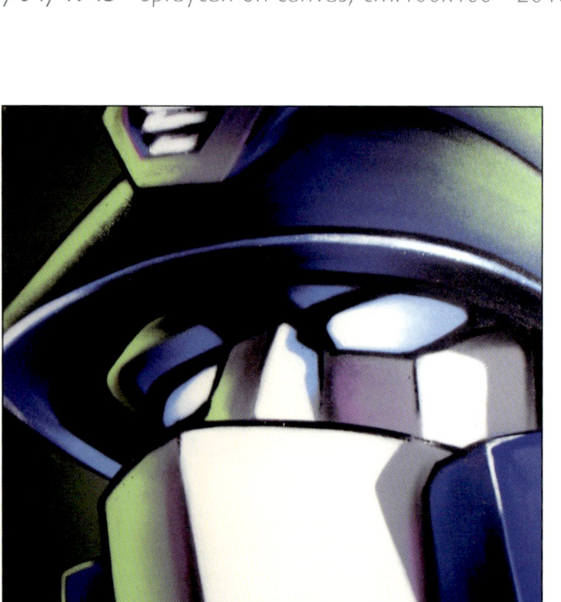

Raptimuz prime - spraycan on canvas, cm.100x100 - 2008

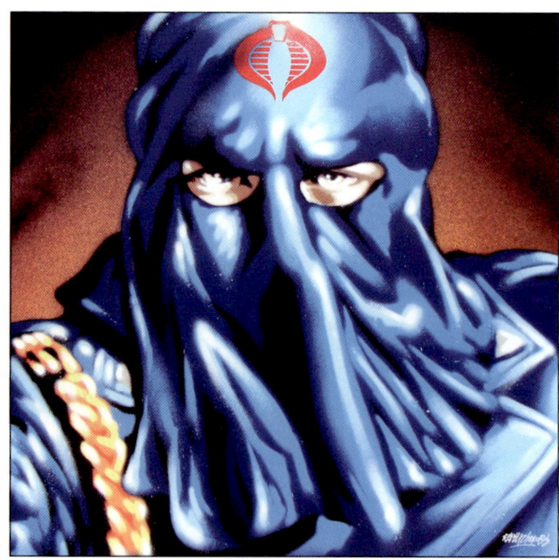

Cobra commander - spraycan on canvas, cm.100x100 - 2011

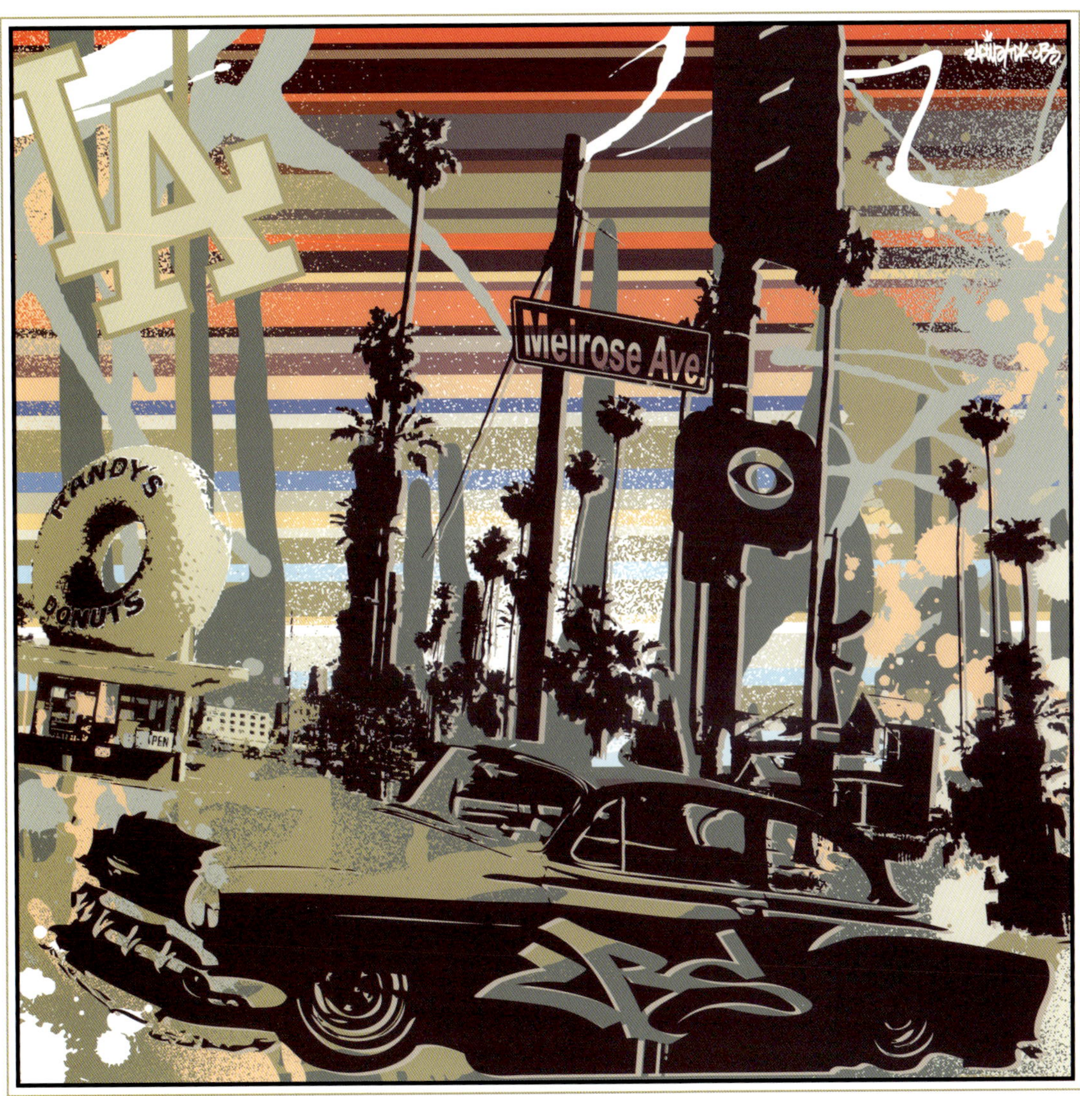

Cant Be Stopped - Limited edition vectorial digital print - 2011

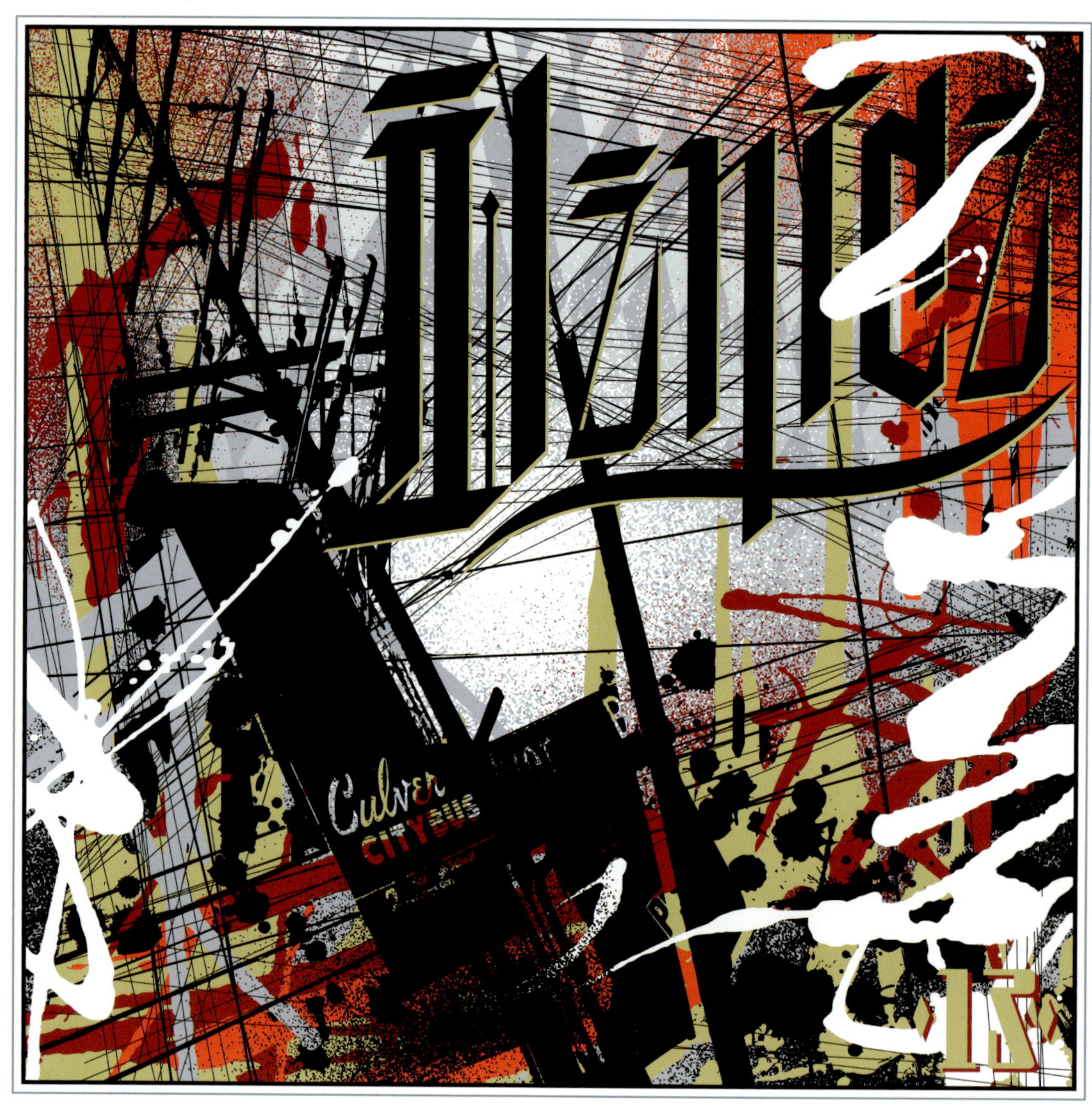

Venice Bloods - Limited edition vectorial digital print - 2011

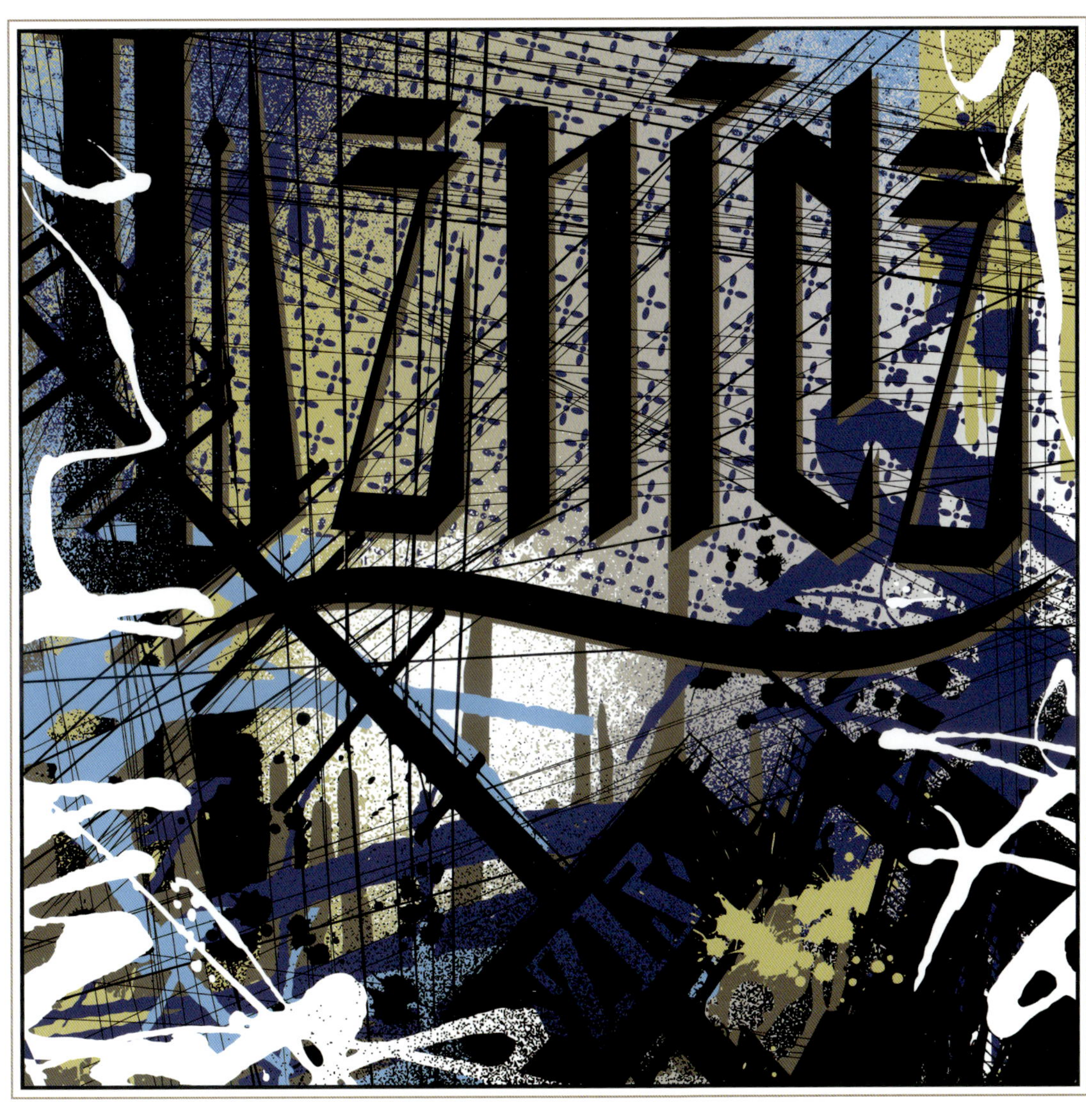

Venice Crips - Limited edition vectorial digital print - 2011

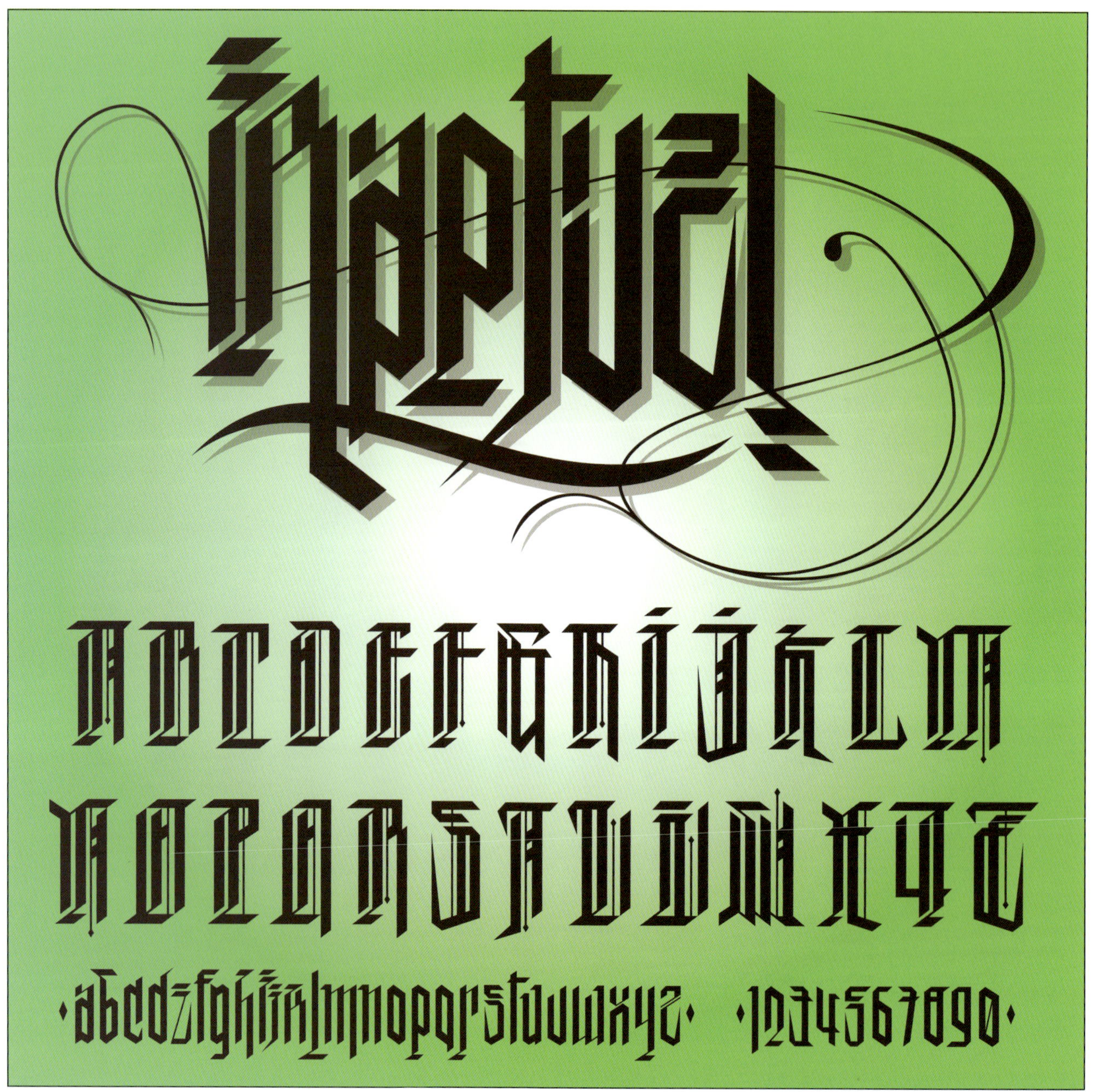

Raptuz Gothic font - ©2007

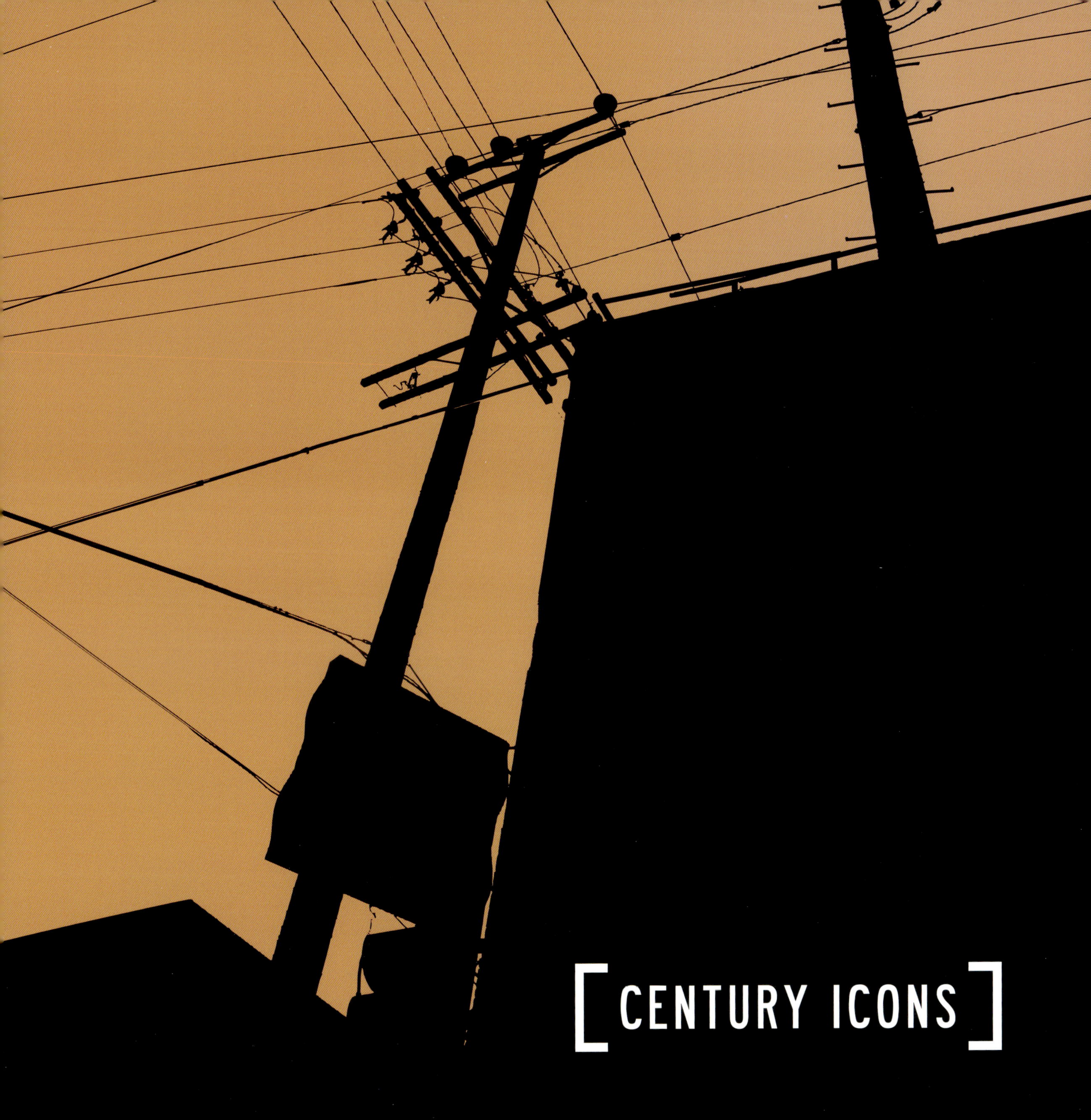
[CENTURY ICONS]

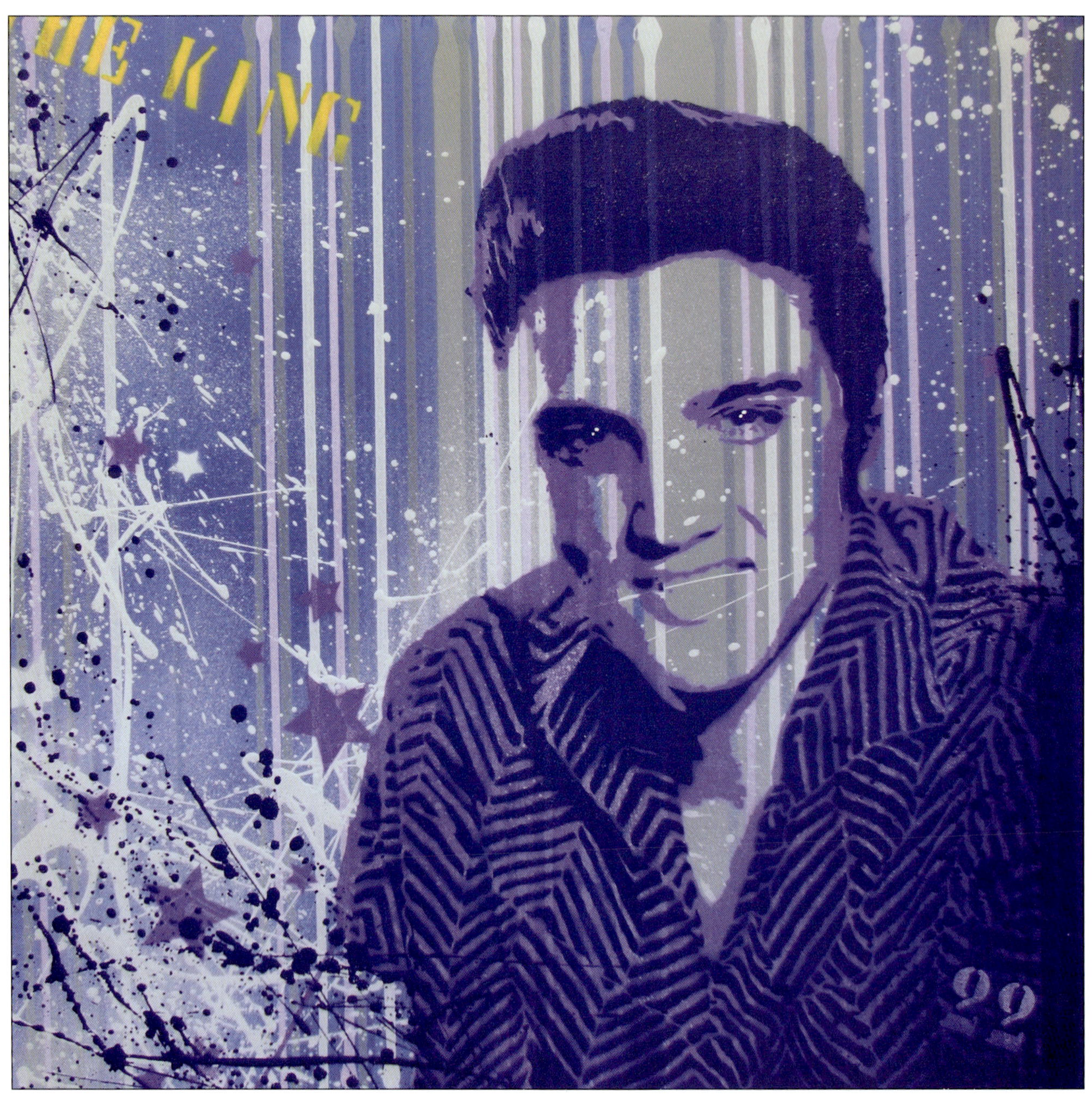

The king - Multilayer stencil & spraycan on canvas, cm.100x100 - 2011

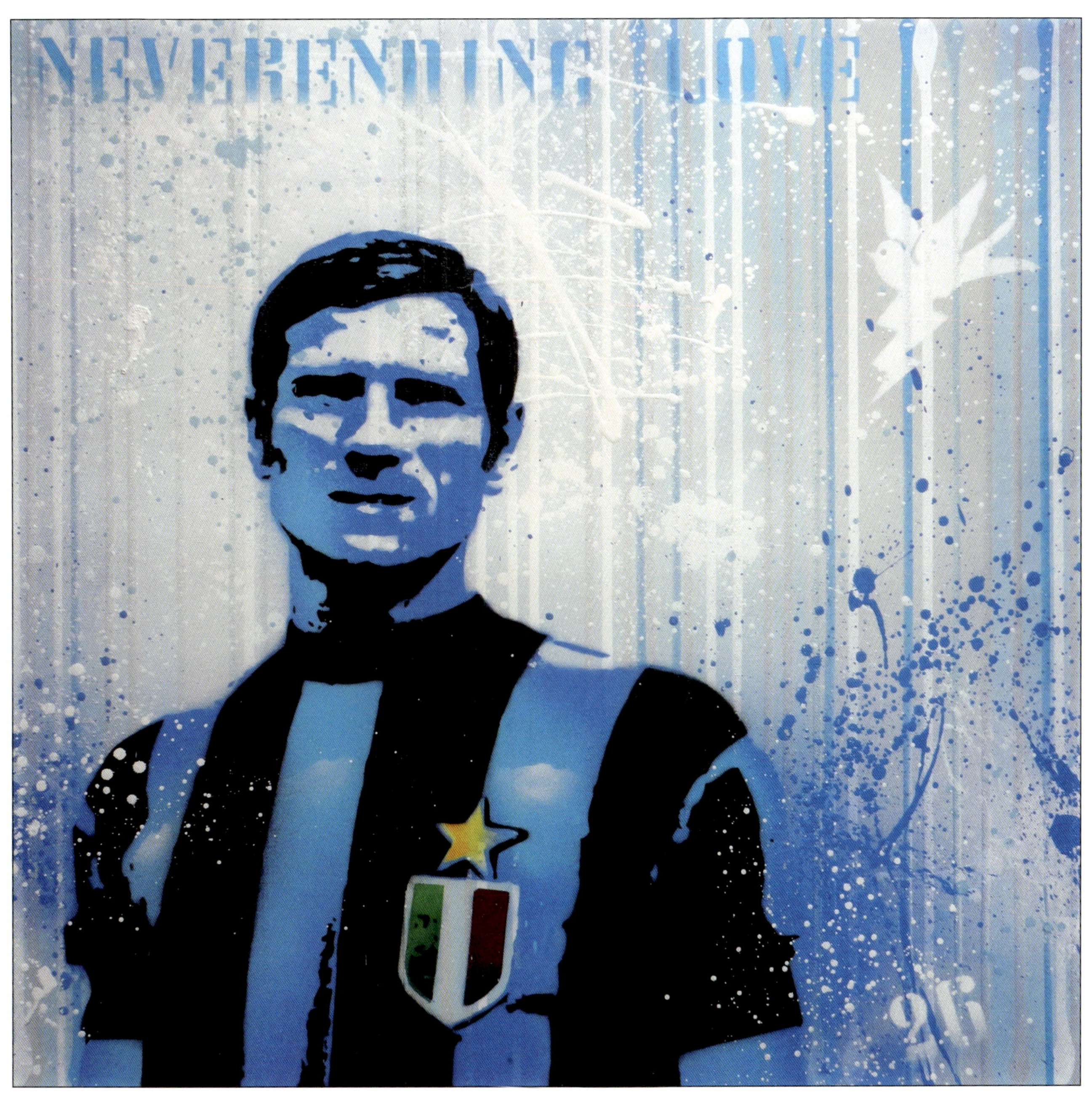

Neverending love (Giacinto Facchetti) - Multilayer stencil & spraycan on canvas, cm.100x100 - 2011

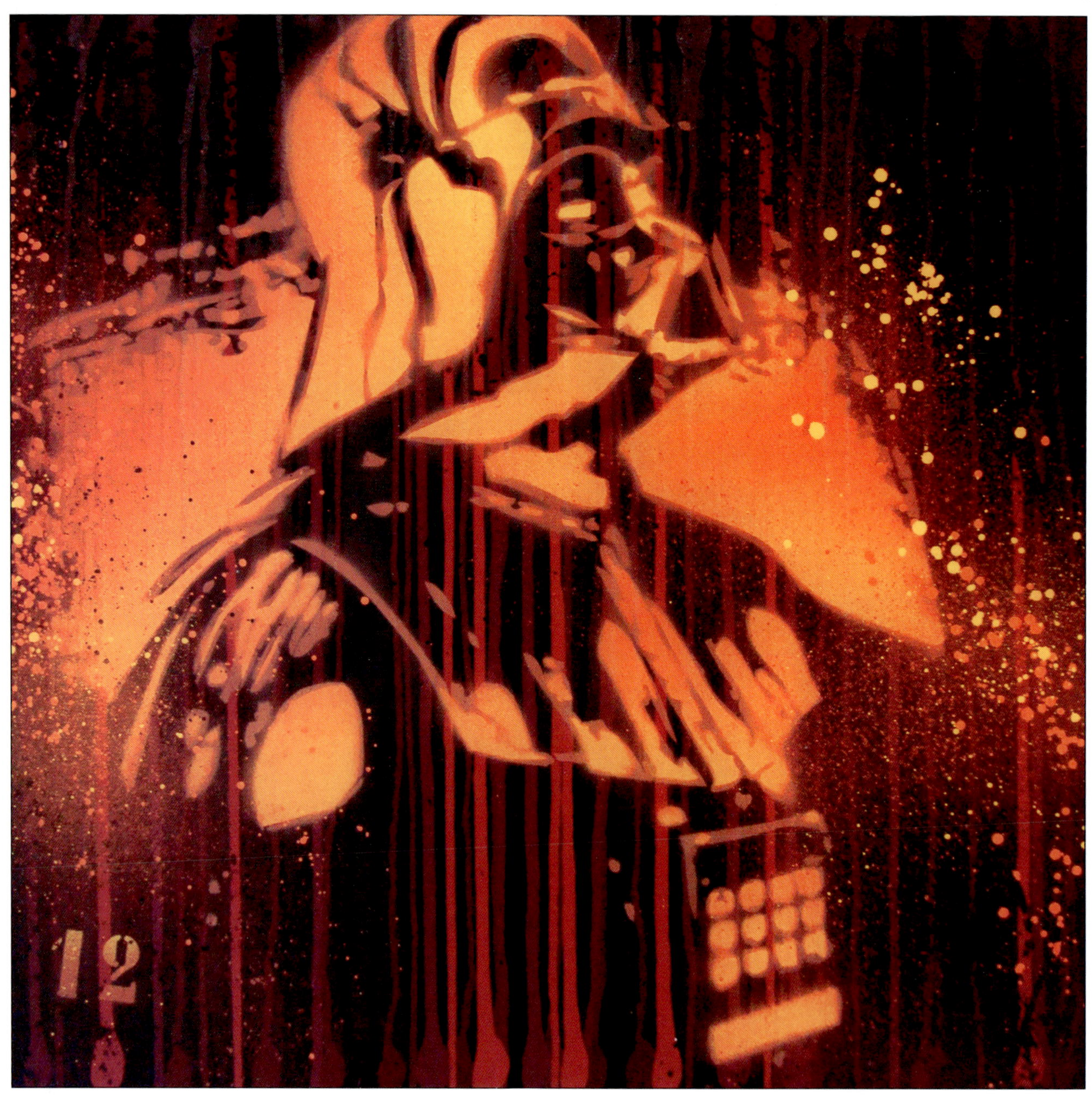

Darth Vader - Multilayer stencil & spraycan on canvas, cm.100x100 - 2011

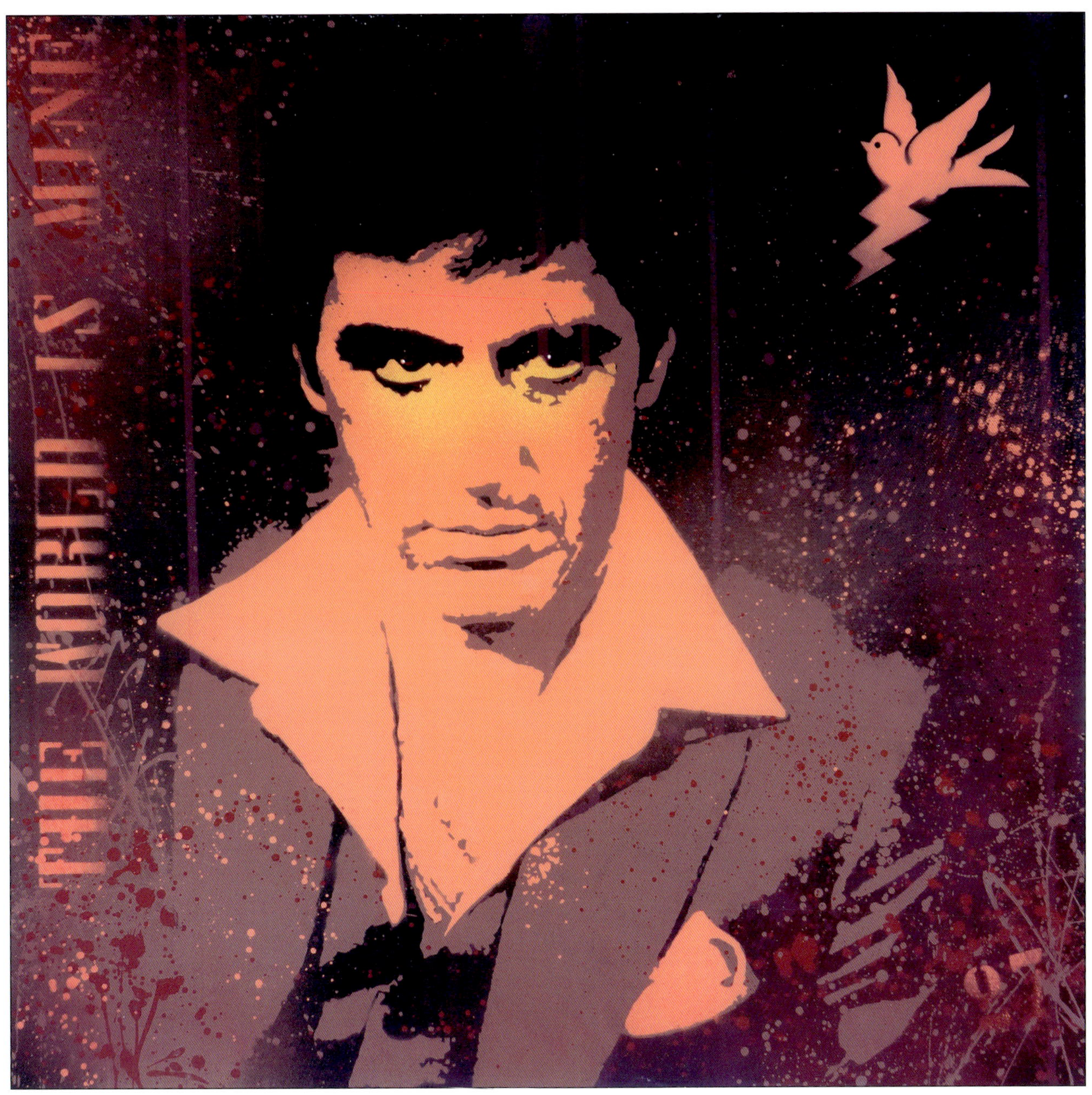

Tony rulez - Multilayer stencil & spraycan on canvas, cm.100x100 - 2011

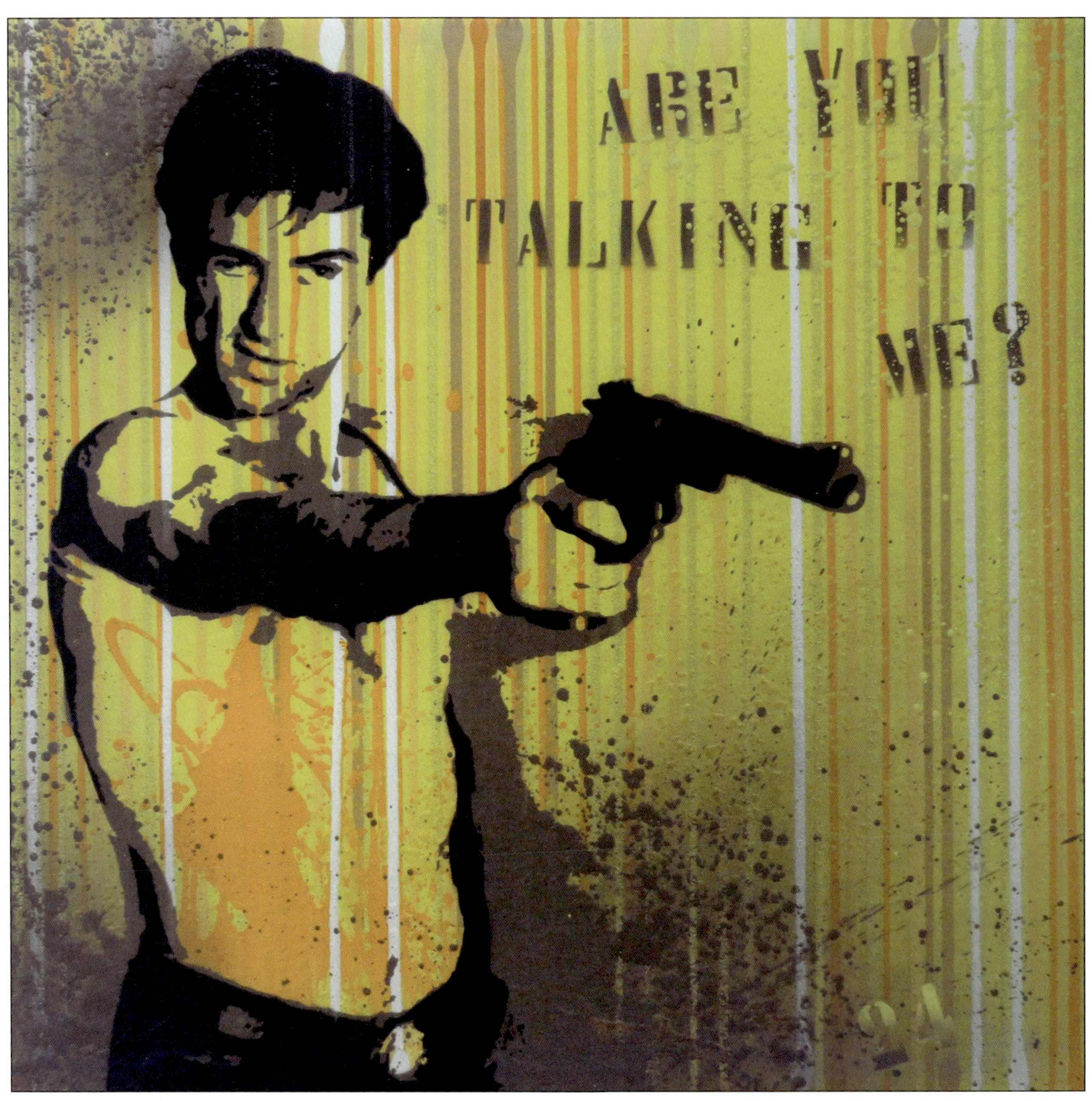

Taxi driver - Multilayer stencil & spraycan on canvas, cm.100x100 - 2011

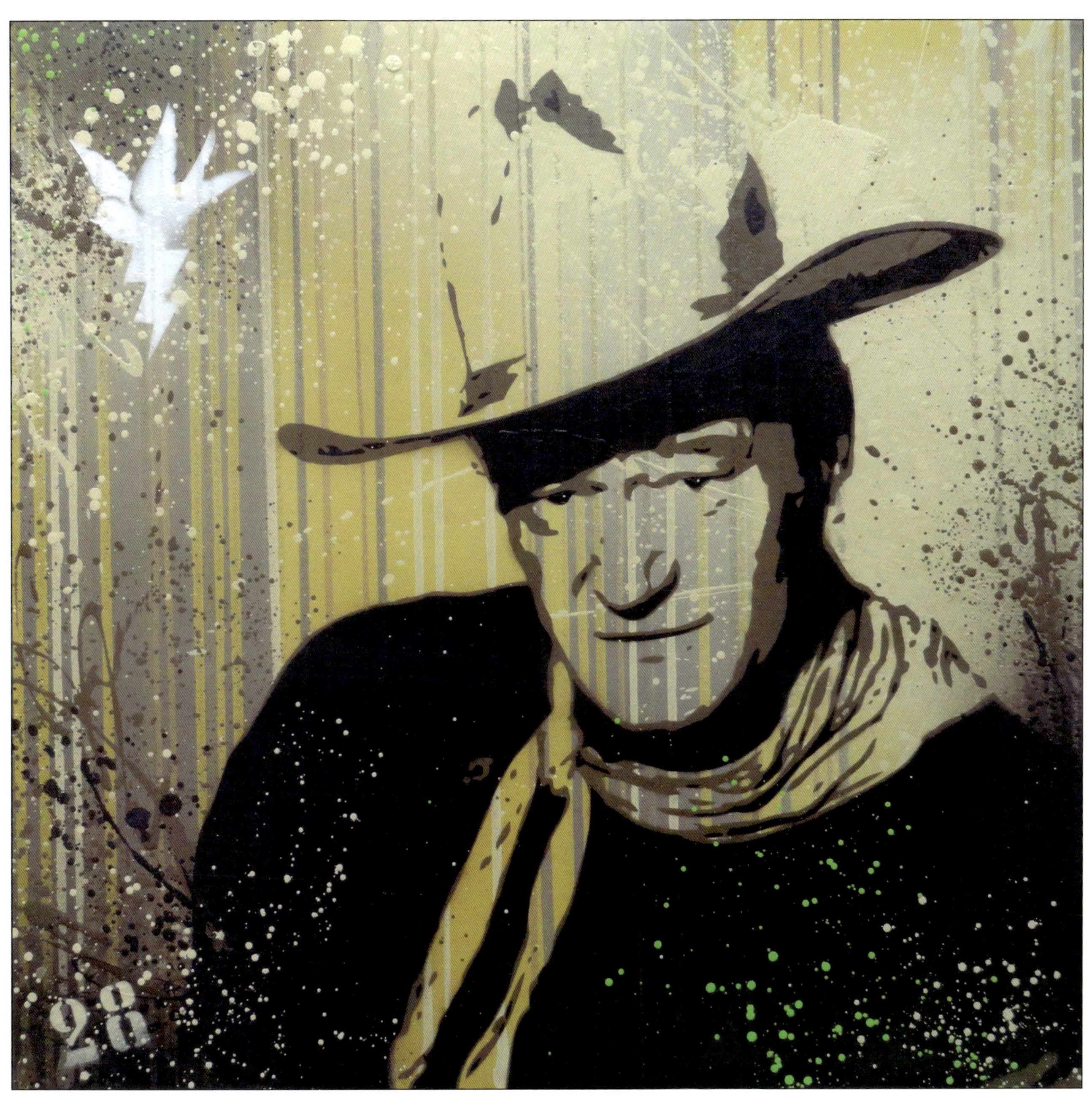

Lone cowboy - Multilayer stencil & spraycan on canvas, cm.100x100 - 2011

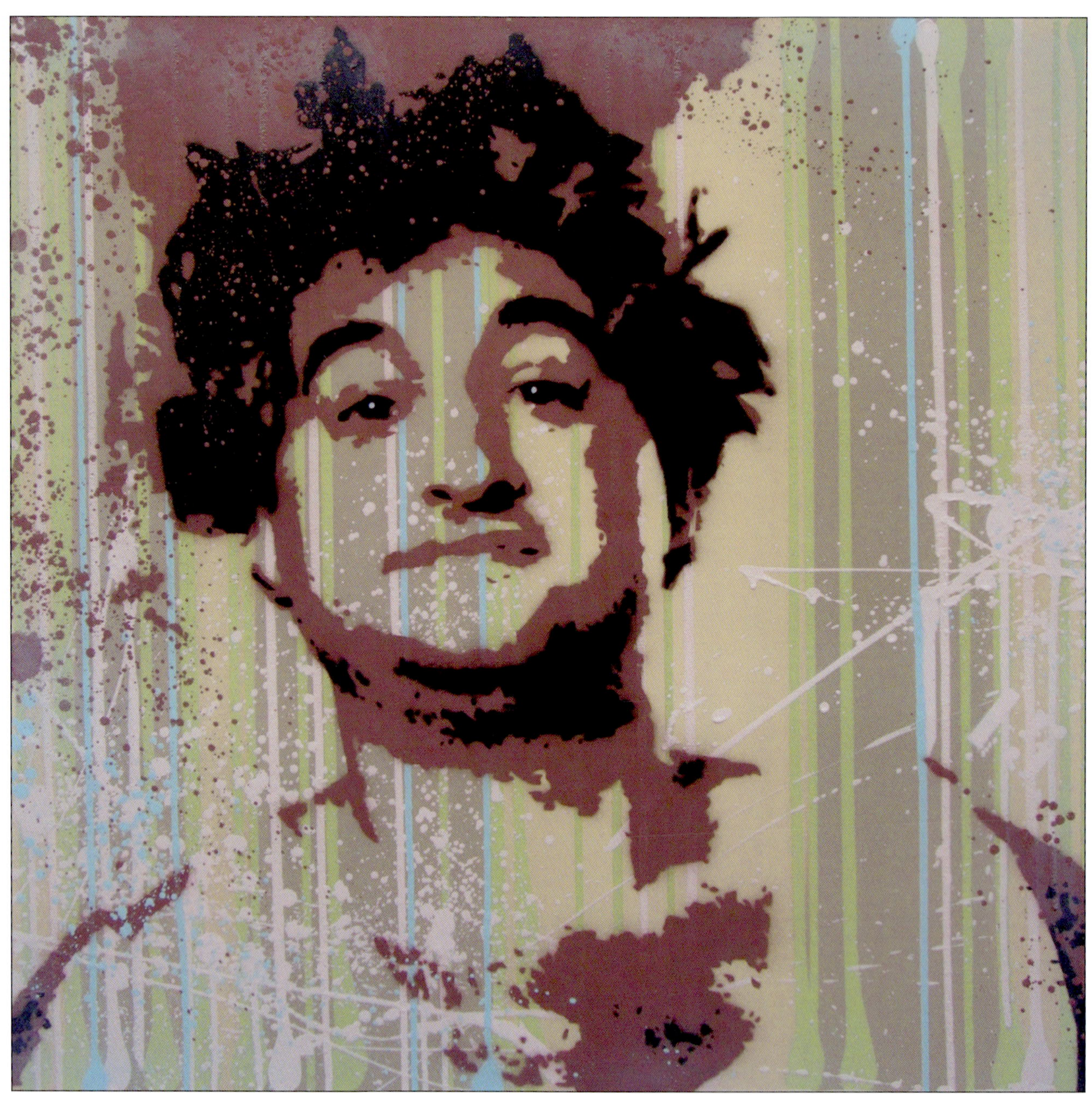

Toga! - Multilayer stencil & spraycan on canvas, cm.100x100 - 2011

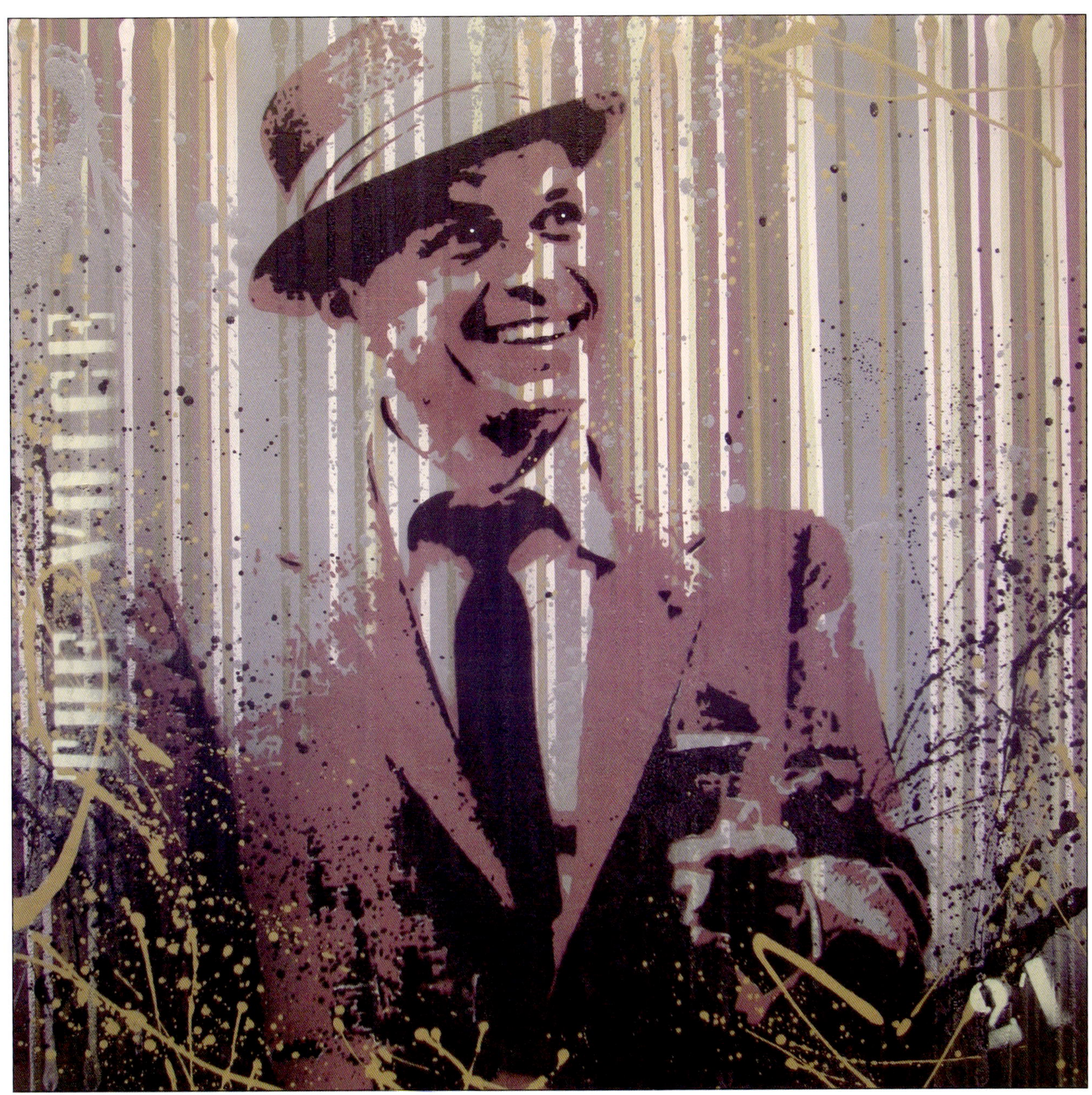

The voice - Multilayer stencil & spraycan on canvas, cm.100x100 - 2011

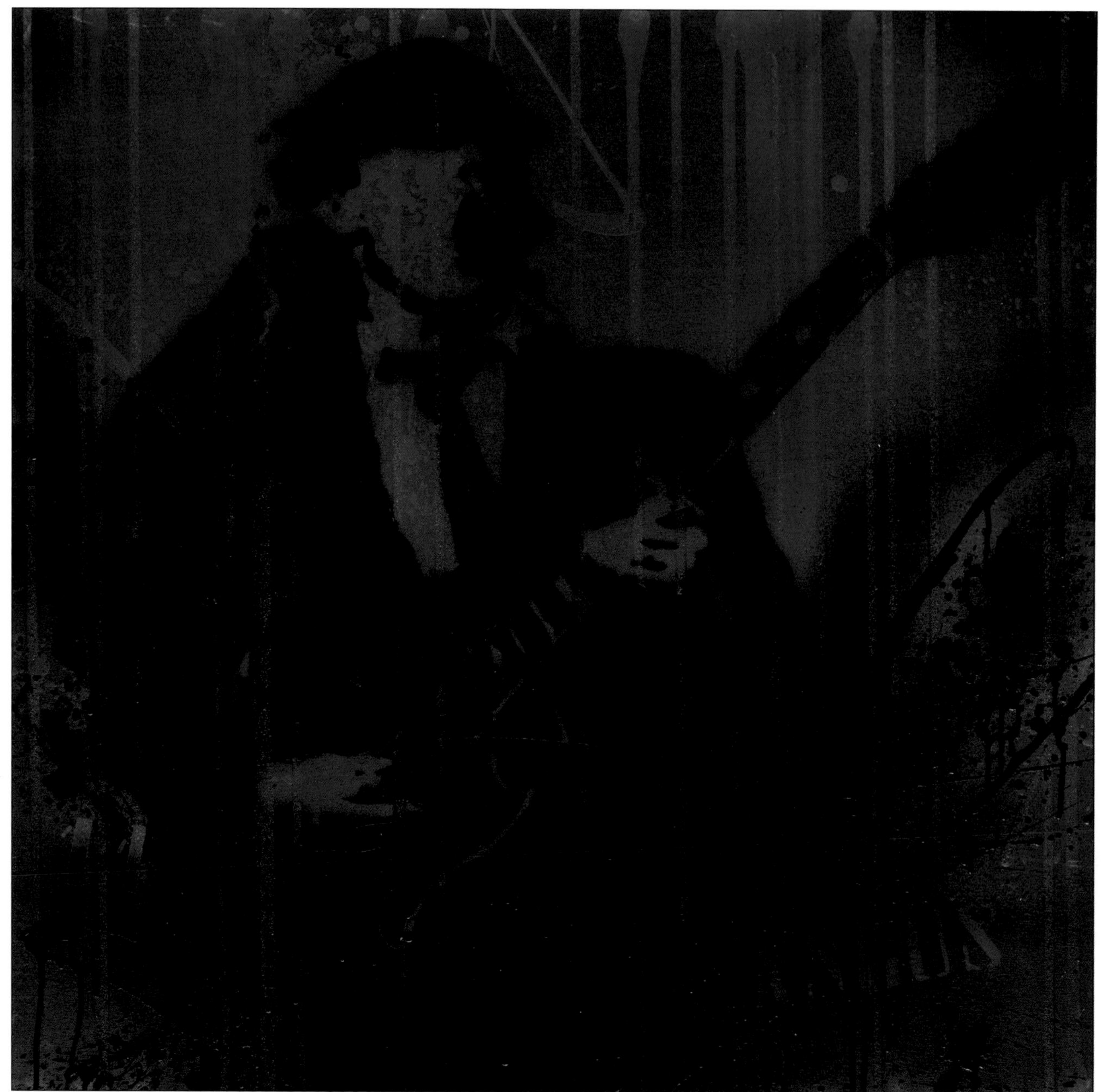

Photo: Daniele Barraco

Back in black - Multilayer stencil & spraycan on canvas, cm.100x100 - 2011

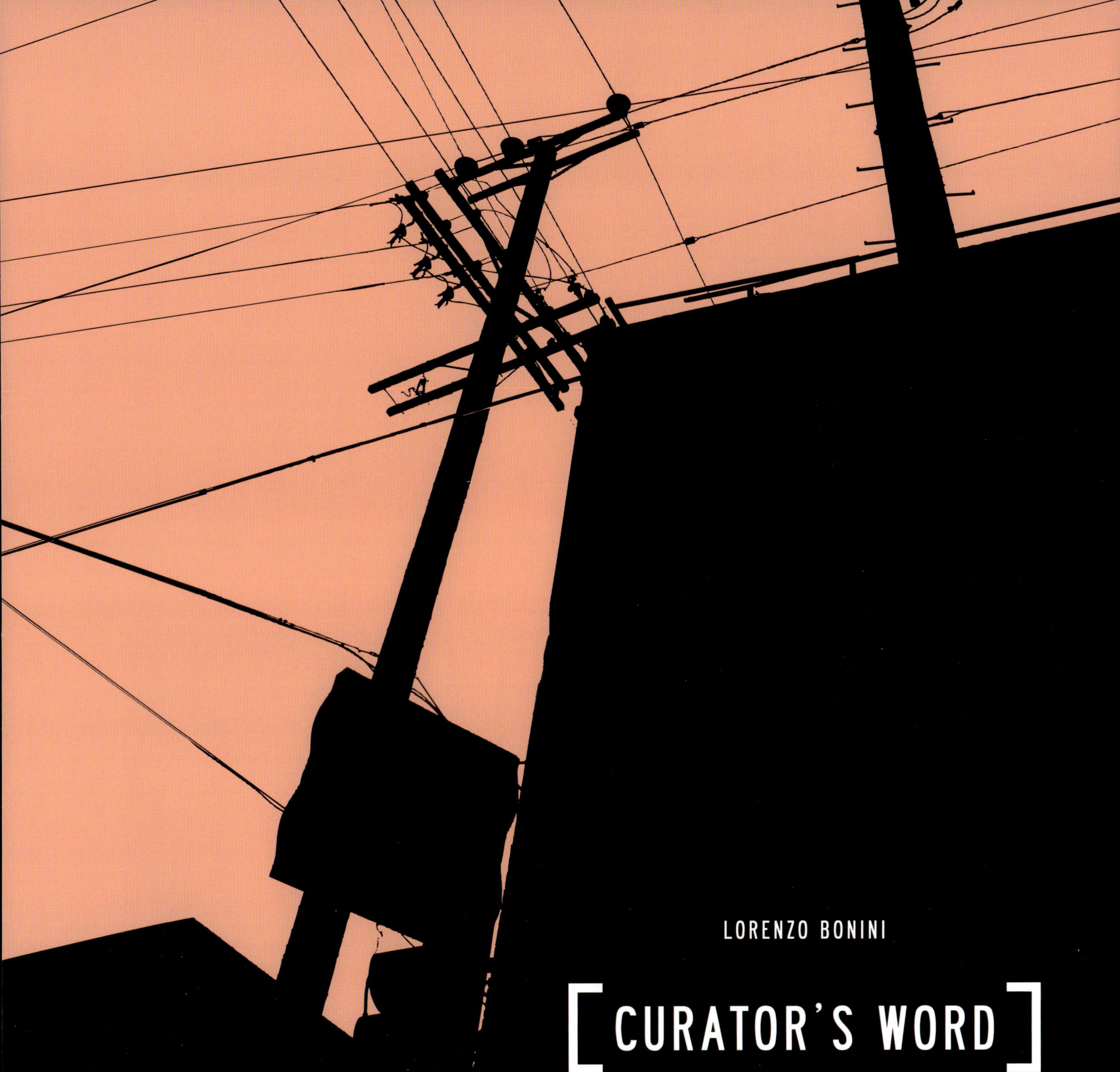

LORENZO BONINI
[CURATOR'S WORD]

Introduction

Popular books often tend to banalize the graffiti phenomenon, perhaps because, at least in the past publishing houses used to hire authors who did not fully know about the topic or who did not get enough information on it, but maybe they are the only ones who show a useful attempt to criticism for understanding the phenomenon and to allow them to mature a personal point of view. Books on graffiti can be divided into two categories, those made by writers for their community and popular ones. The first are certainly considered the best as far as workmanship, quality of information and images, they are often biographies or books that focus on a single aspect of the phenomenon, graffiti on trains, graffiti in a particular city or in a particular historical moment.

Since they are books which were made to be "read" by a community of professionals, many things are taken for granted and they often use an incomprehensible kind of language to ordinary people. They often deal with the story of graffiti in New York, and it is the epic story of young writers who are able to challenge the industrial power of six hundred miles of steel and cars going back and forth througout city, venturing into tunnels and thundering along overheads, for miles and miles of abandon and destruction occupying the spaces of the old council buildings.

Innocent creators of street art, threaded their way through fence holes to illuminate the decaying urban system, by transforming a system which was devastated by poor maintenance into colored surfaces that challenge the common opinion on public space.

Twenty-five years facing the wall and feet on the asphault: *the mirror of our times*

by Lorenzo Bonini.

Our world is an omnivore that wastes us and perpetuates everyday life troubles through a continuous stream of demands and needs. We are made of what we see and assimilate with uncritical obsession, with indifferent necessity, almost like a ritual due to life or to its fiction.

The works of Raptuz appear as the faithful mirror of a certain situation. They appear to us as a lucid metaphor of a behavior that belongs to us and identifies us also in a merciless and palpable existential malaise way. Man is crushed, broken, overwhelmed by things becoming thoughts. It is about food, the poison which is necessary for restarting the daily desire to start over again, to get back on track, to run towards the immediate future of the minutes and hours ahead. In order to document all this, we need an efficaciously chaotic painting and incisively descriptive, symbolistic and recognizable one. Raptuz squeezes his talent, trained since the years of apprenticeship and chopped away during frantic work nights along the road, as he says: "*My background is indisputably connected to the road, I lived half my life on the streets, I painted refining the*

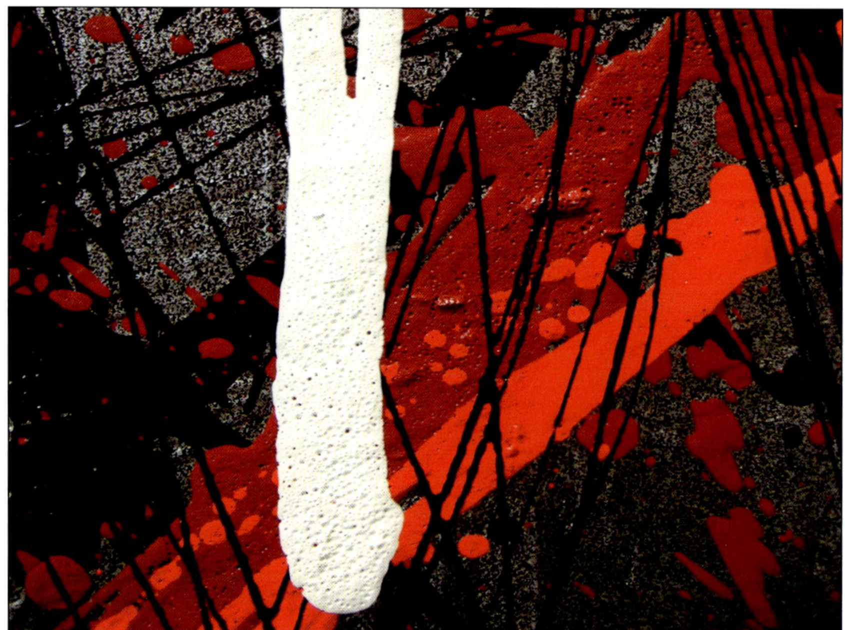

Photo: Daniele Barraco

After having summoned the ghosts of wild expressionism, armed with spray cans along the streets of the world, proceeding on walls and canvas made of acrylic colurs. He renews the time of obsessions and desolation, citing the oppressive emarginating neighborhoods by contrasting arrogance through pop iconographic paintings of popular characters.

Or through dismembered angular views of the neighborhoods of those cities which are considered modern. Seen in a cluster that invades the stage as if under the stimulus of a cataclysm which transforms objects and thoughts, following the results of metamorphic images and concepts in perpetual flux. Shattering and confusing with references to elements belonging to the city and to daily life, where the idea materializes itself and becomes a part of it, replacing the natural view, fueling the overall vision path, through determined pictorial schematic touches, furious and dynamic ones, without hesitation and repentance.

Therefore, he intervenes through the night rhythm of tones chasing now and then yellow, ocher, red with milky whites and brick-like brown lightings. There are recurring great Gothic writings created and produced with a raw, straight and sharp lettering, usually found in his pieces and studio-like works, a recognizable brand that became a symbol of the basic, honest, direct and concrete character as in the paintings. His works are created and born in the oppressive cities of the dormitories, gasometers, in the *promised land* of the outskirts, of the suburbs, where only false reflections of life are offered and the unreal escape of thought while playing in an artificial world, far away, if not absolutely opposed to the solar rumbles of the day and by the enchanting harmony of the ancient city.

This was for Raptuz: "The mother road" (his definition) is that which made him aware of being worth something, of growing up as a man and artist and for this purpose he says: "*The road has given me trouble, but it has also got me out of trouble, from the moment in which I focused on my writing energy rather than on*

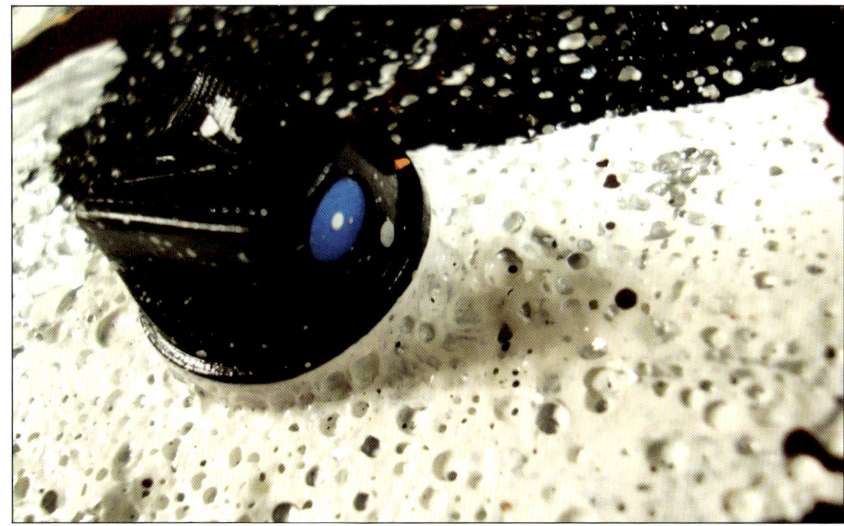

the other thousand bad roads I could have easily turned into.
My "mother roads" were Pioltello Satellite Centre; Rodano; Via Padova; and the Cimiano area in Milan; Santa Ana, West Hollywood, Los Angeles - California - USA. Some of the works which are published in this book are indeed inspired by the network of roads that intersect with Melrose Avenue and all lead towards the alley on which I paint, when I'm in Los Angeles, home and pictorial gym of my historical second family CBS Crew Hollywood (California Bomb Squad)."

The narrative pictorial chaos enhanced by the invention of compostion and by the chromatic combinations is the sysnthesis of a confusion that asails and permeates the perennial run-up of illusions. Techniques and materials are the classics ones of writing, especially: spray paint, acrylics and enamels, hydro-paints, canvases are prepared for simulating the rough wall, often using hand-cut stencils and later destroyed after being used just once.

He does not disdain the use of applying objects that have a symbolic meaning, which are familiar to him and are a part of his experience, such as: brushes, pencils, cardboard, cans, bullets, bandanas and of course talent. Kobra, one of the leading brands of spray cans for writers with whom he collaborates as a consultant and testimonial, has created and dedicated a specific color for the range of greens: kob code 10057 "Raptuz Green", emblematic.

The turbulent crushing in the works published in monograph always refers to that climate of assonance in the union of compositions, where thoughts, torments and fantastic solicitations encounter themselves and combine, materialize themselves in actual fact, giving birth to the work. These are the valid results which show us the reflected painting on our busker, born and raised in the vast suburb of Milan, which also offers us a glimpse, even in a dramatic way, of the story of his life during his twenty-five years spent as a writer on walls, trains, wagons, subways, bridges, underpasses, overpasses, climbing, guards, escapes, breathless climbings with his heart in his mouth, but always looking for the fantastic to surprise and fascinate for love.

I'd dare say - *twenty five years on the sidewalk* - with my head facing the wall and my feet on the asphalt. Seasons came and went, but he was always tough and stubborn, a vagrant on the sidewalks around half the world, always facing the wall and his feet on the asphalt with his imagination among the mesh of research and his back facing the suburban street, over there, down there looking for that Agorà that does not exist, with the illusion and the hope that barrier wall against freedoms, son of other sad walls. He was observed, fixed, scanned, examined, studied, investigated for twenty-five years, then painted, repainted and repainted again... Enough! Hoping he will dissappear by dissolving into a cloud, hoping he will never show up again, or be seen and each time you will meet him, face to face, turn your back on him.

Run away with your eyes facing the road of freedom. Explode angry thought of desolation, crumbling yourself and throw the debris in the ignorance's butt, the mother of idiocy.

U.S. playwright and Nobel Prize for Literature winner William Faulkner, said: "*The aim of every artist is to arrest motion and gesture, which is life, through artificial means and hold it still so that one hundred years later, when a stranger looks at it, it moves again because it is life and freedom*".

Premessa

I libri divulgativi tendono troppo spesso a banalizzare il fenomeno del graffitismo, forse perché, almeno in passato sono stati ingaggiati dalle case editrici autori che non conoscevano a pieno l'argomento o che si sono scarsamente documentati a riguardo, ma sono forse gli unici in cui è presente un tentativo di critica utile per comprendere il fenomeno e far maturare un proprio punto di vista. I libri di graffiti si possono dividere in due categorie, quelli fatti dai writer per la loro comunità e quelli divulgativi. I primi sono sicuramente i migliori per fattura, qualità delle informazioni e delle immagini, si tratta spesso di biografie o di volumi che inquadrano un singolo aspetto del fenomeno, i graffiti su treno, i graffiti in una particolare città o in un particolare momento storico.

Essendo libri fatti per essere "consumati" da una comunità addetta ai lavori si danno molte cose per scontante e si usa un linguaggio spesso incomprensibile per la gente comune. In essi spesso è raccontata la

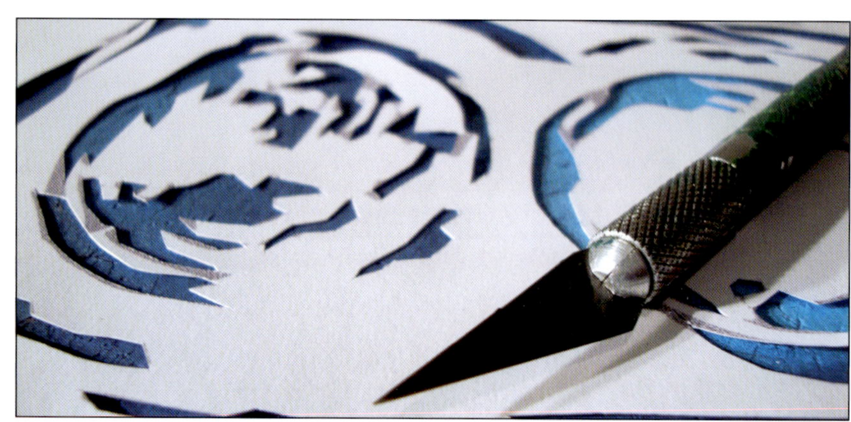

storia dei graffiti a New York, ed è la storia epica di giovani writer capaci di sfidare la potenza industriale di seicento miglia di acciaio e macchine che corrono attraverso la città, avventurandosi nei tunnel e tuonando lungo le sopraelevate, per miglia e miglia di abbandono e distruzione occupando lo spazio dei vecchi edifici popolari. Innocenti creatori di arte di strada, s'infilavano in buchi nelle recinzioni per illuminare il decadente sistema urbano, trasformando un sistema devastato da scarsa manutenzione in superfici colorate che sfidano l'opinione comune sullo spazio pubblico.

Venticinque anni con la faccia al muro e piedi sull'asfalto: *lo specchio del nostro tempo.*

by Lorenzo Bonini.

Il nostro è un mondo onnivoro che ci consuma e perpetua i travagli della quotidianità attraverso un continuo flusso di sollecitazioni e di esigenze. Noi siamo fatti di ciò che vediamo e che assimiliamo con acritica ossessione, con indifferente necessità, quasi come un rito dovuto alla vita o alla sua finzione.

Le opere di Raptuz ci appaiono come lo specchio fedele di una tale situazione. Si propongono ai nostri occhi quale lucida metafora di un comportamento che ci compete e ci identifica in maniera anche impietosa e palpabile malessere esistenziale. L'uomo è schiacciato, spezzato, tra-

volto dalle cose che si fanno pensieri. E sono l'alimento, il veleno necessario per riavviare ogni giorno il desiderio di ricominciare, di rimettersi in pista, di correre verso l'immediato futuro dei minuti e delle ore che incombono. Per documentare tutto questo occorre una pittura efficacemente caotica e incisivamente descrittiva, simbolista e riconoscibile. Raptuz spreme il suo estro, allenato fin dai lontani anni dell'apprendistato e triturato nelle frenetiche notti di lavoro sulla strada, racconta lui stesso:" *Il mio background è indiscutibilmente legato alla strada, in strada ho vissuto metà della mia vita, in strada ho dipinto affinando la tecnica, in strada ho sudato, avuto freddo, litigato e versato sangue (e fatto versare), ma anche molto riso e gioito... alcuni dei più bei momenti della mia vita li ho passati con la faccia attaccata ad un muro ed i piedi ben piantati sull'asfalto*".

Dopo avere chiamato a raccolta i fantasmi dell'espressionismo selvaggio armato di bombolette spray percorre le strade del mondo, procede su muri e tele investite da colori acrilici. Egli rinnova il tempo delle ossessioni e delle desolazioni, citando i periferici plumbei quartieri emarginanti a contrapporre l'arroganza attraverso pitture iconografiche pop di personaggi popolari.

Oppure vedute angolari smembrate di quartieri in città definite moderne. Viste in un agglomerato che invade il proscenio come sotto lo stimolo di un cataclisma che trasforma oggetti e pensieri, seguendo quella deriva

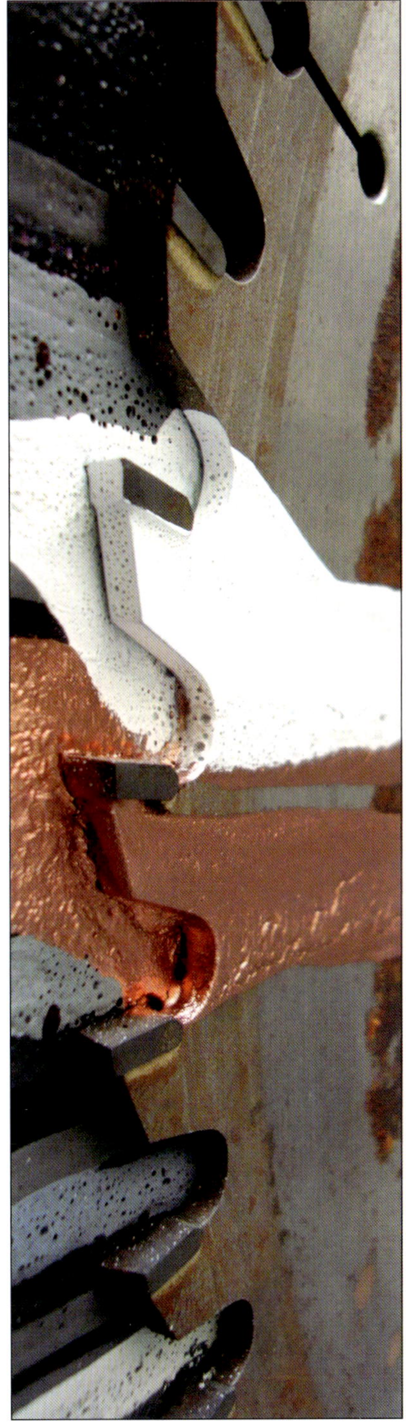

metamorfica d'immagini e di concetti in perpetuo divenire. Frantumarsi e confondersi con richiami a elementi della città e del quotidiano, dove l'idea si materializza e s'inserisce sostituendo la naturale veduta, alimentando il percorso d'insieme della visione, attraverso interventi pittorici decisi schematici, rabbiosi e dinamici, senza perplessità e pentimenti.

Quindi interviene attraverso il ritmo notturno dei toni che inseguono talora accensioni di gialli, ocra, rossi con bianchi lattiginosi e bruni mattonati. Ricorrenti sono le grandi scritte gotiche create e realizzate con un lettering crudo, lineare e tagliente, di solito presenti nei suoi pezzi e nelle opere da atelier, marchio riconoscibile che ne diventa simbolo del carattere basico, sincero, diretto e concreto come nei dipinti. Le sue opere si generano e nascono nelle città plumbee dei dormitori, dei gasometri, nella *terra promessa* delle periferie dei sobborghi, lì dove si offrono solo falsi riflessi della vita e l'illusoria fuga del pensiero nella messa in scena di un mondo artificiale, lontano, se non addirittura opposto ai fragori solari del giorno e dall'incantevole armonia della città vetusta.

Questa per Raptuz è stata: "La strada madre" (sua la definizione) è quella che le ha dato la consapevolezza di valere qualcosa, di crescere come uomo e artista e a tal proposito ci dice: *"La strada mi ha dato guai, ma mi ha anche tolto dai guai, dal momento in cui ho focalizzato la mia energia sul writing piuttosto che sulle altre mille cattive strade che avrei potuto facilmente prendere.*
Le mie "strade madri" sono state Centro Satellite Pioltello; Rodano; Via Padova e zona Cimiano a Milano; *Santa Ana, West Hollywood, Los Angeles - California – Usa. Alcune opere pubblicate in questo libro sono appunto ispirate al reticolo di strade che intersecano con Melrose Avenue e portano tutte al vicolo dove dipingo, quando sono a Los Angeles, casa e palestra pittorica della mia storica seconda famiglia la CBS Crew Hollywood (California Bomb Squad)."*

Il caos narrativo pittorico esaltato dall'invenzione compositiva e dagli accostamenti cromatici è la sintesi di uno sconcerto che assale e permea la perenne rincorsa delle lusinghe. Le tecniche e i materiali sono quelli classici della tradizione writing, soprattutto: vernice spray, acrilici e smalti, idropitture, le tele sono preparate in modo da simulare il muro grezzo, spesso utilizza stencils tagliati a mano e poi distrutti dopo un solo utilizzo.

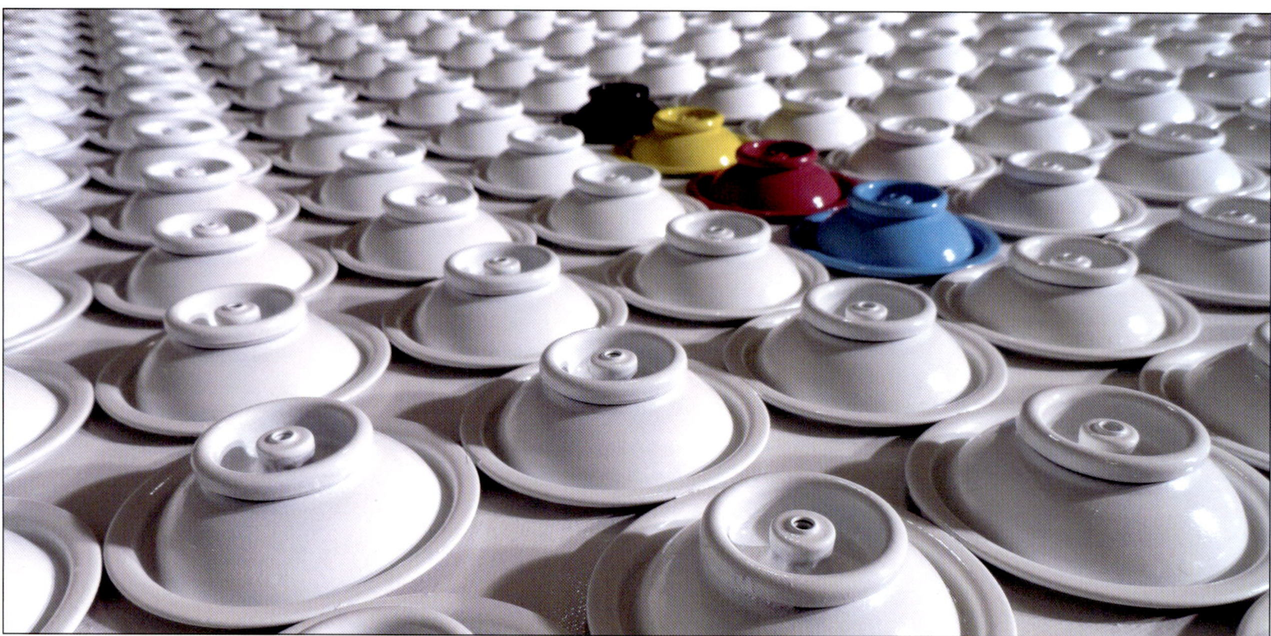

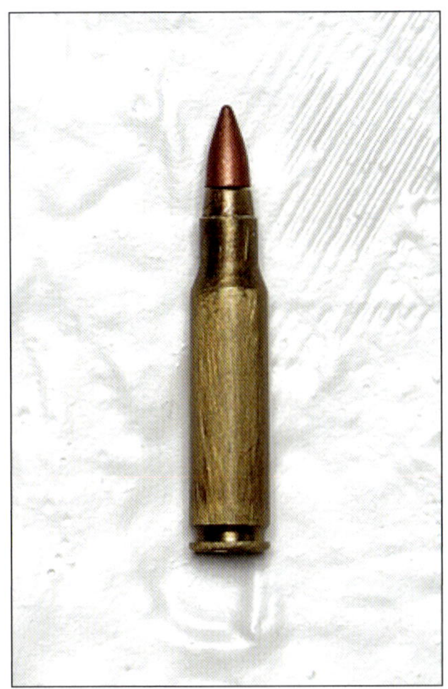

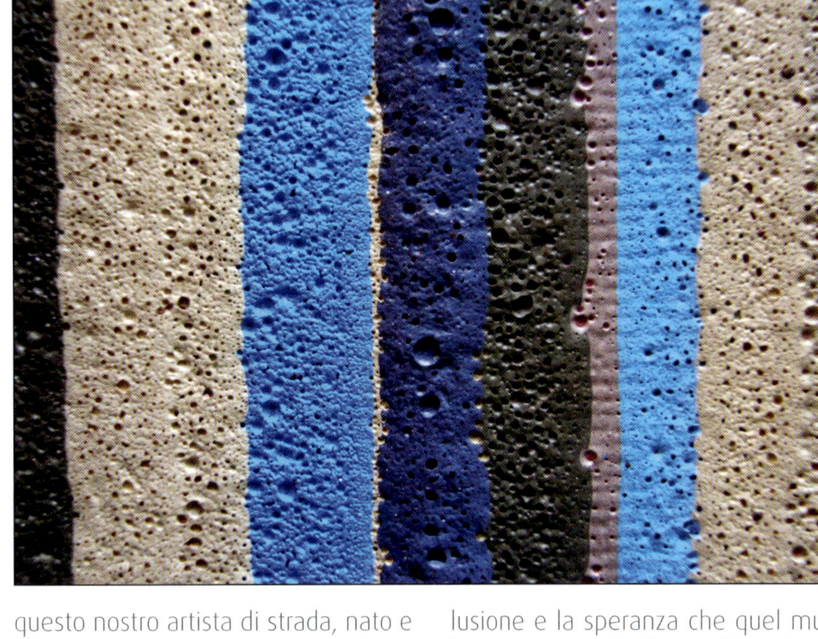

Non disdegna l'utilizzo di applicazioni di oggetti che hanno un significato simbolico, che conosce bene e fanno parte del suo vissuto, tipo: pennelli, matite da muratore, pezzi di cartone, bombolette, proiettili, bandane e naturalmente il talento. La Kobra una delle marche leader di bombolette spray per writers con la quale collabora in qualità di consulente e testimonial, ha creato e dedicato uno specifico colore della gamma dei verdi: codice kob 10057 "Raptuz Green", emblematico.

La movimentata frantumazione nelle opere pubblicate in monografia rimanda sempre a quel clima sicuramente di assonanza nell'unione delle composizioni, dove pensieri, tormenti e sollecitazioni fantastiche s'incontrano combinandosi, si materializzano concretamente dando origine all'opera. Sono questi validi risultati che ci mostrano il quadro riflesso su questo nostro artista di strada, nato e cresciuto nella vasta periferia milanese, che lascia intravvedere anche in modo drammatico la sua storia di vita nel corso dei suoi venticinque anni da writer, di muri, di treni, di vagoni, di metropolitane, di ponti, sottopassi, di cavalcavia, di scavalcamenti, di guardie, di fughe, di arrampicate col fiato corto e il cuore in gola ma sempre alla ricerca del fantastico per stupire e affascinare per amore.

Oserei dire - *venticinque anni di marciapiede* - con la faccia rivolta al muro e piedi sull'asfalto. Le stagioni si succedevano, ma lui sempre arduo e ostinato, vagabondo sui marciapiedi di mezzo mondo, sempre con la faccia al muro e i piedi sull'asfalto con l'immaginazione tra le maglie della ricerca e le spalle rivolte sulla strada di periferia, là, laggiù alla ricerca di quell'Agorà che non c'è, con l'illusione e la speranza che quel muro barriera contro le libertà, figlio di altri tristi muri. Osservato, fissato, scrutato, esaminato, studiato, indagato per venticinque anni poi pitturato, ripitturato e ripitturato ancora... Basta! Che sparisca dissolvendosi in nuvola, non si faccia più vedere, trovare e tutte le volte che ti capita di fronte, muso a muso, giragli le spalle.

Scappa con lo sguardo rivolto alla strada della libertà. Esplodi sdegno pensiero di desolazione, sgretolandoti scaglia i resti nel culo dell'ignoranza, madre dell'idiozia.

William Faulkner drammaturgo statunitense e Premio Nobel per la letteratura, disse: "*Lo scopo di ogni artista è arrestare il moto e il gesto, che è vita, con mezzi artificiali, e tenerlo fermo in tal modo che cent'anni dopo, quando un estraneo lo guarderà, torni a muoversi perché è vita e libertà*".

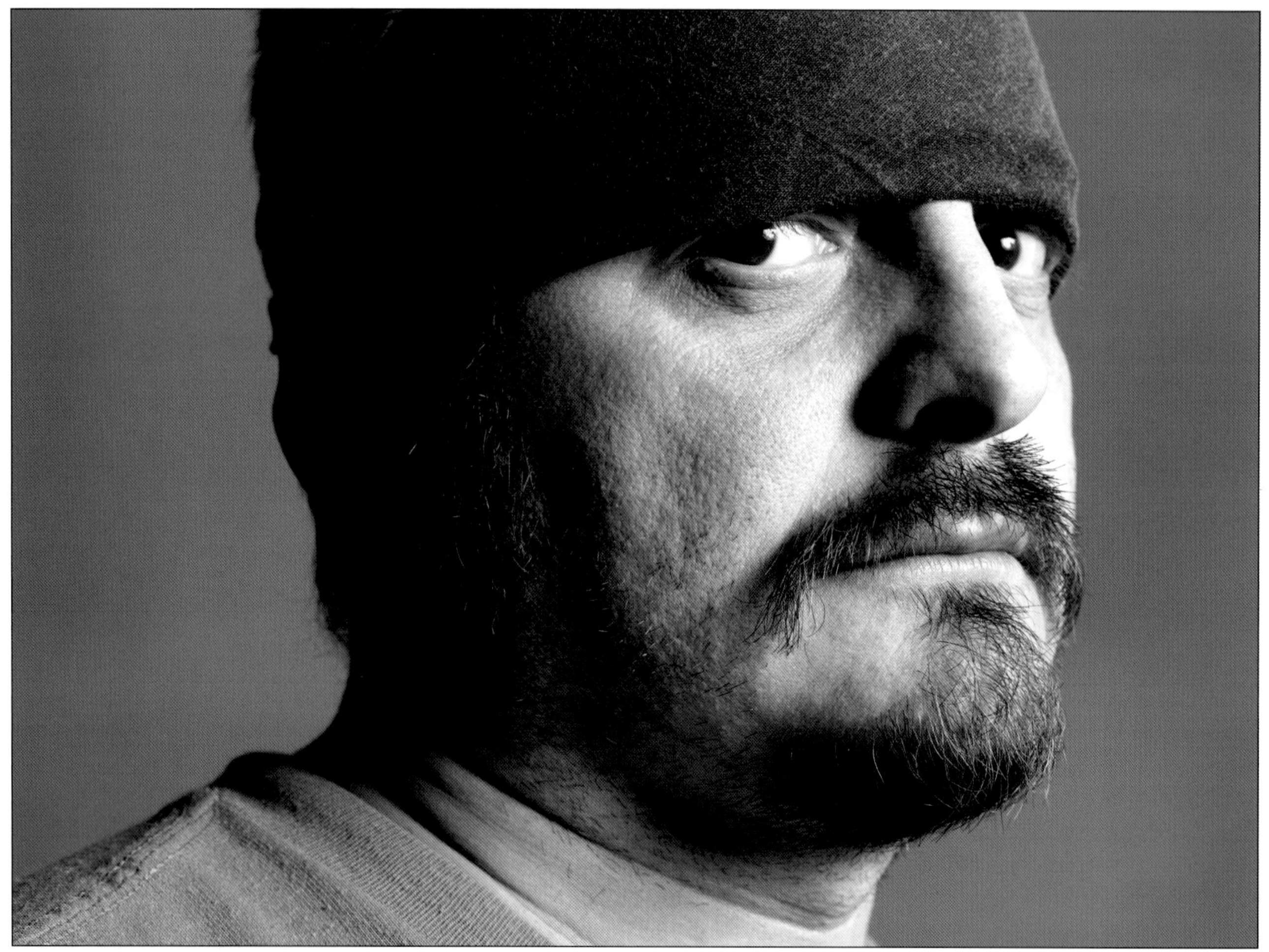

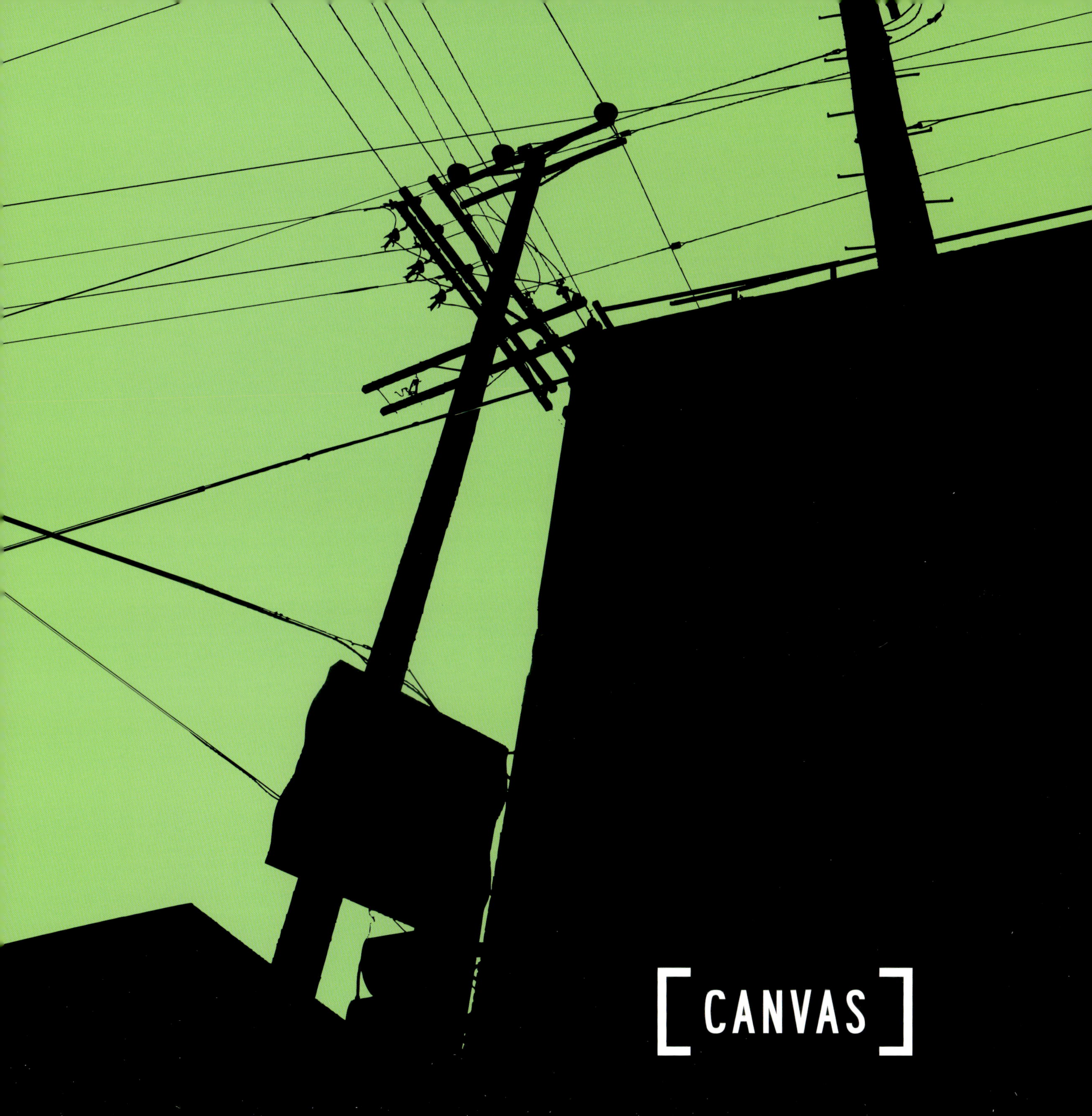

[CANVAS]

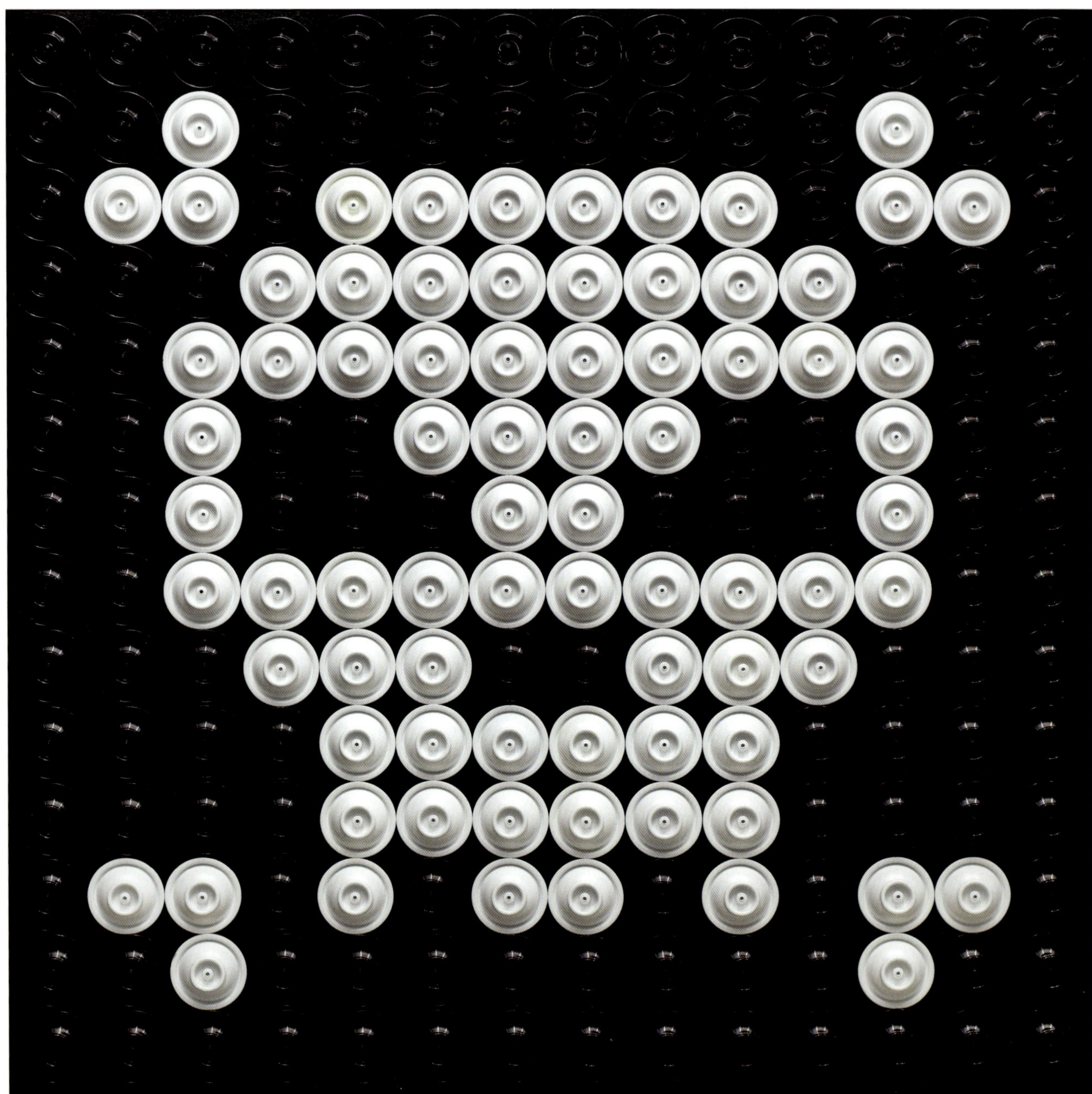

Old skull - Applications on canvas, cm.100x100 - 2011

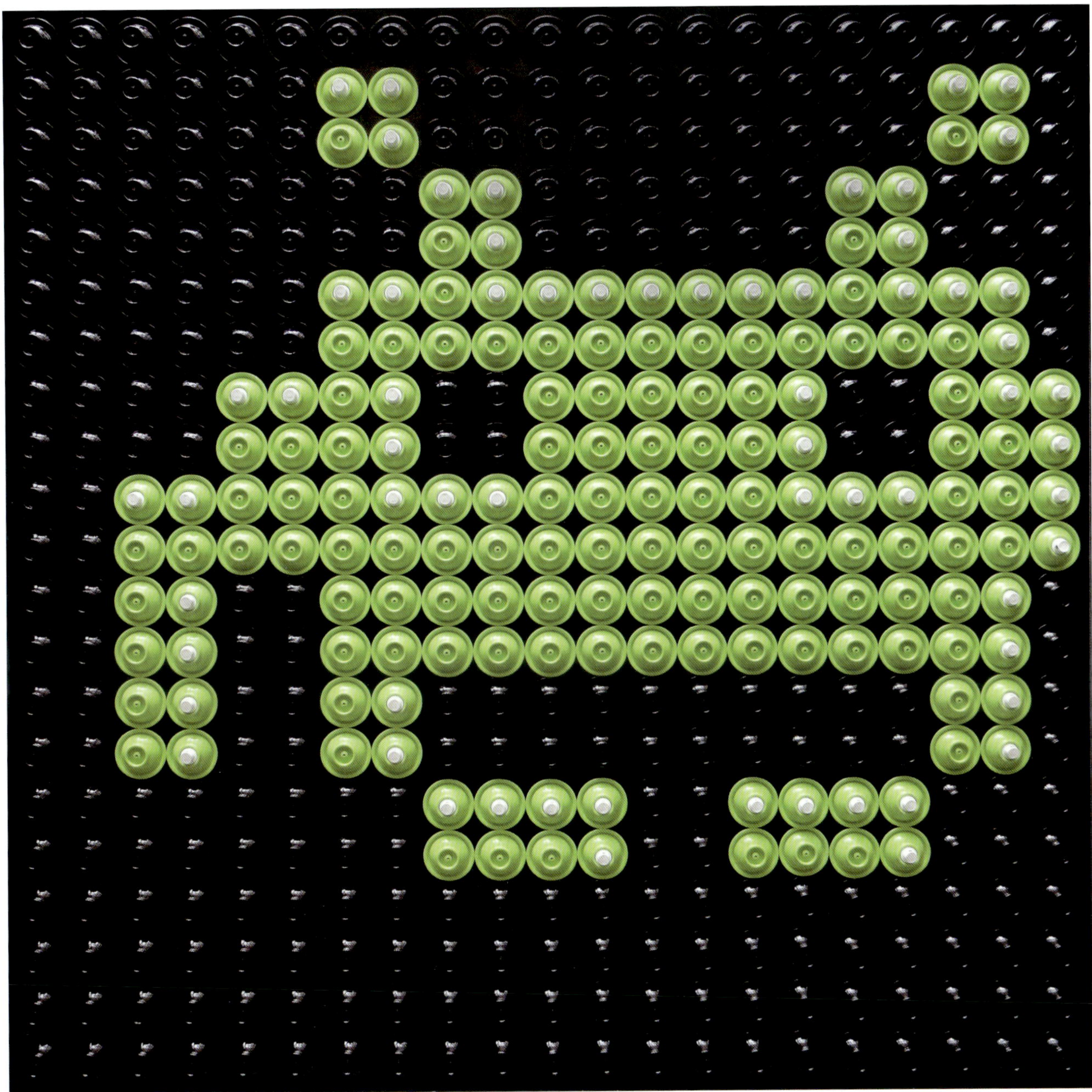

Green invader - Applications on canvas, cm.150x150 - 2011

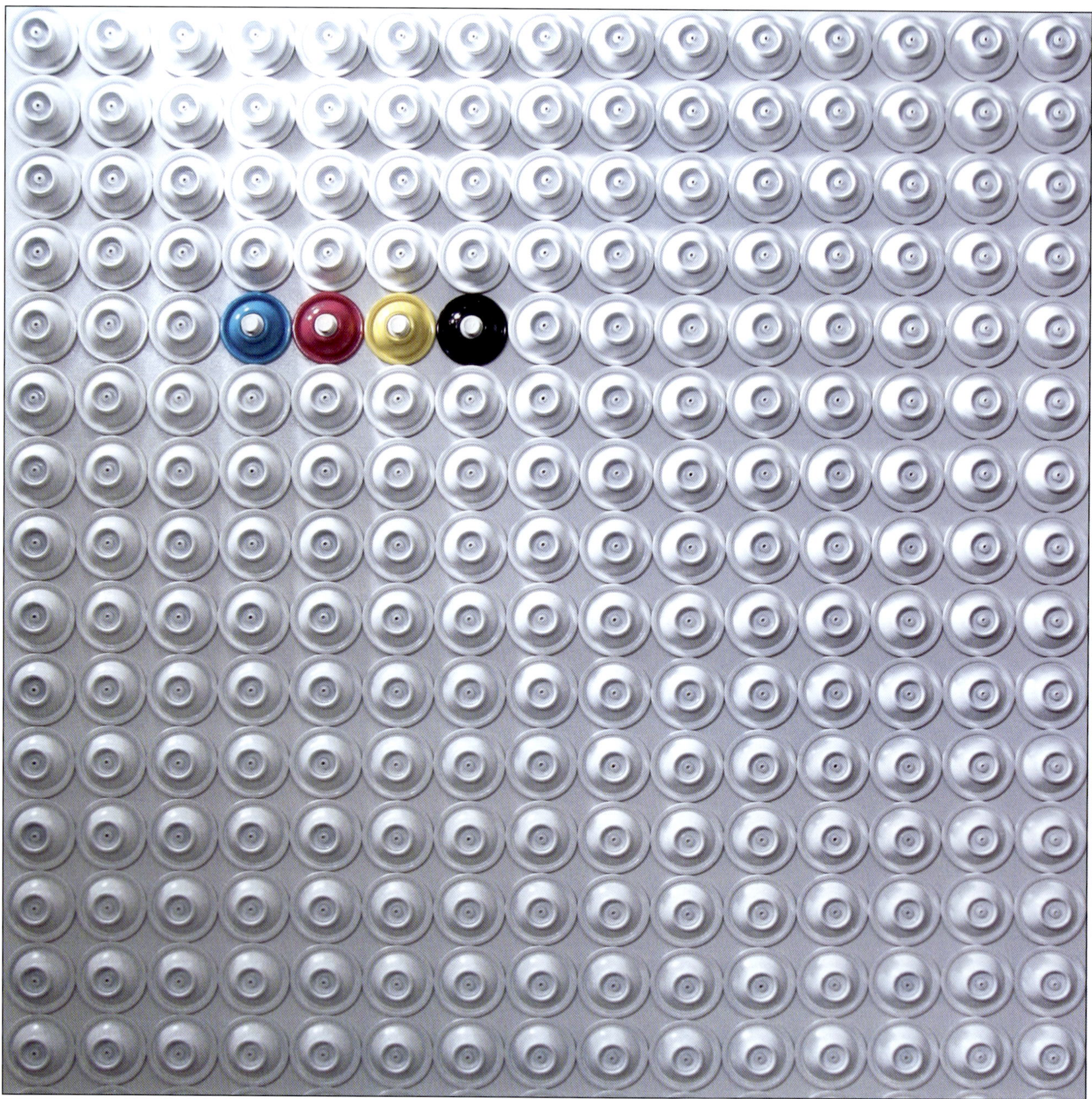

CMYK - Applications on canvas, cm.120x120 - 2011

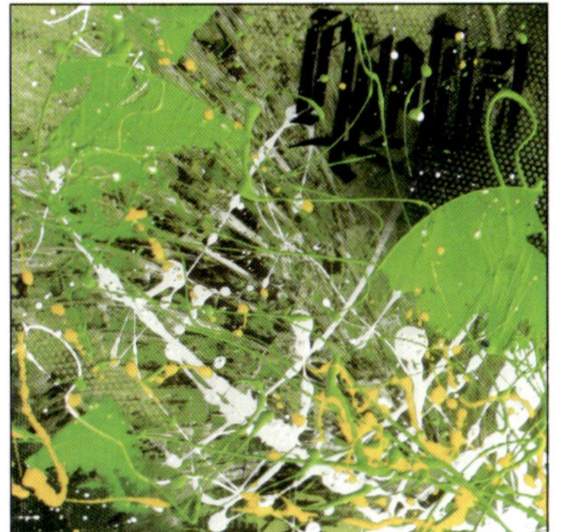 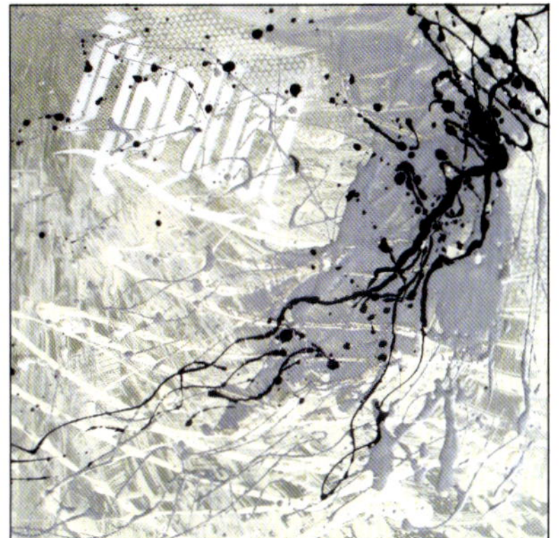 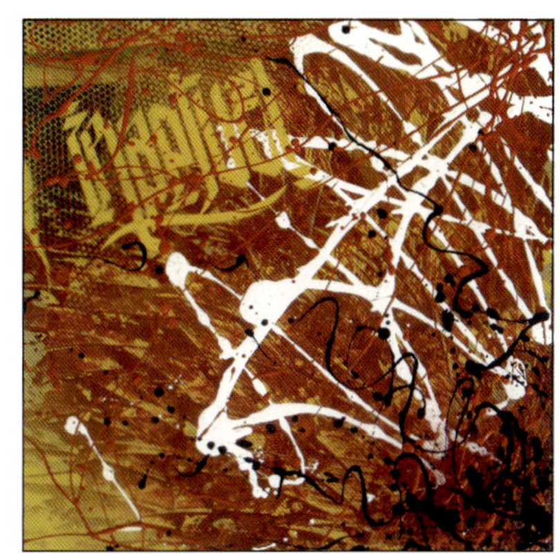

Spring 57, Winter storm, Sangre de toro - Mixed media on canvas, cm.30x30 - 2009

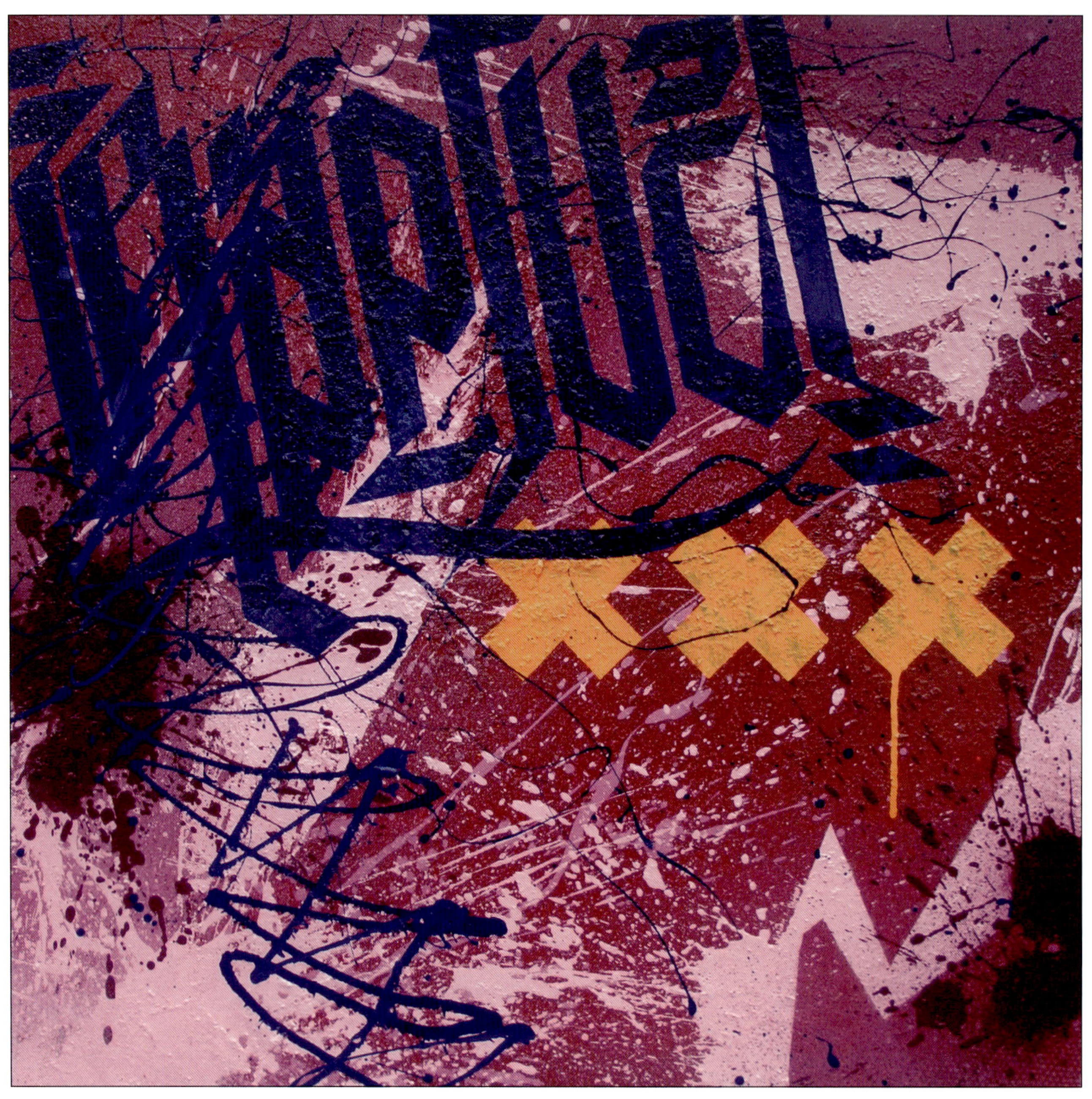

Blue gothic - Mixed media on canvas, cm.100x100 - 2009

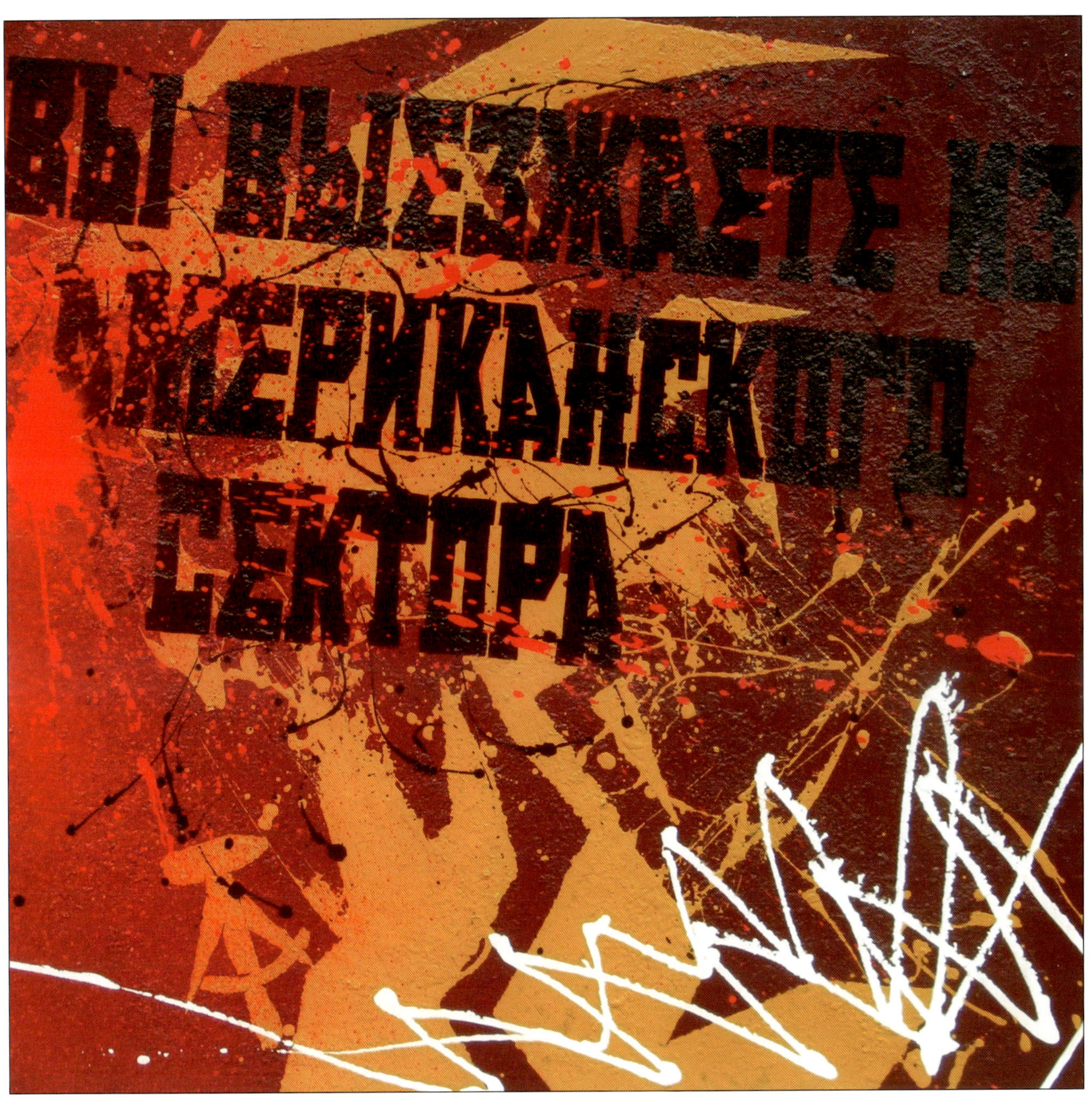

Checkpoint - Mixed media on canvas, cm.100x100 - 2009

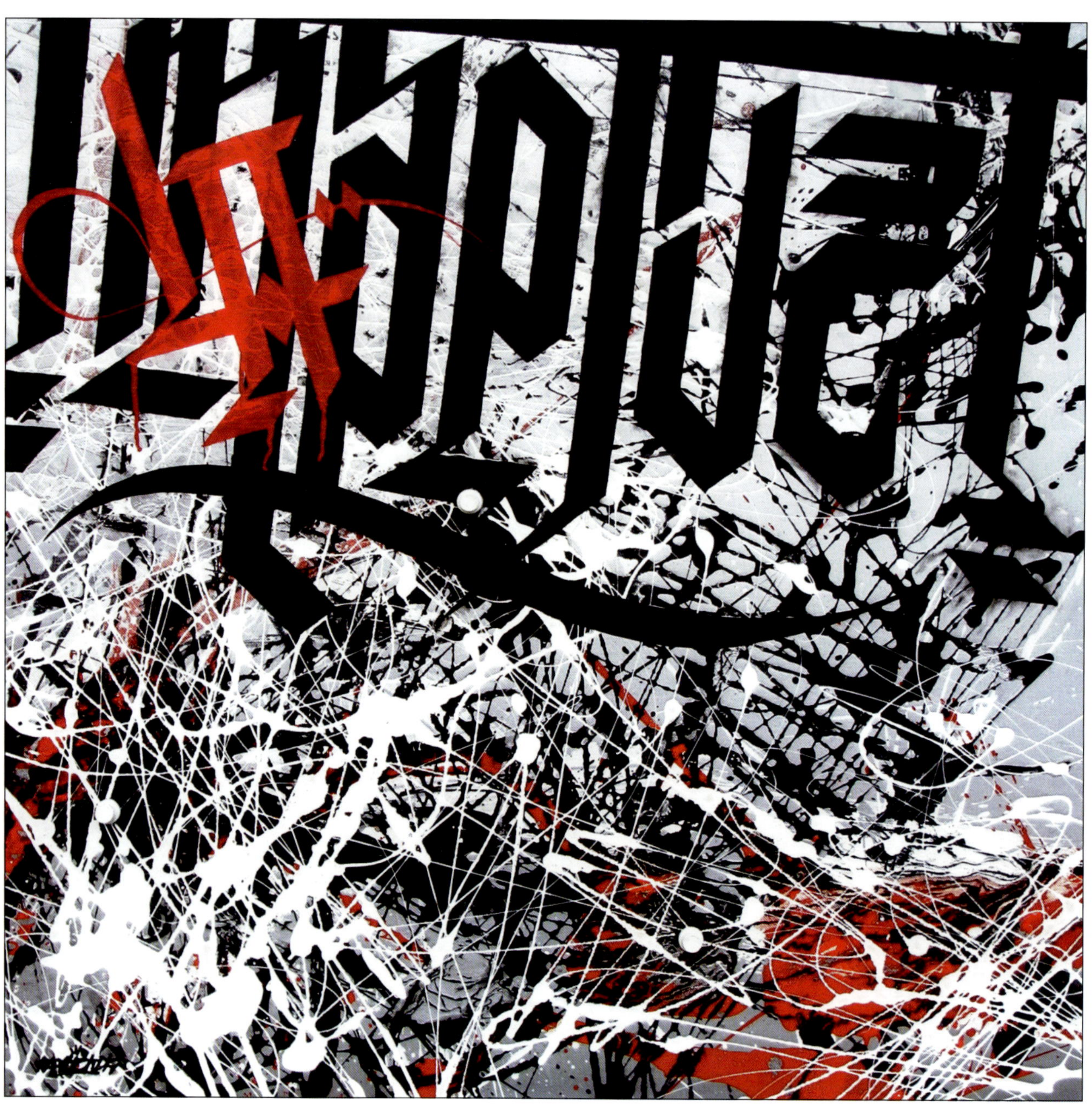

Lost angel - Mixed media on canvas, cm.100x100 - 2010

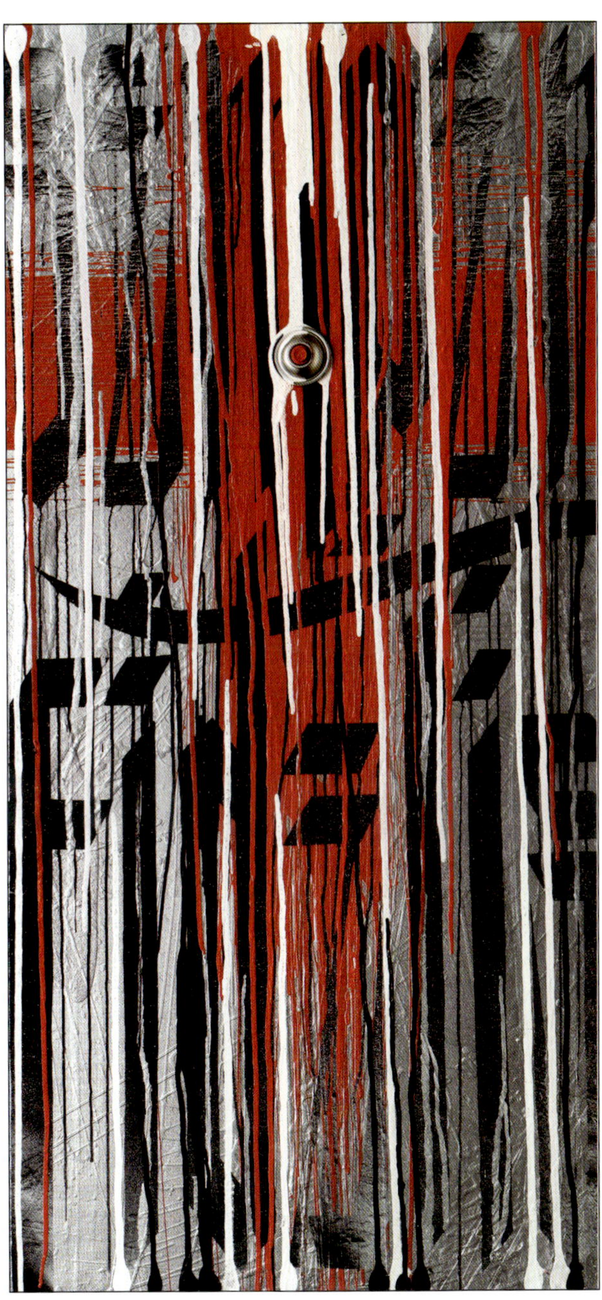

Semper fidelis II - Mixed media on canvas, cm.70x150 - 2011

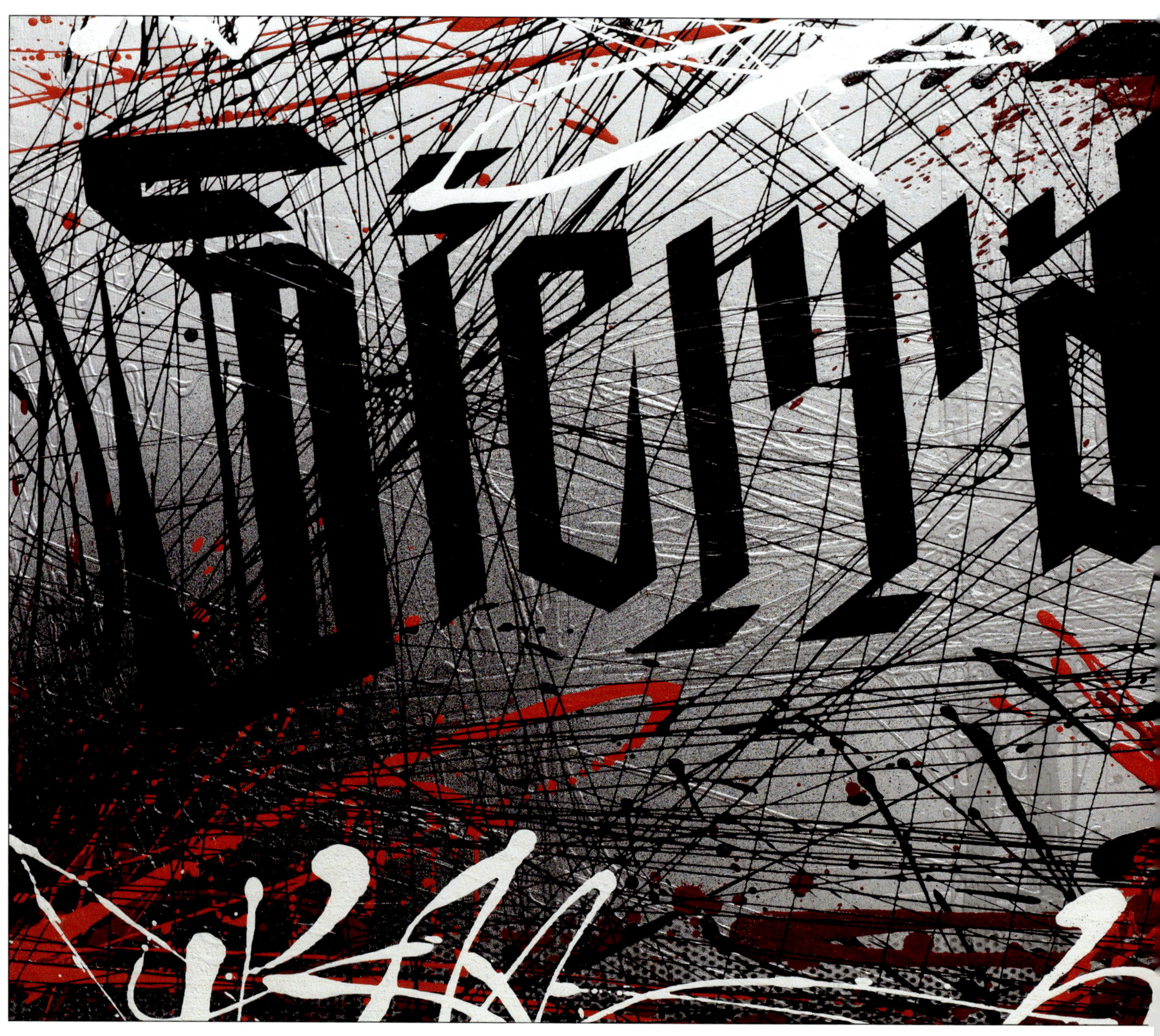

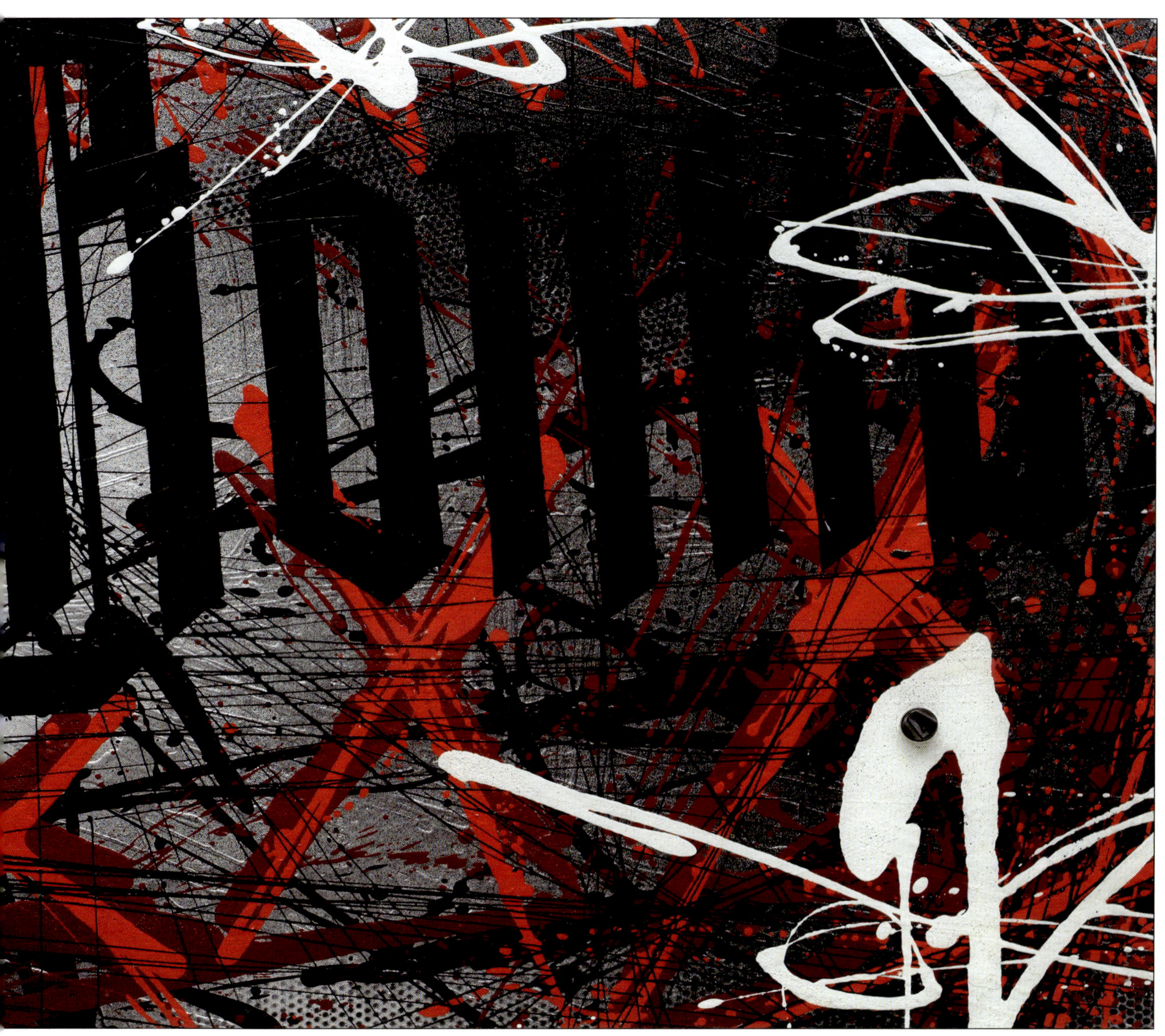

Sierra bonita love - Mixed media on canvas, cm.150x70 - 2010

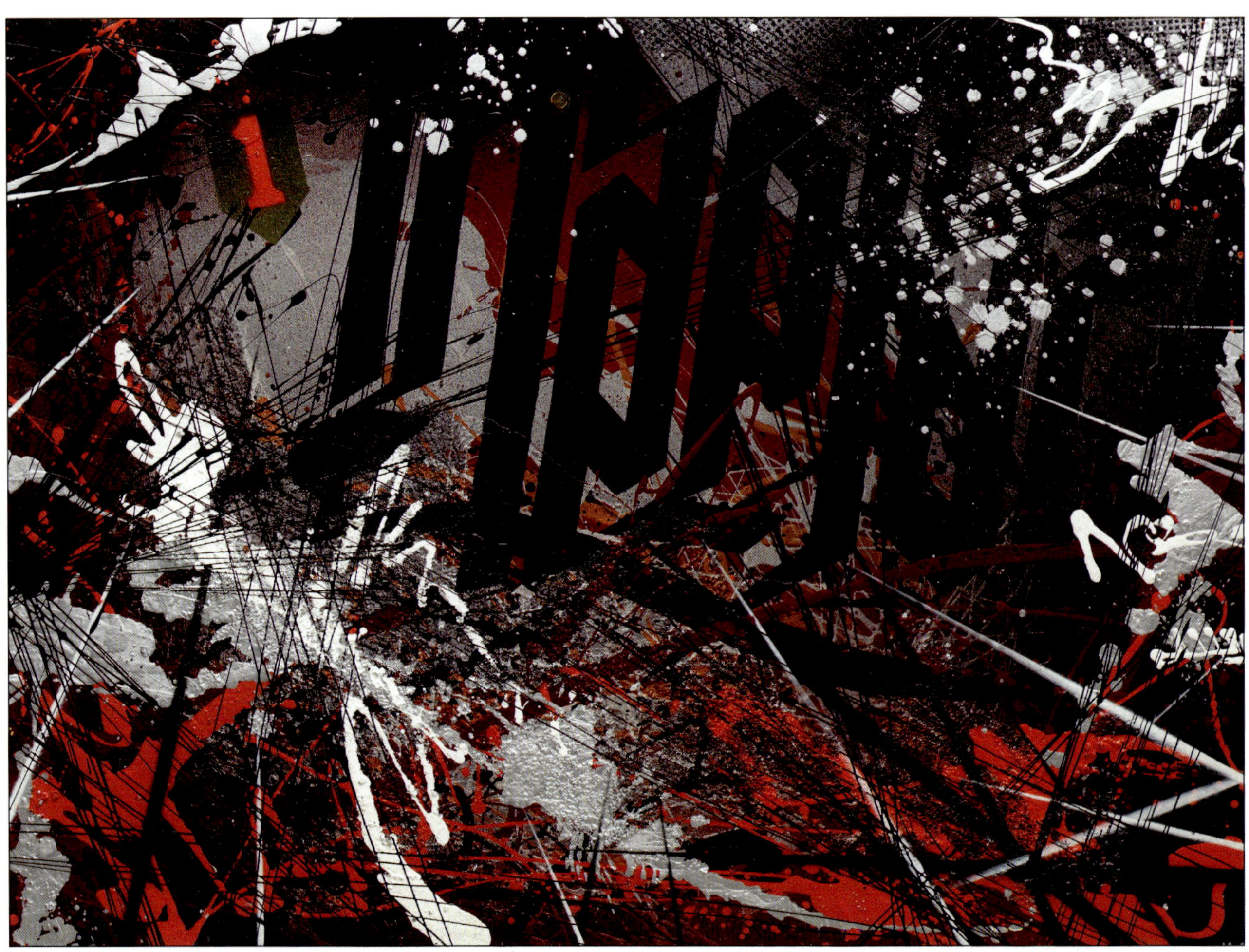

Bastogne memories - Mixed media on canvas, cm.120x90 - 2010

Self justice - Mixed media on canvas, cm.150x100 - 2011

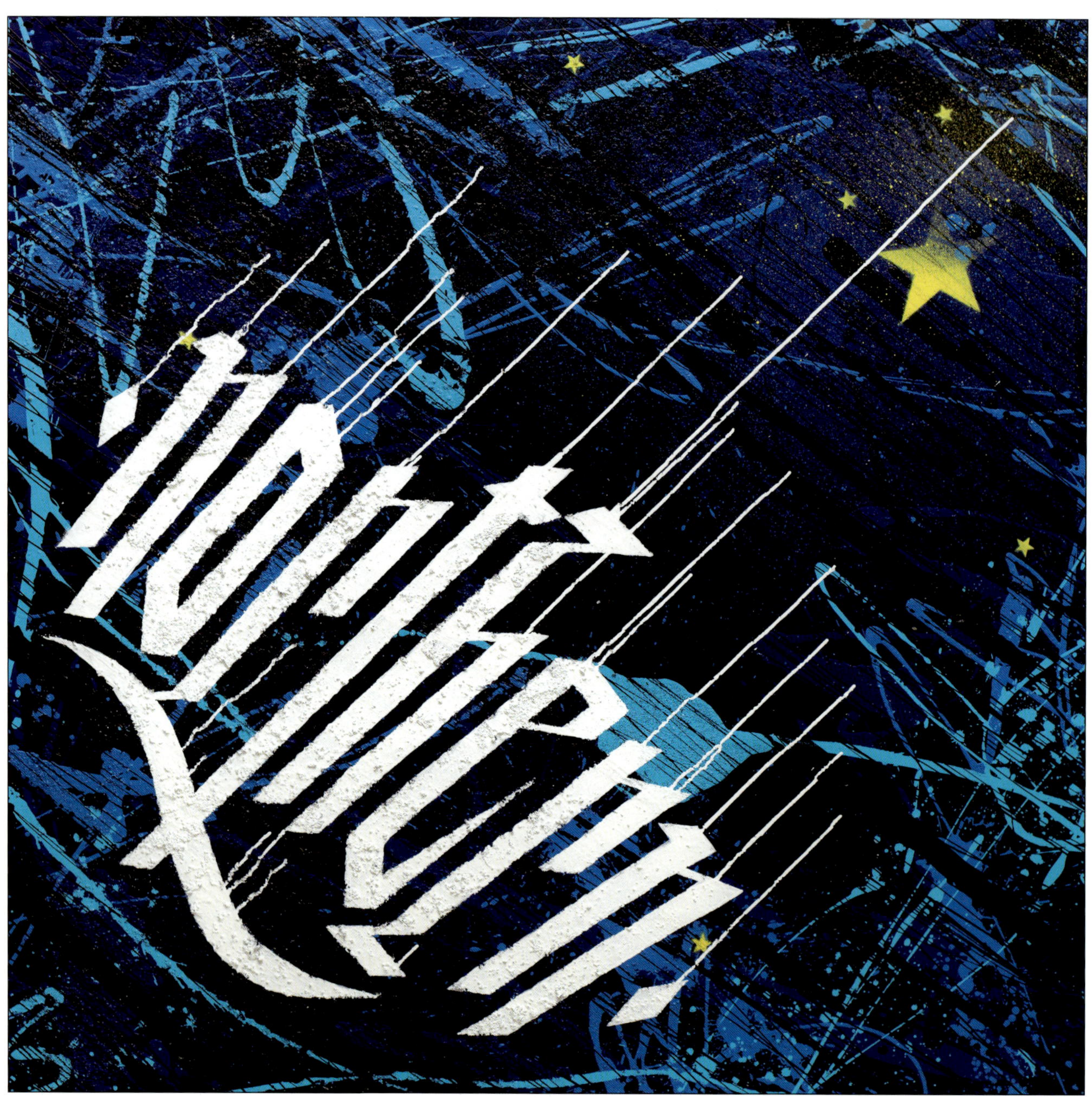

Northern sky - Mixed media on canvas, cm.120x120 - 2011

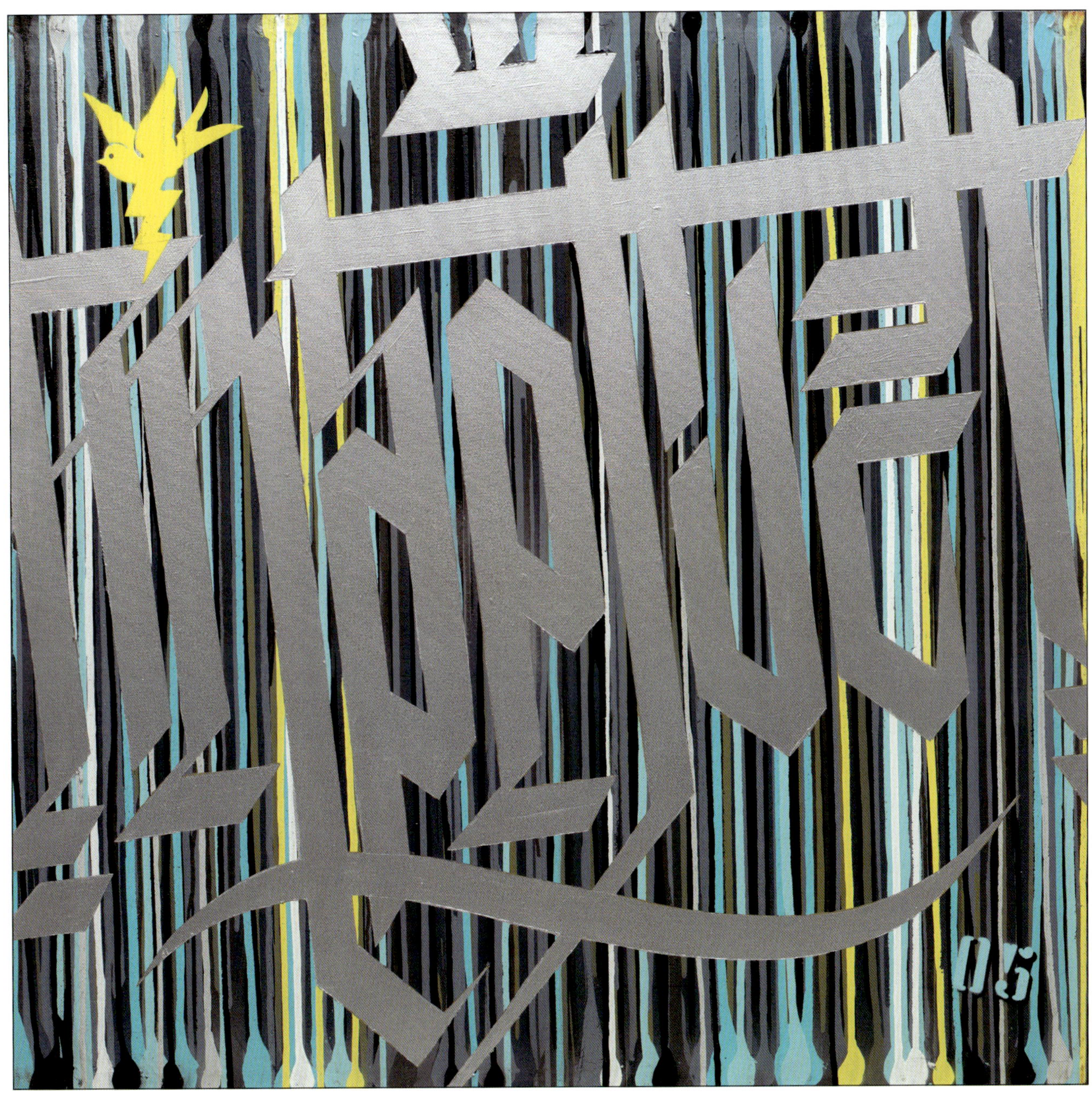

Silver soul - Mixed media on canvas, cm.120x120 - 2011

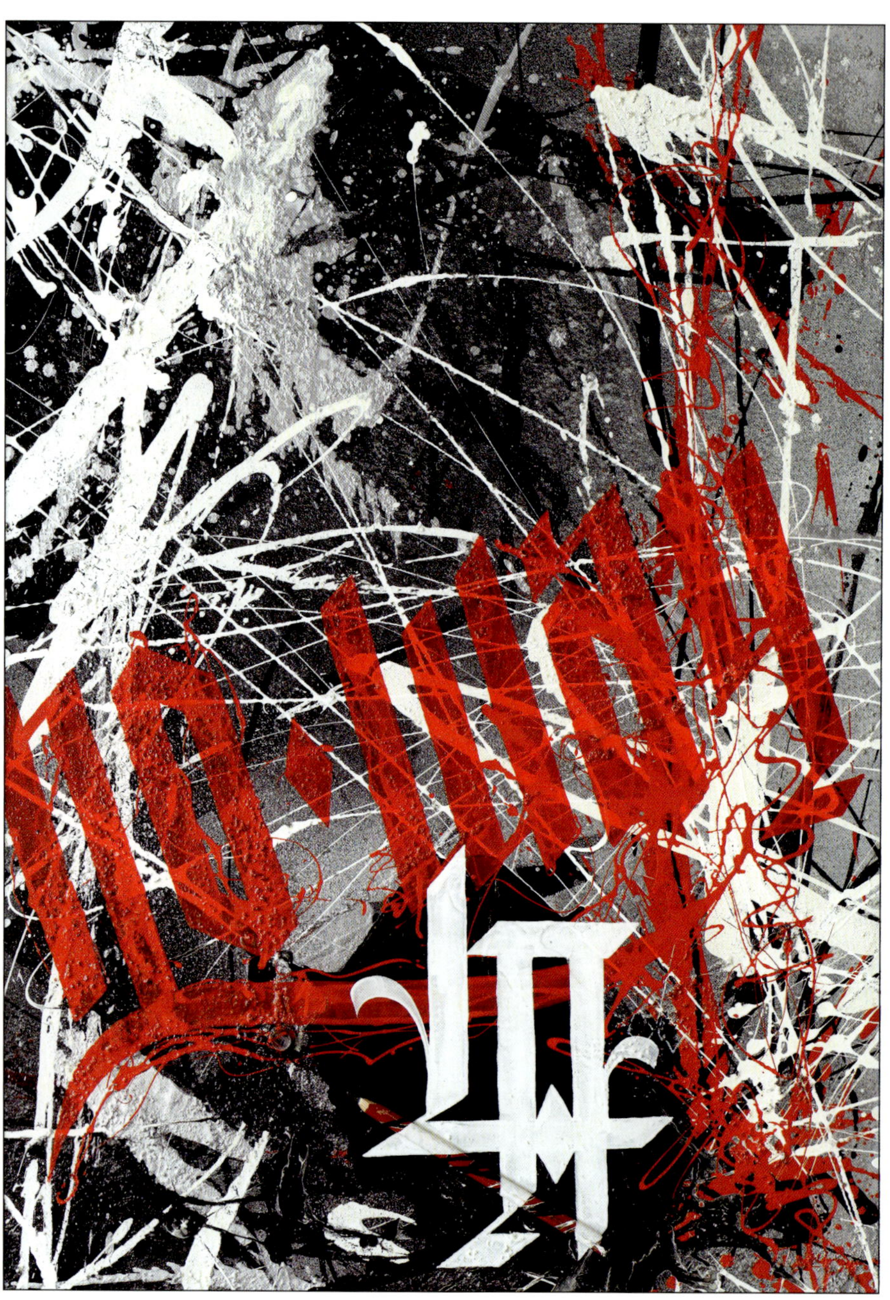

Freedom - Mixed media on canvas, cm.70x100 - 2010

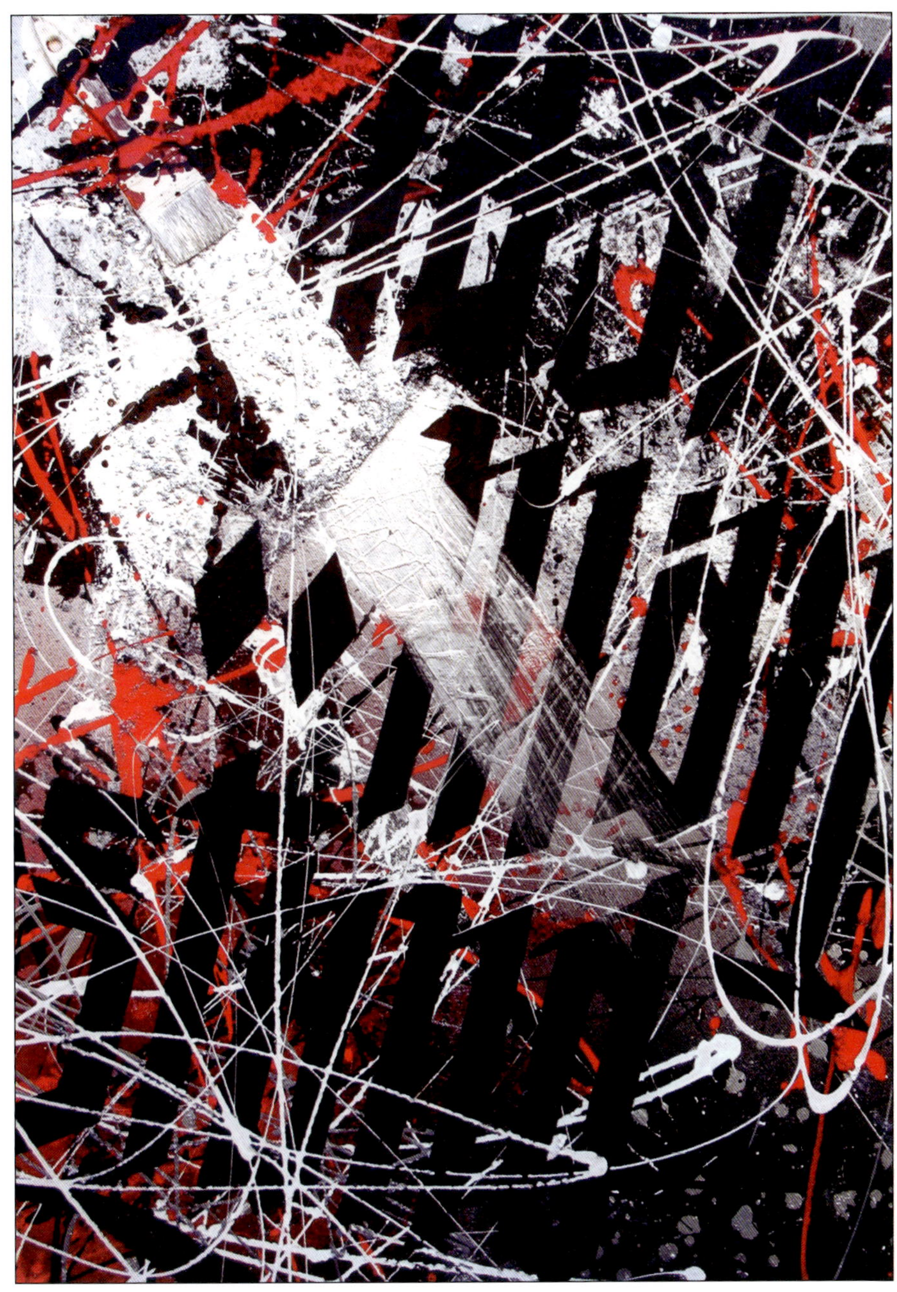

Last man stand - Mixed media on canvas, cm.70x100 - 2010

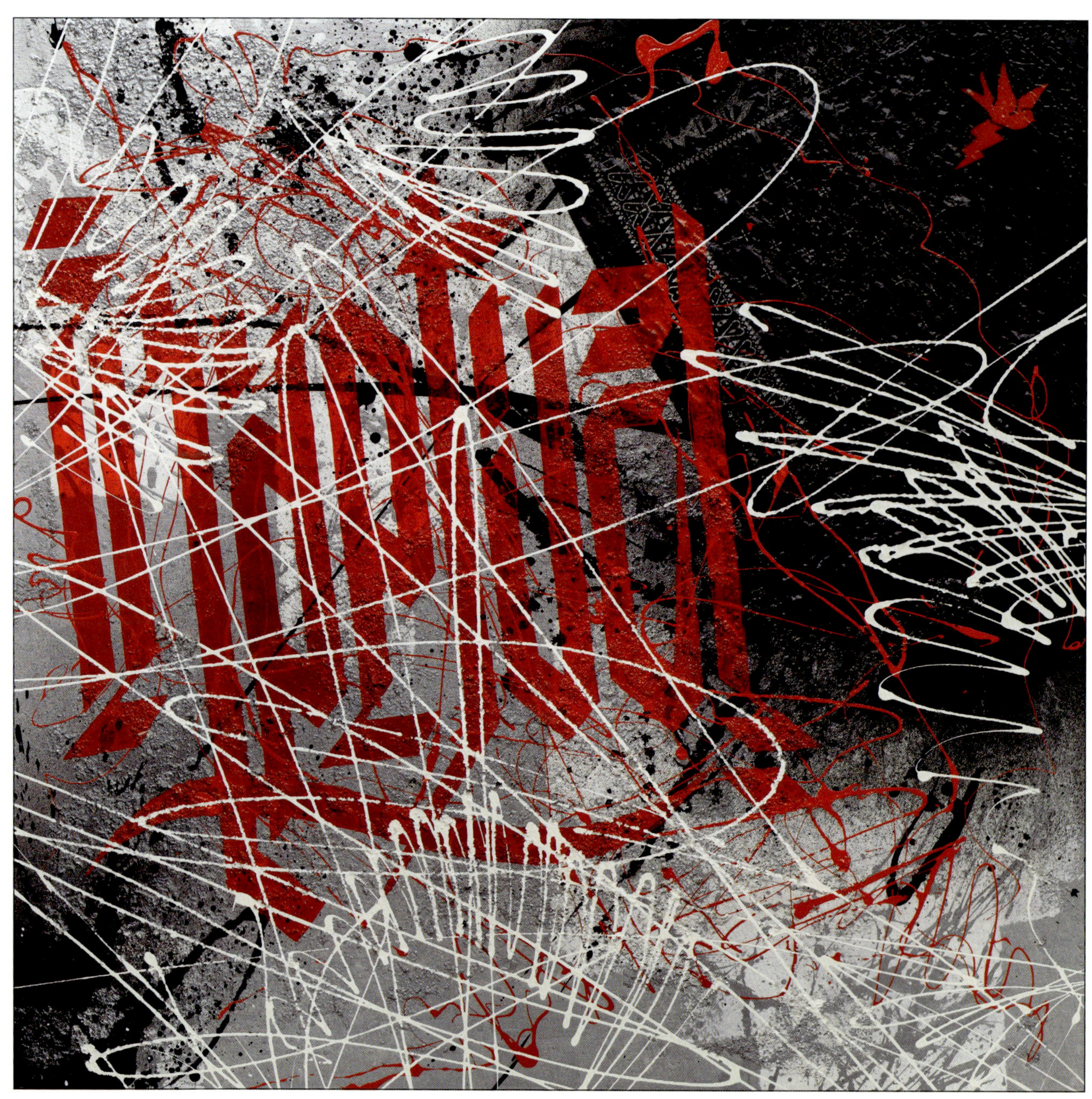

LA Hardcore - Mixed media on canvas, cm.100x100 - 2010

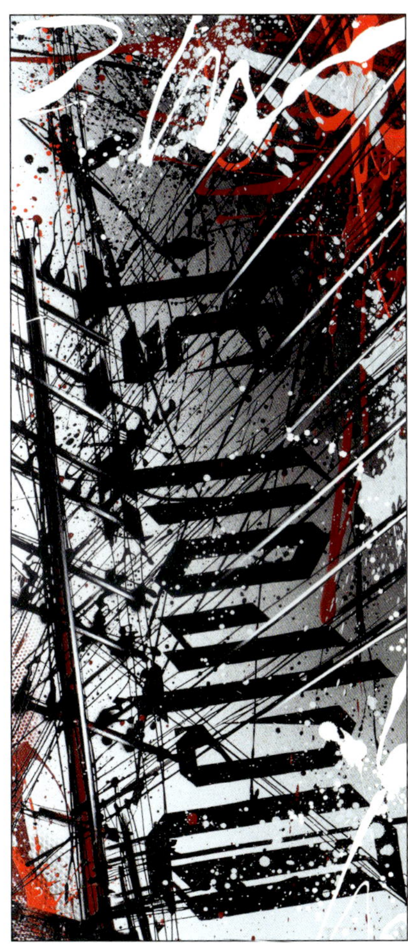 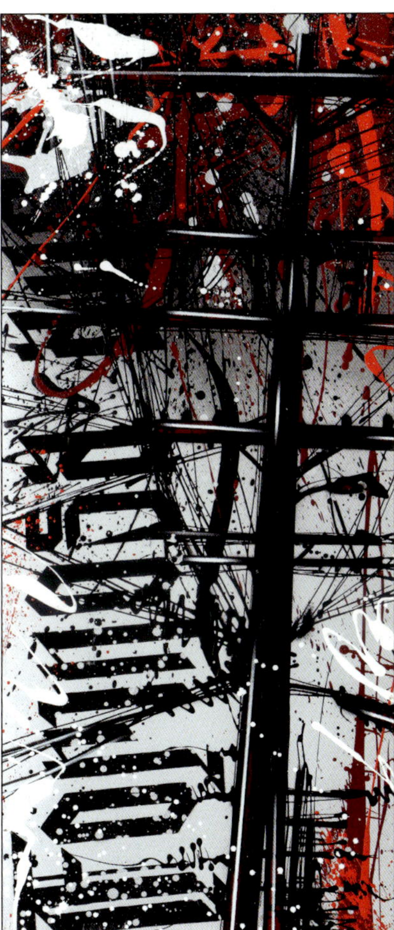 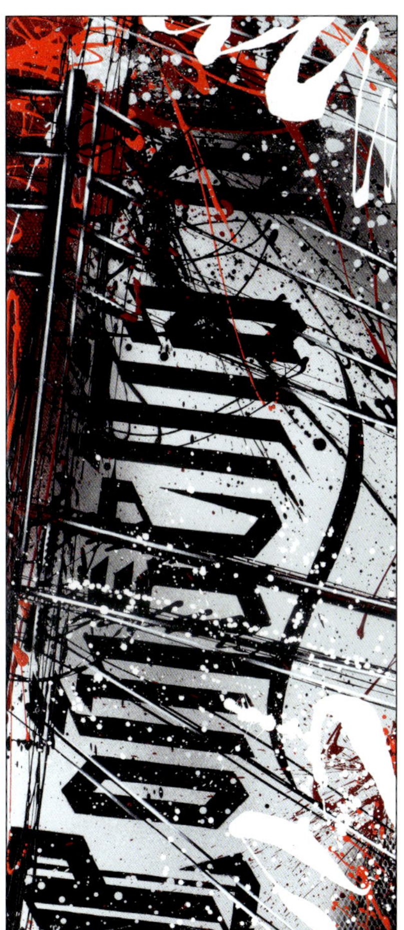

Detroit street, Formosa avenue, Poinsettia place - Mixed media on canvas, cm.60x150 - 2010

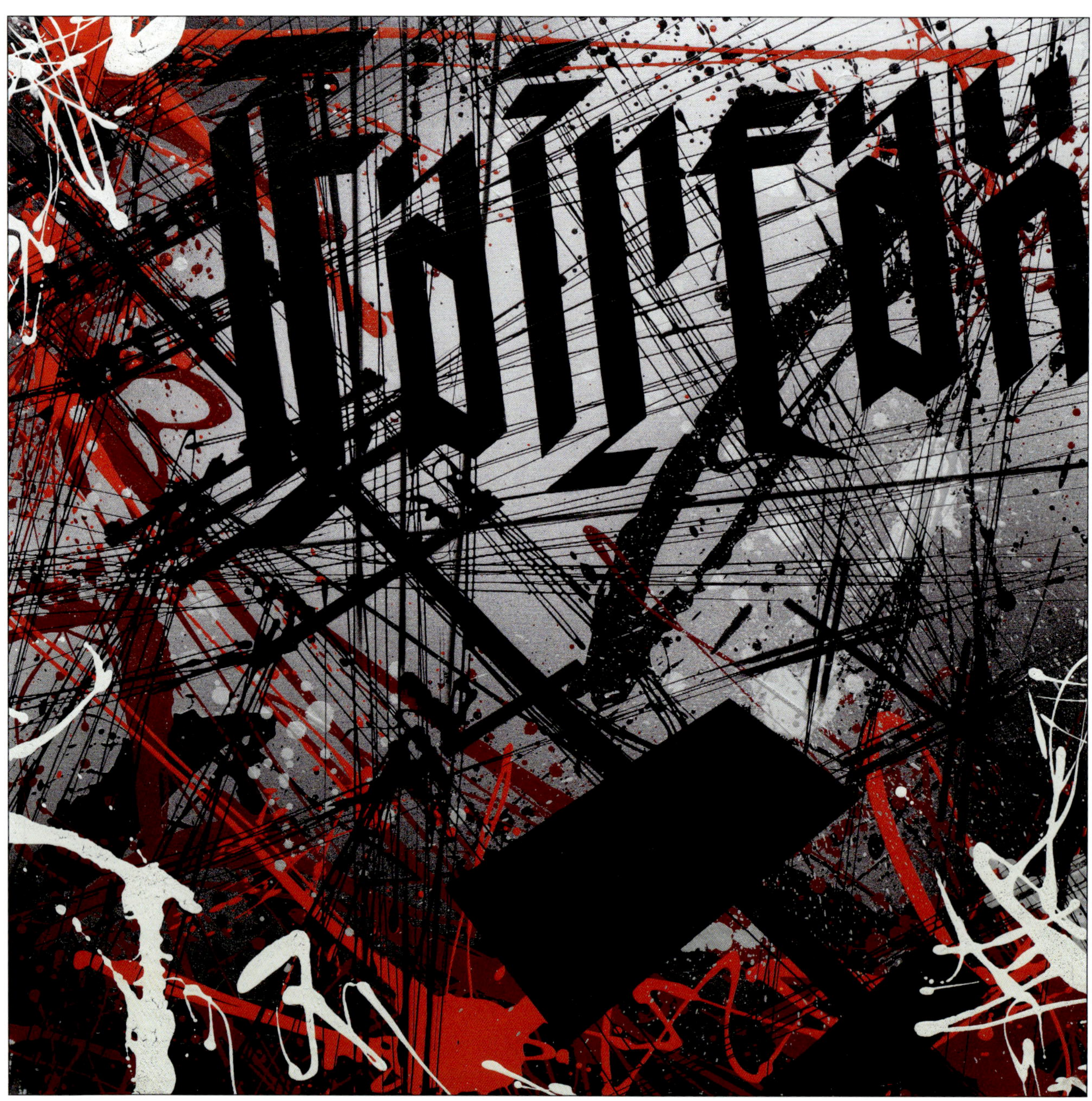

Fairfax rules - Mixed media on canvas, cm.100x100 - 2010

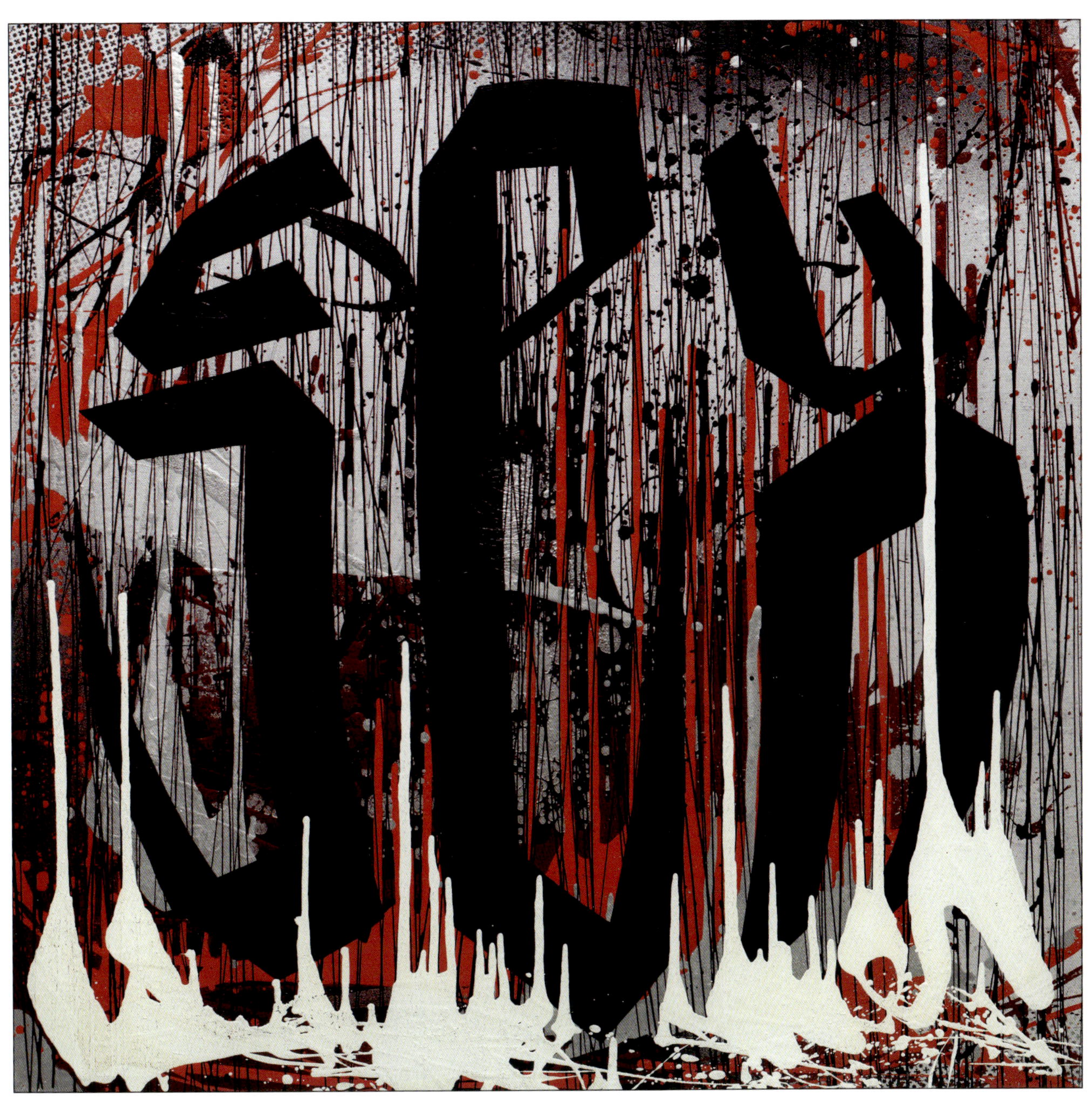

Sex crimes - Mixed media on canvas, cm.100x100 - 2010

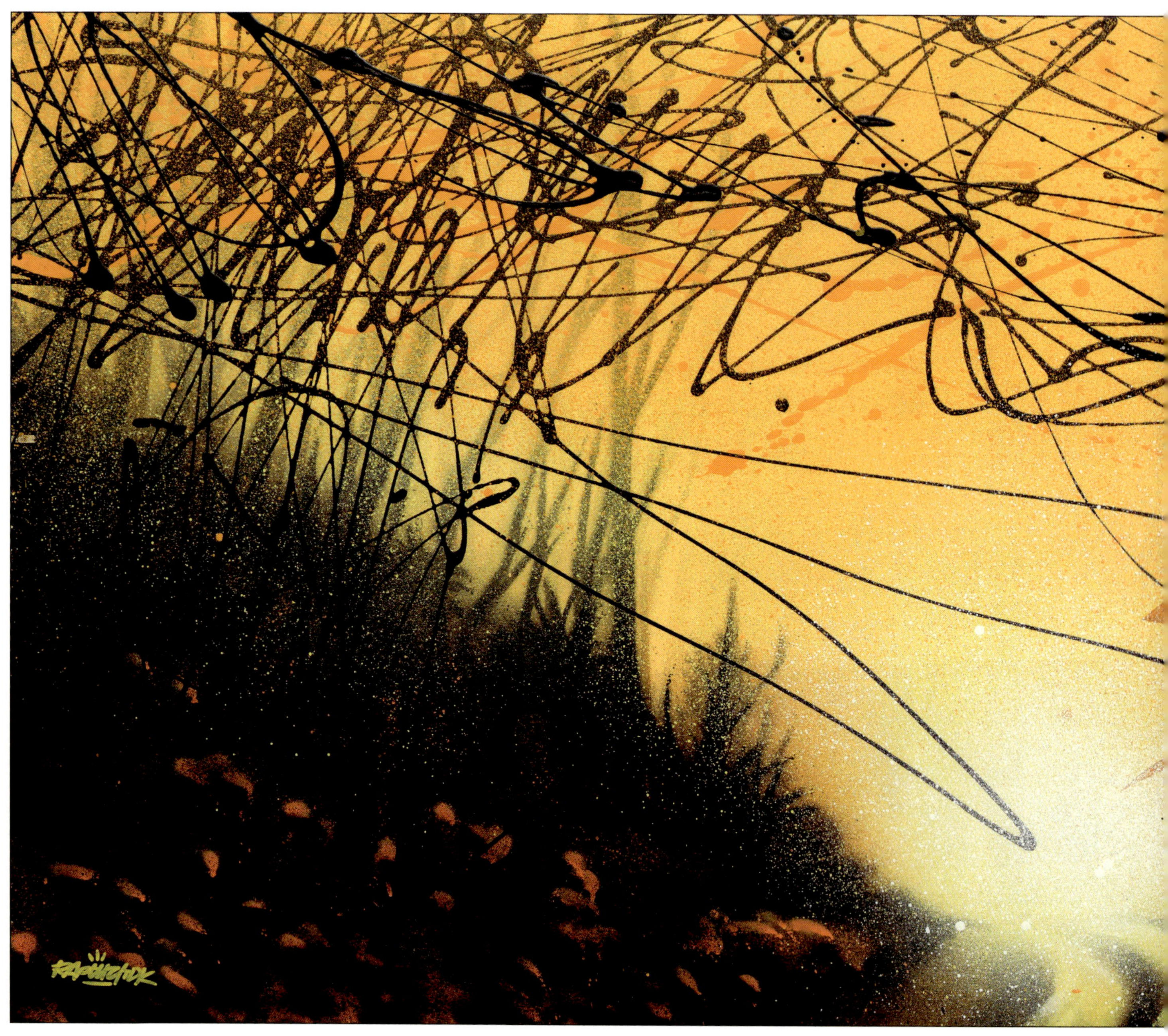

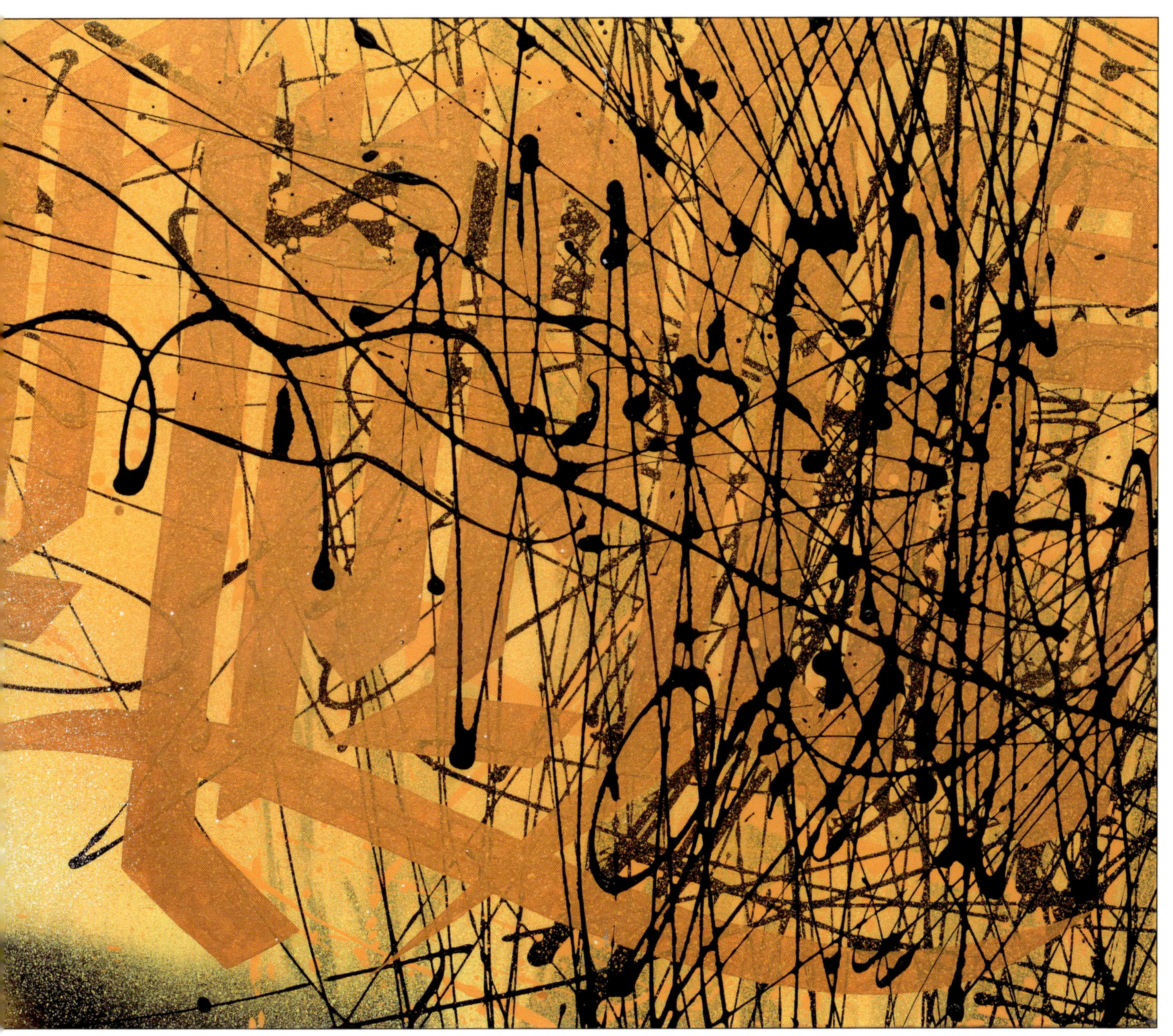

Yellow fog II - Mixed media on canvas, cm.200x80 - 2010

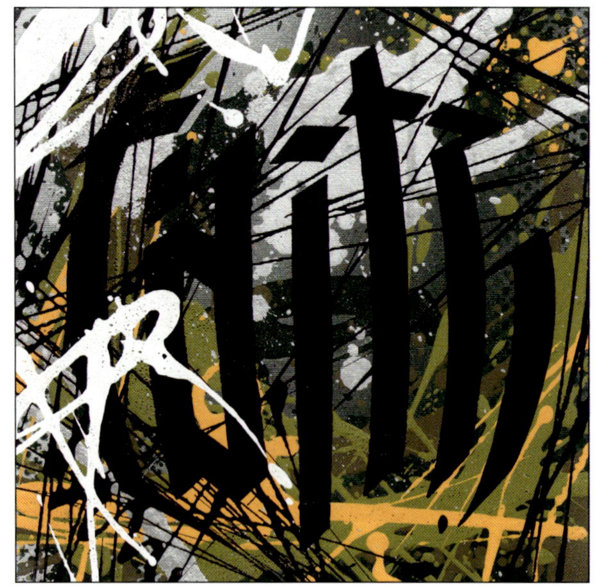 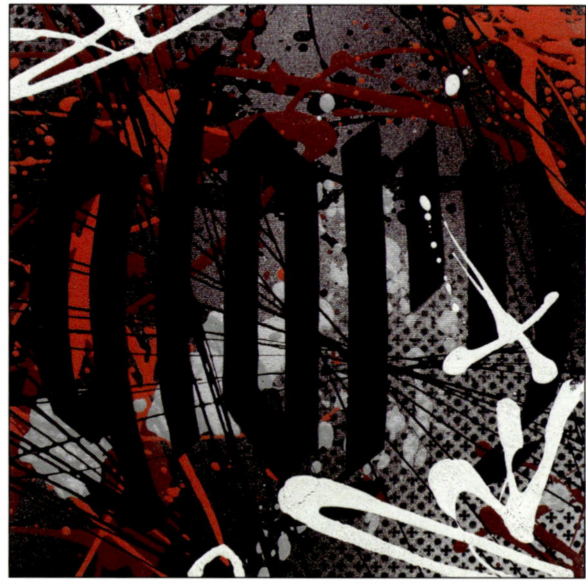

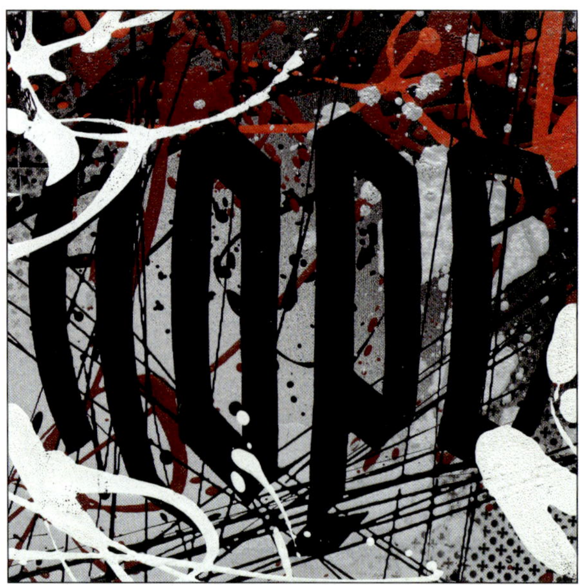 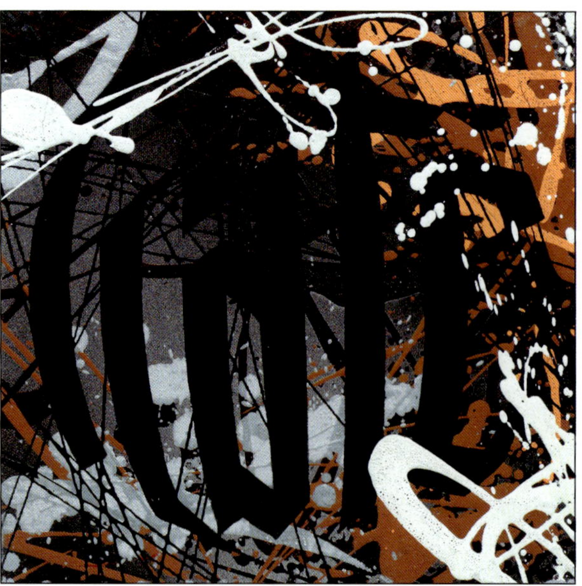

Little faith, Little glory, Little hope, Little hate - Mixed media on canvas, cm.30x30 - 2010

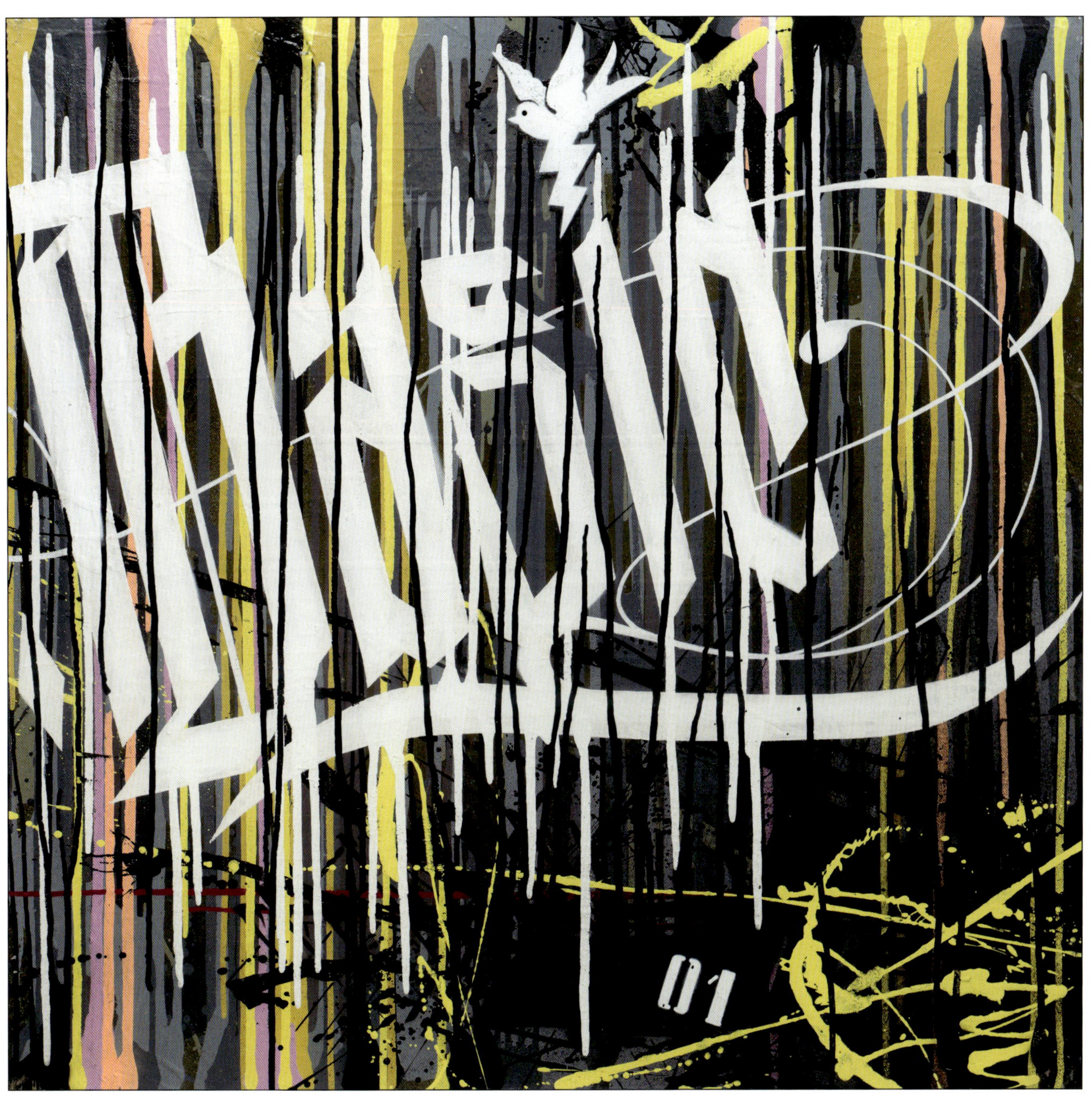

Basic instinct - Spraycan on canvas, cm.120x120 - 2011

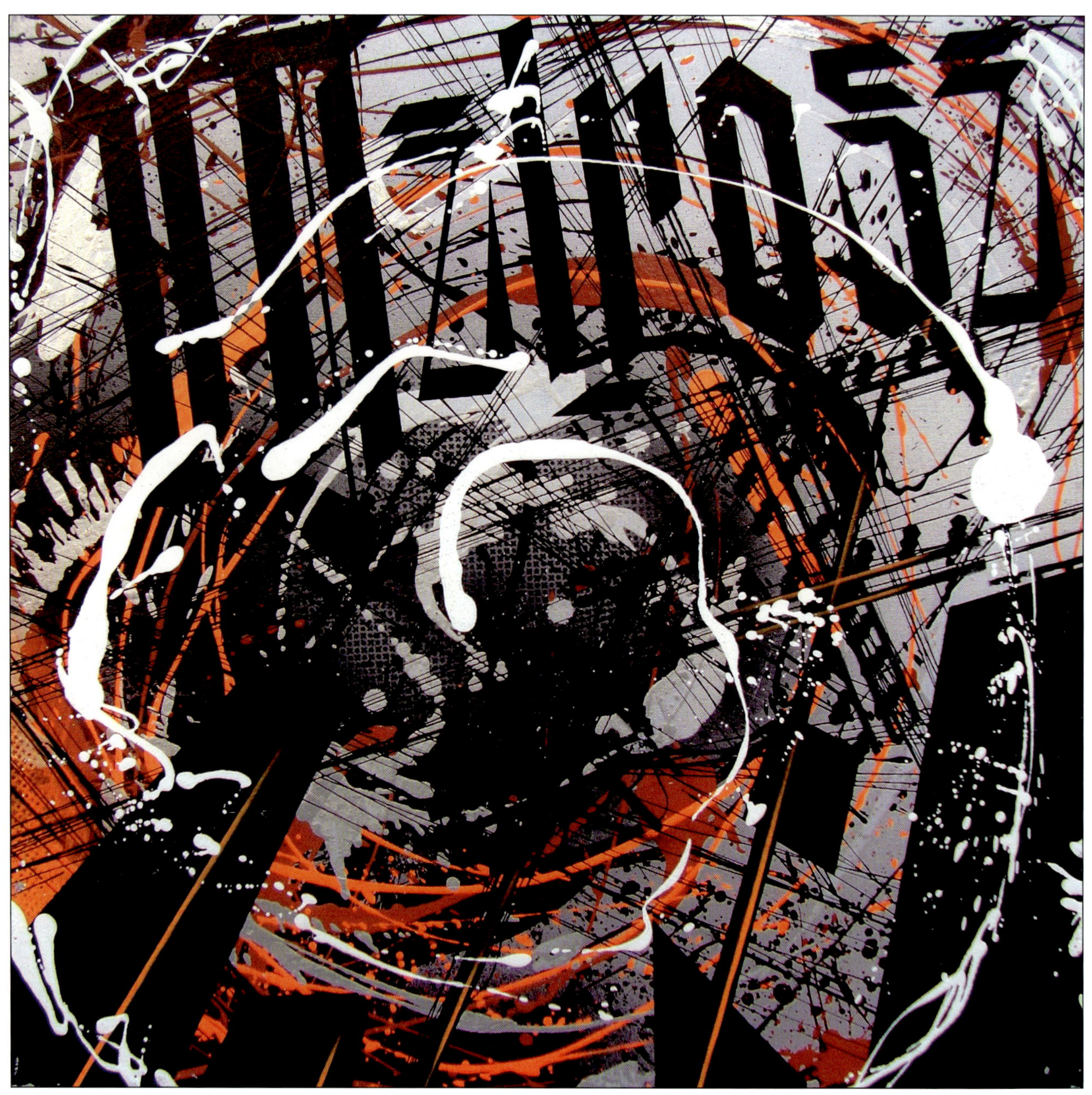

Melrose vortex - Mixed media on canvas, cm.100x100 - 2010

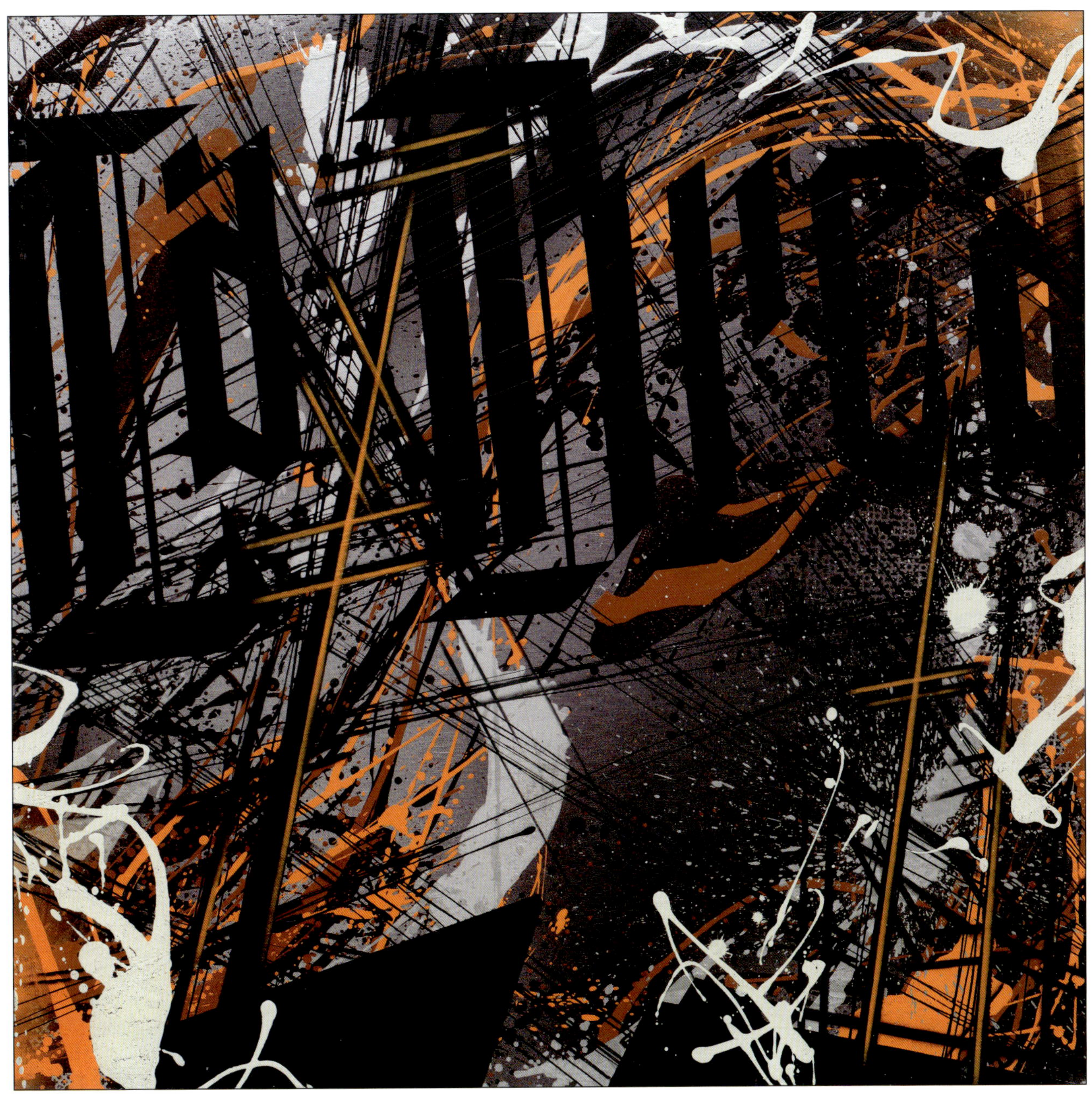

La brea rockers - Mixed media on canvas, cm.100x100 - 2010

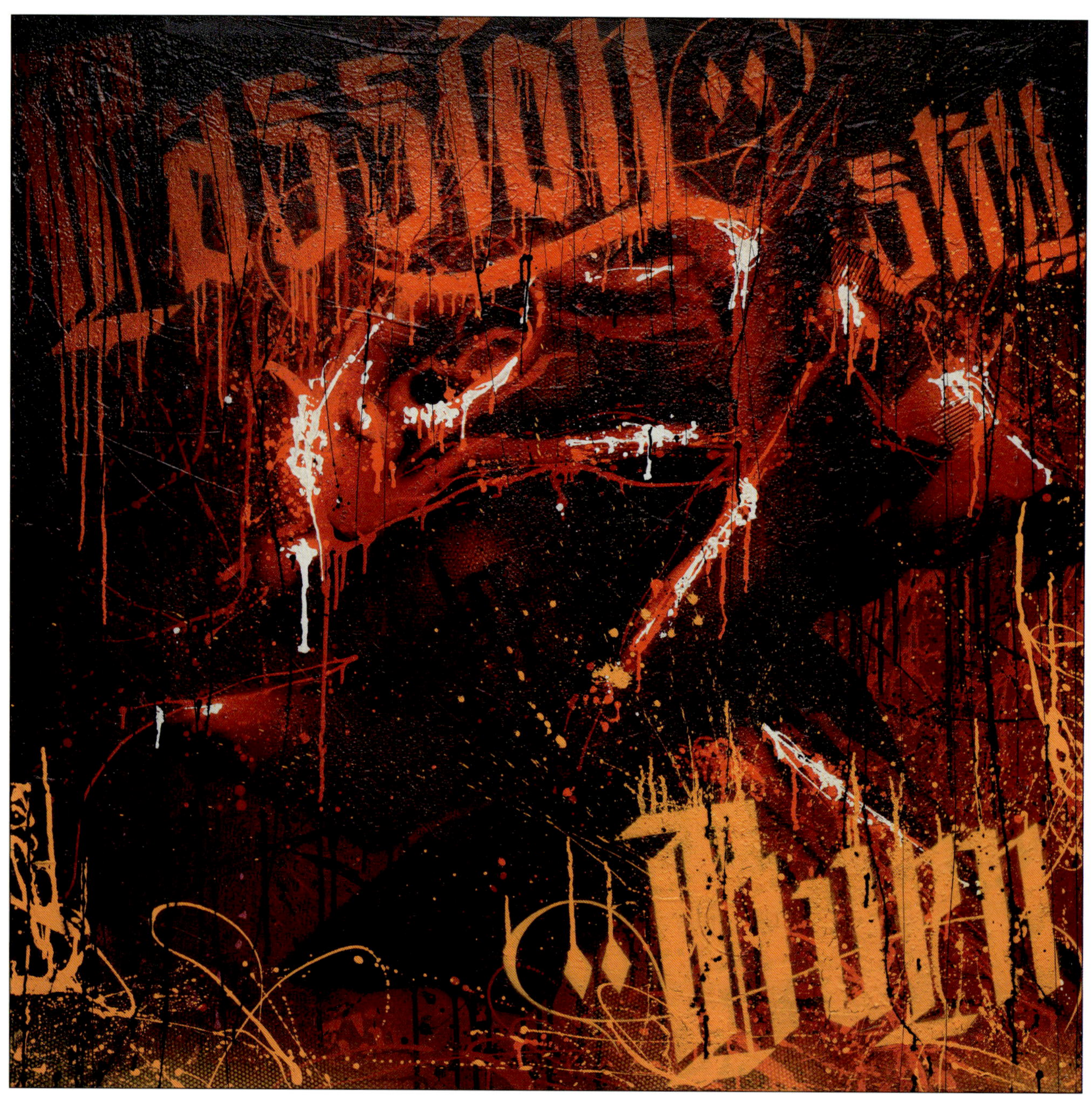

Passion still burn - Spraycan on canvas, cm.150x150 - 2012

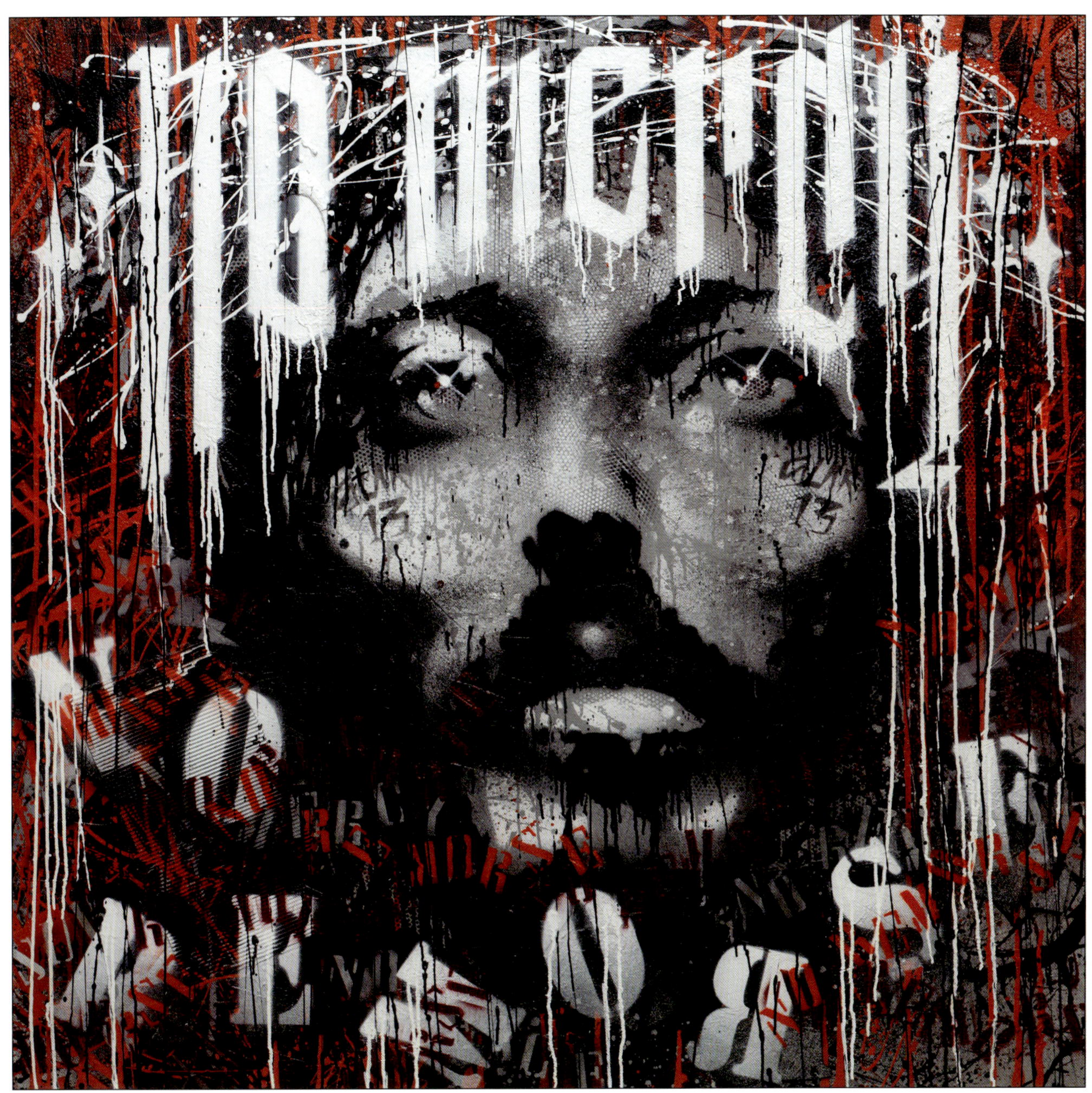

No mercy - Spraycan on canvas, cm.150x150 - 2012

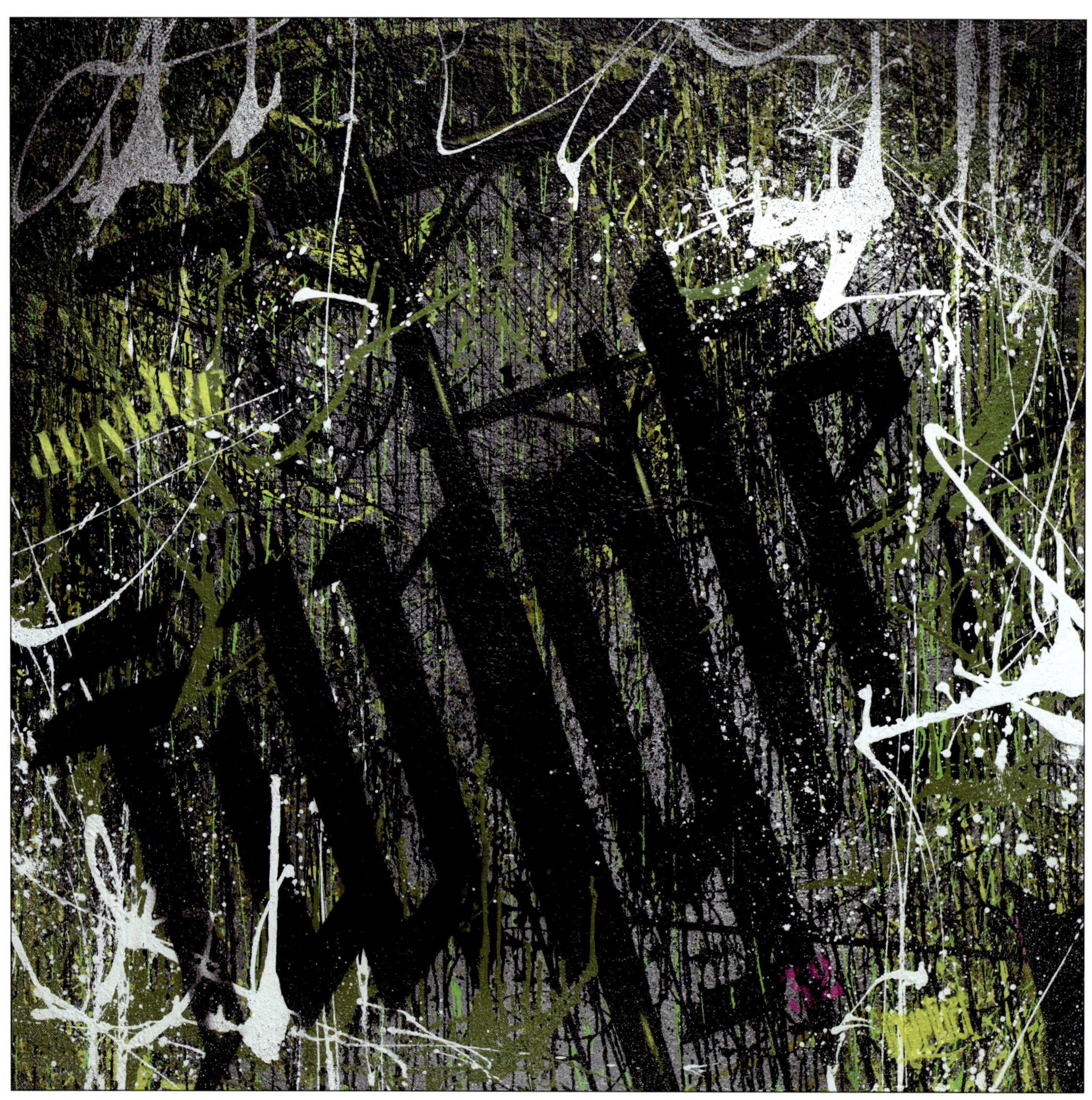

Concrete jungle - Spraycan on canvas, cm.150x150 - 2012

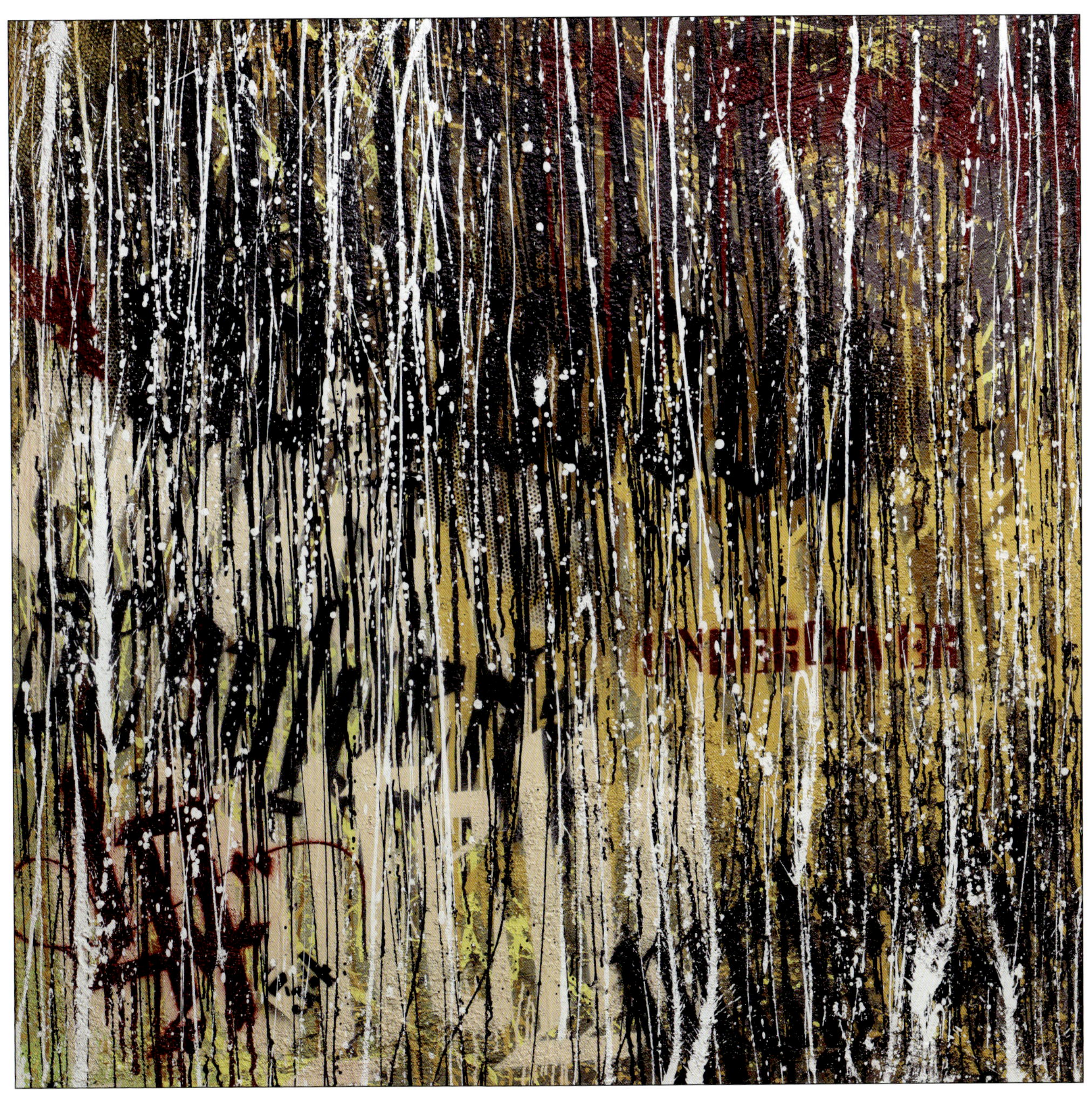

Undercover words - Spraycan on canvas, cm.150x150 - 2012

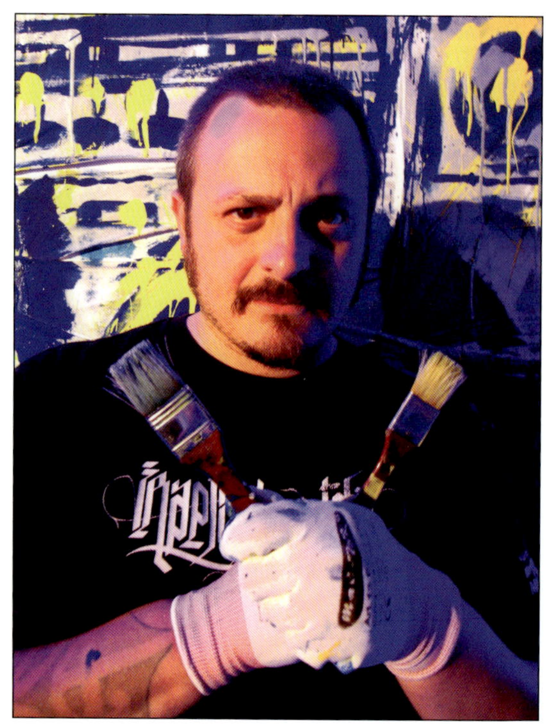